Advanced Praise for Salome Thomas-EL
and
I CHOOSE TO STAY

"This is a powerful story about what an inspirational teacher can do to open new horizons for economically disadvantaged young people."
—William H. Gray, III, President, United Negro College Fund

"Salome Thomas-EL's story should inspire and motivate us all to get involved in public education."
—Pat Croce, best-selling author of *I Feel Great*
and former president, Philadelphia Seventy-Sixers

"Men like Salome Thomas-EL are the perfect prescription for what ails inner-city public education. He was introduced to the world outside his community from public schools inside it. Instead of longing for a way to escape, he longed for a way to share his world-view with the people he grew up around. It's going to take men who care enough to leave the neighborhood and learn how to teach and with enough commitment to bring those lessons back home where they are needed most."
—Elmer Smith, columnist, *Philadelphia Daily News*

"Salome Thomas-EL's life is an inspirational story of one man's determination to make a difference in the lives of children in the inner city. As Salome's former high school teacher, and an educator in the inner city for over 25 years, I am proud to call him a friend and a cherished colleague. Salome Thomas-EL's name is destined to become known by the public along with other heroic and indomitable educators such as Marva Collins, Joe Clark, and Jaime Escalante. But his efforts and successes do not let the rest of us off the hook. I hope those who hear his story will be inspired by his choice to be an educator in the inner city. While he deserves our admiration and encouragement, he needs our support. He cannot do this work alone. We must join in the struggle for a just and equitable educational system which will nurture the potential of all of America's children."
—Marsha Pincus, English teacher, School District of Philadelphia

"As an educator and one privileged to have had the opportunity to know and work with Salome Thomas-EL, I remain inspired by the dedication and courage emerging in his life story. A good teacher is concerned with the present; a better teacher is concerned with the past and its role in the present, but a great teacher is concerned with the future. It takes a leap of faith, a strand of hope, a measure of civility, a good deal of patience, and a resolute tenacity to plant that tree under whose shade you are not likely to stand. But such is the work, the testament, and the

covenant of the few whose responsibility it is to recognize that children are everybody's future."

—Dr. Richard W. Leland, professor,
Department of Communication Studies, East Stroudsburg University

"The story of Salome Thomas-EL should be an inspiring one for all of us who believe that educating our kids well is the number one challenge facing America. He shows how one dedicated educator who believes in the potential of all of our kids can make a huge difference and how, under the proper circumstances, urban education can work."

—Edward G. Rendell, Governor of Pennsylvania
and chairman of the Democratic National Committee

"Salome Thomas-EL demonstrates the power of knowing by showing through his uncompromising commitment to the promise and potential of urban children. As he sees himself reflected in his students, and he is aware of the love, support and high expectations that boosted him to success, he has chosen to remain a reliable and dependable anchor for the next generation of leaders."

—Deidre R. Farmbry, Ed.D., former Chief Academic Officer,
School District of Philadelphia

"Salome Thomas-EL is a serious, industrious, caring, compassionate and committed individual who truly believes that he can make a difference in the lives of his beloved students. Mr. Thomas-EL's story must be told because it may inspire others to follow his example and become teachers in the inner city."

—Germain E. Francois, Ph.D. Professor and Chair,
Department of Academic Enrichment & Learning,
East Stroudsburg University

"This is an uplifting and inspirational story. Though the setting is Philadelphia, its message reaches out across the country. We have to let our young people know that we are there for them and we will not give up. Mr. Thomas-EL is to be admired and, hopefully, emulated."

—Congressman Chaka Fattah (D–PA)

"I want to offer my enthusiasm for Salome Thomas-EL's book on improving public education from within and impacting the lives of inner city children. No one understands this better than Thomas-EL or is in a better position to help inspire others to fight the same good fight."

—Zachary Stalberg, Editor, *Philadelphia Daily News*

"I Choose to Stay *is a real story—written by a real Philadelphian! Salome Thomas-EL tells it like it is!"*

—Ukee Washington, KYW-TV News, Philadelphia

I CHOOSE TO STAY

A Black Teacher Refuses to Desert the Inner City

Salome Thomas-EL
with Cecil Murphey

KENSINGTON PUBLISHING CORP.
http://www.kensington.com

DAFINA BOOKS are published by

Kensington Publishing Corp.
850 Third Avenue
New York, NY 10022

All Kensington titles, imprints and distributed lines are available at special quantity discounts for bulk purchases for sales promotion, premiums, fund-raising, educational or institutional use.

Special book excerpts or customized printings can be created to fit specific needs. For details, write or phone the office of the Kensington Special Sales Manager: Kensington Publishing Corp., 850 Third Avenue, New York, NY 10022, Attn. Special Sales Department. Phone: 1-800-221-2647.

Library of Congress Card Catalogue Number: 2002112563
ISBN 0-7582-0186-9

First Printing: March 2003
10 9 8 7 6 5 4 3 2 1

Printed in the United States of America

IN MEMORY OF MY BELOVED MOTHER
DORIS THOMAS-EL
(AMENA HOTEP)
1936–2002

Thank you for giving me life and teaching me how to live it.
I will always remember your everlasting message:
Every teacher is not a parent but every parent is a teacher.
I will forever love and cherish you. . . .

ACKNOWLEDGMENTS

To our fallen educational heroes: My sister-in-law, Delores Brown, and my good friends, Sylvia Abdul-Haqq, Don Grillet, Tony Irving, Rev. Wilkins O. Jones, Laura Marshall, Thomasina Smith, and Ella Travis. You gave your hearts and lives to the children of Philadelphia. Your memory lives on.

To my students who died too young: I will continue to pray for you and your families. We will someday meet again and unite in the classroom as we always did. I love you and cry for you everyday.

To my wife Shawnna: Your patience and understanding throughout my career and this book project has been tremendous. Your ability as a wife and mother is amazing. Thank you for allowing me to give so much of myself to our community and its children.

To my beautiful two-year-old daughter Macawi: You have given me the opportunity to be the type of father I wished for every night as a child. Your love of reading and learning will give you eternal life. I think you can work a little harder on your Spanish lessons. I love you.

To my friends Cecil Murphey (co-writer) and Deidre Knight (my agent): Your guidance and literary mentorship with this book has allowed me to communicate my story and understand my purpose in life.

To my editor at Kensington, Karen Thomas: Your dedication, passion, and creativity should be mandatory at every publishing house.

To Steven Zacharius and everyone at Kensington Publishing: Thanks for believing in me and all of the other hard-working educators in the United States. We deserve your respect, and you have been most honorable in your work.

To Arnold Schwarzenegger: Your love for children through the Inner-City Games is relentless. Thanks for supporting the kids and me. Your personal visits with the students will never be forgotten.

To Dr. Deidre Farmbry and Mrs. Marsha Pincus: You have both been my teachers and mentors for over twenty years. If I can save one half the number of the children you have given life and hope to, I will have been successful.

I would like to thank the following people for supporting the chess team, my students and our schools: The wonderful teachers and staff members at Reynolds Elementary School, Vaux Middle School, University City, Simon Gratz, and Strawberry Mansion High Schools. My brother and friend, Ishmael Al-Islam, Cathy Hensford and Elvin Wilson for developing the hearts and minds of the young ladies and men on the chess team. To my wonderful secretaries Edith Bridges and Debbie Banks, and my assistant principal, Octavia Lewis, Ellie Deegan (Lecture Bureau), Jill Eisenstadt (Full Picture), Liora Mendeloff and Donna Frisby-Greenwood (Inner-City Games). To Harold Adams and all my fellow brothers of Kappa Alpha Psi Fraternity Incorporated, for working with me through the tough times. A special thanks to Laurada Byers, Elmer Smith and the entire Daily News family. To my pastor and teacher,

Sean Wise at Calvary Baptist Church, and Miller Memorial Baptist Church, Sharon Baptist Church, Haven Memorial United Methodist Church, and Wayland Temple Baptist Church for your support. Thanks also to Doug Brantz and the crew at Garden Fresh Deli (for feeding my staff and students when we didn't have money). We are blessed to have the Men of BACA, Delta Sigma Theta and Alpha Kappa Alpha Sororities, and the Vaux Alumni Association. To Cecil Martin and Hugh Douglas of the Philadelphia Eagles: Thanks for giving books to our entire school and reading to the children. I owe a lot to the staff, students and alumni of Hampton University, East Stroudsburg University, Nichols College, Depauw University, Cheyney University, Lehigh University, Bucknell University, and the Lee County schools of Ft. Myers, Florida. To BOTA, continue our fight.

To my seven brothers and sisters: You all have helped to shape me into the man that I am today. I am blessed to have had you by my side every day of my life. Thanks for your support Karen and Dexter Hamilton.

To Julius (Dr. J.) Erving, Maurice Cheeks, Pat Croce and Marc Zumoff: Thanks for always encouraging me to pursue my dream to become a teacher and principal. Charles Barkley, what can I say? Only you could make me smile about being a teacher and happy that I am not a millionaire. Thanks for being such a good friend to Tony Irving.

To my boyhood friends: Quentin (Ice) Isom, Derek Sharp, Kevin Compton, Rob Powlen, Dion Harris, Stewart and Sean Sharpe. It was tough but we made it! To Jeff, Freddie (Bean), and Artrice, thanks for the Fathers Matter meeting.

To the numerous other individuals who have touched my life: There isn't enough space for me to thank you for your love and support. Please know that I am grateful for you and that you are forever in my heart and mind. And by the way, thanks for the excellent advice, Grandma.

A portion of the royalties from the sale of this book will help support the college education of the students featured in this book.

To Our Nation's Teachers

" 'Our deepest fear is not that we are inadequate. Our deepest fear is that we are powerful beyond measure. It is our light, not our darkness, that most frightens us.' We ask ourselves, Who am I to be brilliant, gorgeous, talented, fabulous? Actually, who are you not to be? . . . Your playing small doesn't serve the world. There's nothing enlightened about shrinking so that other people won't feel insecure around you. We are all meant to shine, as children do . . . And as we let our own light shine, we unconsciously give other people permission to do the same. As we're liberated from own fear, our presence automatically liberates others."

—Nelson Mandela
Recreating the words of Marianne Williamson
at his Presidential Inauguration

CONTENTS

FOREWORD

by
Arnold Schwarzenegger

Salome Thomas-EL and I come from different countries, different backgrounds and different experiences, but we both believe that breaking the cycle of violence, teenage pregnancy, drugs, dropouts, gangs and illiteracy is the only way we can ensure that the next generation of Americans have the opportunity to experience the "American dream."

The foundation for achieving my American dream started long before I came to this great country. I had two caring and involved parents who were there for me after school. I had long days of classes with very strong teachers, incredible mentors and coaches encouraging me, pushing me to do my best, spending quality time with me, telling me that I was a winner and helping me to set goals and accomplish them. When I joined ex-President George Bush's administration as the Chairman of the President's Council on Physical Fitness and Sports in 1990, I traveled the country and saw firsthand that many kids today do not have those influences at home and some do not have them at school. That is why Danny Hernandez and I started the Inner-City Games Foundation—to bring hope, support, competition, build confidence, provide education, culture and a safe haven for underprivileged kids after the school day ends. The Inner-City Games now reaches over 250,000 kids across the country and has proven to be a great partner program for Salome Thomas-EL, Harold Adams and the fantastic teachers, administrators and volunteers at the Vaux Middle School in Philadelphia and fourteen other cities.

This book about Salome Thomas-EL is about courage. It is a story about determination, about compassion, love and the ultimate fight. This is the fight against the odds, against the "system" and years of cultural, social and economic factors that would have allowed this group of inner-city kids to become nothing more than another set of statistics—victims of gang violence, teenage pregnancy, death, drugs and a life on the street. But Salome Thomas-EL would not let that happen. He would not give up. He saw the potential in them and he fought for them. He used a board game as his weapon in this fight.

Chess is a game requiring skill, planning, strategy, determination and courage. This was his secret to teaching these kids confidence, showing them hope and creating a recipe for success they had never known before. He chose to stay when many would have given up. He believed in them and, more importantly, he made them believe in themselves. Because of Salome, Mr. Ishmael, and the Vaux Administration these kids knew that they could be winners, that they were smart, that they were talented, and that they had earned the right to compete with the best because they were the best. And Salome proved that even against the greatest odds, one man, with the support of others like him, can make a great difference.

Vaux has set the standards high with a great example: opening up its doors for parents, creating a community center, and encouraging everyone to get involved. I have great memories of the time I spent at Vaux Middle School playing volleyball with the kids and watching them when fencing, but my best memories are with the chess team. Salome introduced me to the Chess

Club when visiting the Inner-City Games Summer Camp Vaux in 2000. There was one incredible girl, Denise Pickard, who was about thirteen years old. She had worked so hard to master the game and was so determined to beat the Terminator. So I challenged her to try to win, with all the cameras rolling. She had trained to be a champion, and while I would normally be upset to lose—to anyone—even I was happy as I heard her say, "checkmate." I was so proud and so happy that this young girl was a winner because of Vaux, because of Salome and because of Inner-City Games. This chess team went on to be the national champions because someone cared enough to encourage them, and teach them, and mentor them, and inspire them, and that is what this is all about.

We say that kids are our future, but very often those words are just that—rhetoric without action. Time and time again we adults have let kids down by not living up to our promises and expectations in terms of setting the proper foundation for kids to grow and prosper. It is our job, our most important responsibility to take every step necessary to ensure that kids from all walks have a fighting chance. These kids at the Vaux Middle School Inner-City Games Program could have continued the cycle—becoming the next generation of disadvantaged minority adults with shattered dreams, minimal education and living on welfare. They might never have had the chance to see or experience life beyond the inner cities. Salome Thomas-EL believed in those kids; he believed that if he stayed he could break that cycle. He chose to stay and he made a difference. He has touched many people in this lifetime, and his work and efforts will affect many more in the generations to come. For all of that, I thank him.

1

The Choice

That morning of November 20, 1997, began like any other Friday. Yet within the next hour, my life would drastically change. In some ways it was like reaching the fork in the road, and I had to decide which way to go.

For me, that choice presented no problem.

Long before that Friday, I had decided—I just hadn't realized it.

I walked into the Roberts Vaux Middle School. It's located in Philadelphia's inner city at Twenty-Fourth and Master Streets. All of the eight hundred students lived in the inner city; most were African-American, with a sprinkling of Hispanics.

By the time I entered the main office, as I did every day, the morning's business had already started. Children's voices filled the hallways and the doors opened and closed. Even before I could see her, I heard one of the secretaries, Ms. Stanback, explaining to a parent that the principal didn't meet with people without appointments.

My principal, Harold B. Adams, usually busy with other duties, was in the office, obviously waiting for me. After he greeted me, he said, "Come into my office, Mr. EL."

Something about the way he invited me into his office made me know something was wrong. Why did he want to see me? Neither his face nor his voice gave any indication that he was upset, but I sensed that he was.

Adams had been the principal since 1990. We had worked well together and I respected him. He had been in education for more than forty years, with more than twenty of them as a principal. This was his second stint at Vaux. He had been the assistant principal in the early seventies and was well known in the community as well as in political circles.

What had I done wrong? As I followed him past the secretaries' desks and into his office, I wondered if a parent was sitting in his office after registering a complaint against me. Maybe a student had been hurt. Had I forgotten any forms to fill out or failed to make requests for my chess team?

As soon as he opened the door, I saw the assistant principal, who was already seated. She nodded at me, but she didn't say anything or greet me. Now I knew something was terribly wrong.

"Have you heard anything from FitzSimons?" Adams asked.

"FitzSimons?" That was another inner-city middle school. Confusion must have filled my face. Before coming to Vaux, Adams had been the principal there. "No, I haven't heard anything. Why would I?"

He stared at me, his eyes boring into mine as if he didn't believe me. "You don't know anything about FitzSimons requesting you to become an assistant principal in their school?"

"No, I do not." Now I felt really confused. "Why would I hear from them?"

I was a teacher at Vaux with the title of Small Learning Community Coordinator. My primary duties were handling discipline and assisting teachers with instructional programs. I coordinated assemblies, schedules, parent conferences, and taught two classes. At the time, I was teaching math to sixth graders.

If he had asked, I would have said, "I have no interest in FitzSimons. My goal is to become the assistant principal—right here at Vaux." I had been at this school since 1989—one year before Mr. Adams came back—and I didn't want to leave.

"You are sure about that?"

"I've heard nothing from FitzSimons."

"That is strange, because this morning I received a call that you're to report to FitzSimons as their assistant principal. You're to be there Monday."

Today was Friday. I had never heard of such a swift promotion.

"I don't know anything about it and it sounds peculiar. Why would they call *you*? Why wouldn't they call me first?"

He shrugged. "Steve Bailey asked for you."

Now I felt an even greater surprise. Bailey was the principal at FitzSimons. He, Adams, and I knew each other, but I had never asked Bailey for a position. I had no idea that he was even remotely interested in having me come to his school.

"It's because of the chess," Adams said.

Then I knew what was coming, and for the first time, I smiled.

"You've built a national championship chess program here," Adams said, "and everyone knows that. Now they want to steal you away and take you over to FitzSimons to build a championship program at their school."

I stared directly into Adams's eyes as I said, "You have nothing to worry about because I'm not leaving."

I'm not positive he believed me, because his eyes didn't look reassured.

"There's no way that I would leave these students and leave Vaux at this time to take an assistant principal job at another school."

"It's a promotion to vice principal—"

I shook my head.

"And a raise of twenty thousand dollars."

"Really?" I asked. Immediately I realized what this meant. I would have responsibility—I already had that—but I would also have more authority. And twenty thousand dollars increase in salary could make a lot of difference for me. Then I thought of the children of Vaux Middle School. I couldn't leave them, no matter how much money they offered.

"You have nothing to worry about," I said. I didn't explain my reason for turning down the promotion. It was the first time I had been offered an opportunity to move up the professional ladder, and I wanted to move upward, but not at FitzSimons. I knew, however, that most teachers would have grabbed the opportunity.

I don't know why, but the promotion offer put me on the defensive—as if I had to explain my innocence and lack of knowledge. Something about Adams's tone of voice made me think that he felt I might have orchestrated or been involved with creating the opportunity for the promotion.

"I'm telling you the truth. I haven't received any calls. I haven't received anything in writing. I don't understand how this—"

"All right," he said, dismissing me. "If they call me, I'll let you know."

"I still don't understand," I said as I turned to leave.

"You'll get a phone call or a letter. I was under the impression you already knew."

"I don't know anything," I said. Again I assured him that I had no interest in leaving.

The assistant principal didn't say a word the entire time.

"So if you'll excuse me," I said, and went to my office and began preparing for the school day. I had a math class first and I wanted to look over some material.

Each classroom has a telephone in it, and about an hour later, my phone rang. "It's the chief of staff's office," the secretary said. "Will you hold, please?"

I asked the secretary, Ms. Rochester, to transfer the call to my office. After waiting perhaps a minute, I heard a woman's voice say, "Hello, Salome. This is Marilyn Moller." We had met before but we didn't know each other. She worked with the superintendent of schools.

Before I said more than hello, she told me the reason for her call. "A few minutes ago I spoke with your principal. I want to assure you that Steve Bailey and the staff at Fitzsimons have been extremely happy and quite excited about your coming there as assistant principal. They really want you, but your principal said you aren't interested."

"That's correct—"

"It's normal procedure for us to speak to the teacher directly to find out if that's what you want. Mr. Thomas-EL, this is a good opportunity for you, and I would urge you to take it. You do know, don't you, that you'll also get a raise?"

"I appreciate the opportunity," I said. "I really do. I took a deep breath and said, "At this time I decline the offer."

"May I ask why?"

"I can't leave my students like this. I work with these kids every day. I tell them to start something and then I urge them to stick with what they're doing. They've seen me here every day for almost ten years. What happens if they come in on Monday and I'm not here? You know what they'll say? They'll say, 'He left because of the money.' And I don't want them to think that way."

"Yes, that's quite commendable—"

I had started and I couldn't hold back now. "I've talked to these kids about the importance of education. I've tried to tell them that respect outlasts money. The one thing—if I could have nothing else—the one thing I want is the respect of my students."

"Yes, I understand."

"And another thing is about being a role model." I was nervous as I spoke and realized that I was probably killing my chances for advancement, but I wanted her to know how I felt. "I'm the only male role model many of these kids have. A lot of them have never met their fathers. Men come and go—they're in and out of their lives—but they don't have any that stay. I want them to know at least one black male who is committed to stay."

This time she didn't respond when I paused. Now I was really worried. "I hope that this doesn't affect my future with the school district."

"No, in fact, just the opposite. I have the utmost respect for you for making that choice. Quite frankly, when they hear about this, many, many other principals will want you to work for them because you are dedicated and committed to your children. That's a rare quality. We need more principals like you, Salome."

After I hung up the phone, I sat at my desk and rethought everything that had gone on since I had walked into the school at eight that morning.

Had I made the right decision? Twenty thousand dollars could make a lot of difference to my wife and me. We had bought our first home and hoped to have children. I thought of the things we could do to improve the house. Then I thought of the Vaux students again. My wife would understand my commitment—that was one thing I could always count on—her understanding and support.

Shawnna would realize that I wanted to stay for the sake of the children. I thought of several of them who had had the opportunity to leave Vaux, but they chose to stay. They said right to me that they wanted my guidance and would continue to follow the principles I taught. Parents had respected me and wanted me to help with their children. This was my chance to prove to them that I meant more than words and tossing out slogans. Again, I was reminded that I was the only positive male that many of them had ever interacted with.

"You made the right choice," I said to myself.

By lunchtime, the word about the job promotion had spread all through the school. Somehow everyone—including the children—knew that I had been offered the assistant principal position at FitzSimons. I smile as I think back because two rumors had raced through the building. One was that I was going to leave and the other was that I had turned it down—and somehow the money figure had doubled by the time it made the rounds.

Within the space of an hour, four teachers came to me and said, "We're happy for you, but we're also sad because you're leaving." I dispelled that rumor.

Naively, I assumed everyone would applaud my turning down the offer. To my amazement, two staff people didn't see it that way.

"You're a fool," one said. "You should have taken it."

"You can do more good by becoming an assistant principal," another said. "You sure made a big mistake in turning that down."

"Maybe—"

"And furthermore, you've killed every chance to get asked again. You know that, don't you?"

To both of them I could only say, "I did what I thought was best."

Although those who criticized me were the minority, it hurt that they didn't understand. It made me wonder why they stayed at Vaux if they felt that way.

"We're happy you decided to stay," was the response from the majority.

"I'm glad I chose to teach at this school." Those words came from one of the teachers I had recruited to teach at Vaux. "I'm glad because I know I'm working with someone who is committed to the school and to the community." She pecked me on the cheek. As she pulled back, I saw tears in her eyes.

Yes, I had made the right choice.

During the afternoon, I thought about my days at Vaux. Many afternoons I left with a heavy heart and drove home sad and depressed. Have I made a difference? Does it matter what I do? Every day wasn't like that, of course, but there were enough bad ones to push me to examine myself and my life.

By two o'clock that afternoon, I had started to second-guess myself. If I had accepted the position, I could teach the children to take full advantage of every opportunity presented to them. I'd been trying to instill in them that when others are willing to help you move ahead, let them. Had I really made the right choice?

All afternoon I wavered. A nagging voice inside my head kept whispering and telling me how wrong and how stupid I had been. Despite Marilyn Moller's assurance, that same voice said, "You've blown it. She was being diplomatic. Face it: You'll never get another chance."

That afternoon, as soon as we dismissed the children, I went down to the basement where my children played chess every day.

One of the chess players, a sixth-grader, rushed up to me, her arms outstretched. "Mr. EL! Mr. EL! I'm really, really, really glad that I came to this school, and we're all glad that you're staying."

As those small arms struggled to hug me, I smiled. "I'm glad too," I said.

About seven that Friday evening I locked the school door. Three of the chess players had raced for my car and tumbled inside. Most nights I had to take two or three of them to their homes. As I started walking toward my car and saw the smiles on their faces, I knew I had done the right thing.

For the next six months, I'd think about that decision many times. Yes, I would think about it, but I wouldn't doubt.

I had made the right choice.

I had chosen to stay.

2

Earlier Times, Earlier Choices

I felt strongly that I needed to stay and be a mentor to the inner-city children at Vaux. When I asked myself the reasons, the answers, even to me, began to be complex.

One main reason was because I wanted to give to others what I had never received. Or maybe it's a way of saying I wanted to pass on to others what I did receive. Both of those principles operated in my life.

I never had much of a relationship with my father. Neither did most of the kids I grew up with. We needed those male figures in our lives to guide us, but they weren't there. Not having a dad around, I realized from an early age the impact that situation had on me. I've also learned that we have a drive within us that causes us to search for relationships and love that we didn't experience in childhood.

Unlike a lot of kids I knew, I didn't get into much trouble; however, I saw kids who did. For them, the father figures were gang members or drug dealers. All of us were open, eager, and responsive to anyone who reached out to us. Some kids went down the wrong path because bad people came into their lives and showed them attention.

Although I didn't get into trouble, I did miss a lot of the normal, middle-class things that many kids experience with their fathers. My dad wasn't there to teach me to shoot a jump shot, hit a baseball, catch a football, or ride a bike.

I learned how to do those things, but not from him. At times, like most of the kids in our neighborhood, I felt abandoned. Unwanted. Unloved.

I do have one special memory. My maternal grandmother lived in Harlem in New York City and we went there every summer. Dad would pull up at the house, honk the horn, and we'd all rush outside. Somehow our family loaded everything into one station wagon—I'm not sure how we did it, but all ten of us got inside along with all of our clothes. That's the one thing I remember Dad doing—driving us from Philadelphia to New York City every summer. After we returned, it might be weeks or months before we saw Dad again.

Other than our annual trip to New York City, I don't remember that Dad was involved in anything else. He never attended any of my graduations. Not once did he ever show up at a basketball game when I played. When I acted in school plays, I'd peer at the audience, hoping that he'd show up and surprise me. He never came to any of them.

No matter what I accomplished, Dad never seemed to be a part of it; and he certainly wasn't there when I celebrated. He didn't even come to my wedding!

Sure it hurt. I've tried to hide it or pretend it didn't. All kids want their daddy's approval—or at least his appearance at the things that mean the most in their lives. Dad was always absent.

When he died in 1995, I cried—and I must have cried for several hours.

I had never expressed how I felt to him or to anyone else. But at the funeral, I couldn't hold back. While he was still alive, there had always been the possibility of developing a relationship. After he died in a car accident, I had to face reality: We would never develop the relationship I had longed for.

Too many of us grow up like that. Fortunately for me, three strong, caring female teachers—Mrs. Petit, Mrs. Porter, and Mrs. Pincus—and my mother strongly influenced me, and they took away part of the sadness of not having a father around. Even though I resisted and rebelled sometimes, I wouldn't be where I am today without those women.

I remember these details, because this is what shaped me. Somewhere in my teens or early twenties—and I can't pin this down to a specific moment or event—I decided that, as much as possible, I'd become a positive male figure for other black kids.

My twin brother Elihu (we've always called him Eli) took the lack of a strong father figure harder than I did. Of the eight of us, Eli had been the closest to Daddy. When Daddy didn't come to special occasions at school or do anything for our birthdays, it affected Eli the worst. Maybe he was a more sensitive kid. I know that whenever my father didn't show up for special occasions at school, he was the one who felt hurt the most. Sometimes he would cry.

I felt it; I think we all felt it, but I never said anything. I grew up accepting that things never bothered my dad. I accepted it. My father, William Thomas, was a truck driver for a sanitation company. And as a part-time job he drove cars for a leasing company. He died long after we were grown. I'm sorry that I never really knew him or felt close to him the way we kids wanted to.

My mother tried to be both parents to us—which was impossible, but she tried. I know that when I needed anything, she was the one I went to.

I dedicated myself to being there for the kids who had absent fathers or no fathers. Even when I was a teenager, it amazed me how many of my friends had no strong male person in their lives. I've tried to be that kind of father—by being the best teacher and example I can be, but most of all helping kids know that I care about them.

I've tried to show that kind of caring in simple ways. I've driven more than a hundred miles to pick up a college student because his father wouldn't. As a teacher and principal, whenever children stay late after school, I make sure they get home safely.

My mother gave birth to Eli on October 21, 1964, at Philadelphia General Hospital. She didn't know she was having twins and neither did the doctor. In the delivery room, she had one son born. Then they wheeled her gurney into the recovery room.

Mom had already had five babies, so this was nothing new to her. But something didn't feel quite right.

"Something's a little funny about this," she said to the nurse. "I feel—like I'm having another baby."

The nurse examined her more closely and discovered she did have another baby. So I'm a twin, born about five minutes later than Eli. As I tell the story, I sometimes add, "They almost left me behind."

I was the seventh child. Beginning with Jonathan the oldest, then came George, Winifred, Carol, William, Eli, me, and finally the baby, born one year after me. His name is Ravanna, but I never remember calling him anything but Ray.

Like most people who try to remember their earliest childhood, I have only fragments to draw from. I remember that we lived in the toughest part of the inner city of Philadelphia during my earliest years in the Diamond Street Projects. Maybe I heard the stories so often from my mom and my siblings, I think I remember. Mom says we moved to North Nineteenth Street and York Street later.

The only vivid memory I have is that our father wasn't with

us and I realized my parents had separated. At times Dad did come around—but not often—and he never stayed long. Our situation wasn't all that different from our friends, but I knew something wasn't quite right about it.

Even when I was young, I appreciated all the hard work Mom did for us. She worked in the outpatient clinic at Temple Hospital.

By the time I started school at Pratt-Arnold Elementary School, my older siblings and my mother remember me as a smart-mouthed kid who knew the answer to every question— or thought he did.

I do remember the other kids running to the house and yelling to Mom, "You need to get your son to come in the house because he's out there trying to teach everybody. He talks like he knows everything."

Mom says they called me the news reporter—probably the nicest name—and some others like "Know-it-all," "Smarty-Arty," and "Teacher's Pet."

That's probably the way I handled not having a dad around. As an adult looking back, I realize that I was trying to prove to everyone that I was worthwhile. A lot of kids around, including me, had very low self-esteem and we displayed it in all kinds of ways. Mine was sounding like someone who knew things. Most of the time I made up answers. Apparently, however, I was good enough that the neighborhood kids thought I knew what I was talking about.

In school was where I decided to shine. My teachers liked me and they regularly told me how smart I was. I'd hear my teachers talk kindly to my mother about us. My brothers and sisters were "cute" or "nice" or "good students." When they mentioned me, it was "He's such a smart little boy."

Those words didn't mean much to me. Maybe I knew it or maybe because I'd been called the news reporter for so long, I thought I had everyone fooled into thinking I was smart. I do know that all my teachers liked me and I didn't have any trouble understanding or doing the schoolwork. A couple of my siblings would have difficulty and they'd resent my knowing answers or trying to explain to them—and they were older—how to do a math problem. I caught on to things easily, especially math. I even helped my older brothers and friends with their homework. It was something I understood and didn't have to work hard at.

When I was nine or ten, I helped my brother George with his paper route, which was a Sunday only delivery for the *Philadelphia Inquirer*. He was about sixteen at the time, and he got tired of delivering newspapers—I think he was getting more interested in girls than in working—so he turned his route over to me.

I kept delivering those papers until I was at least seventeen. I didn't stop delivering until I went away to college. My younger brother Ray got his own paper route, so I didn't have anyone to turn mine over to.

I had a cart, which we kept in our backyard. Early every Sunday morning, I'd fill the cart and deliver the *Inquirer* from door to door. When they got to be teenagers, most of the kids in our neighborhood didn't want to be known as paperboys—they wanted to focus on girls as my older brother had done. I didn't like the title either, but I couldn't give up the route. It was the time to date, and several girls wouldn't go out with me because I was a paperboy—somehow that sounded as if I wasn't old enough for girls. So why did I stay with the newspaper route so long? That's easy to answer—the customers.

Between helping my brother and carrying my own route, I was a paperboy for ten years. I never missed one Sunday in all those years. My customers counted on me. Many of them were old ladies who couldn't get out to the store and some of them never left the house. Sunday morning was a big event and they waited for that delivery to get there before eight o'clock. I took a lot of pride in that. No matter what kind of weather, whether rain, snow, sleet, hail, I was on the streets with my cart and I made sure I delivered those papers.

A few times the delivery truck didn't get the paper to me on time and I felt so sorry for those old women. When that happened—and it sounds a little silly—I went to the corner store. For some reason they got their papers even if the delivery boys didn't. Then I'd buy two dozen papers for those elderly women and delivered them right to their front doors.

At Christmastime, just about every elderly woman on my route gave me a gift of ten dollars or more because of my faithfulness. That kind of recognition and reward taught me invaluable lessons during my growing up years. I learned a valuable work ethic. But that also gave me a strong sense of community—of belonging and having a vital part to play in my own neighborhood. I learned about responsibility. If I didn't deliver their papers, they wouldn't get them.

In late 1999, the *Philadelphia Daily News* ran an article about me and about my standing in the community. A few days later, they printed a letter from one of those elderly women, Dorsha Mason, and I didn't even know she was still alive. She wrote to the paper and told them I was her former paperboy and how faithful I had been in delivering her paper.

After I read that letter, I felt so touched I went by to see her. She was bedridden by then, but she still read her paper every day.

"I'm so proud of you, Salome," she said. "I've always been proud of you. I knew you'd amount to something, and you proved me right."

Our family had an interesting religious background.

My mother was a Christian when she was growing up, but she became disenchanted with the way the church failed to address several critical social issues in the late 1950s and 1960s. By contrast, Black Muslim leaders were talking about empowerment and dealing with issues people faced every day such as poverty and racial discrimination. I didn't realize it as a child, but my father was mentally and physically abusive to my mother and to us kids. It was only after Mom embraced Islam that she was able to free herself from him and his hold over her.

Although she never left the church, Mom started to study Islam. As she learned more about her cultural history, she changed her name. She had been Doris Jenkins before she married my father. She changed her name to Amena ("mother of the faithful") Hotep ("peace"). She also added EL—("God is with us") and spelled it with both capital letters—to our surname of Thomas to become Amena Hotep Thomas-EL. Dad never embraced Islam and didn't add EL to his name. In fact, the few times he mentioned Islam, it was always with anger—I think he resented the changes in my mother.

I was born while my mother was heavily involved in the Muslim faith. My dad never did accept EL on the end of his name because he remained a Christian.

That means I had a rather diverse religious upbringing. Mom raised us with Muslim beliefs during my early years and we went to the mosque every week on Friday. Because she didn't leave the church, she took us to activities at Bethel Presbyterian Church, located on the corner of the block where we lived.

The people at Bethel, including the pastor, Reverend McClain, never became as political as the Muslims, but they played a large role in the community. That church made me feel I belonged, and I knew they wanted to help us as much as possible.

As I got older, Mom took us to services at Bethel Presbyterian Church. Although she followed many Muslim principles, we were frequently involved in activities at Bethel Church. Mom was there to help in the bazaars or anything that she could do.

My brothers and I liked Bethel because of the sports activities they offered, such as basketball. During the summer, we seemed to be at the church just about every day. The leaders would pray with us, sometimes give little talks with a Bible study, and then they'd let us play. After school, it was the place to hang out and play stickball. Sometimes a bunch of us would go and sit and shoot the breeze on the church steps on York Street.

My mother eventually drifted away from Islam, although she kept the Muslim name and deeply respects their teachings. I have that sense of respect as well.

In one sense I've always been part of the church. Although it didn't become a matter of true, inner faith until after I was married, I respected the teachings of the church.

One of my most vivid memories of my teachers was my third-grade teacher, Mrs. Pettit. She liked me a lot and was one of those who told me regularly how smart I was. What I remember most about her was during lunch—we had a free-lunch program. As I remember it, she made sure I had extra food. Although I can't recall the details, I do recall being in a room with Mrs. Pettit, and the other kids would be outside. She'd go out and come back with extra juice for me. Sometimes she'd bring me crackers or cookies. Maybe she felt sorry for me. Or maybe it was her way to reward me for being a good student. I never knew.

I know that I've never forgotten her. After I became a teacher, I tried to locate her, but I never did. She stands out as the first teacher who was important to me. She was important because she cared. I've forgotten the lessons we had in third grade, but I haven't forgotten her kindness. Sometimes I think maybe I was a little kid who needed someone—anyone—to reach out to him and show him special attention. Mrs. Petit, a white teacher, made me believe that I was important. She was the first person who did that for me.

When I entered fourth grade, my teacher was Mrs. Porter. I assume Mrs. Pettit had talked about me, because before the first week of school was over, Mrs. Porter also told me how smart I was.

I don't mean to minimize those words, but I think I had been hearing them from so many people that they didn't mean much. So I was smart. So what? The one negative thing about all of that is that at times I felt alienated from my siblings. I loved them, but I felt different, even at times that I didn't belong.

Mrs. Porter got me involved in a school drama group. We put on plays at school and at local colleges, and I always seemed to have a large role, maybe even the largest. I remember that when I performed, I loved it and appreciated it when everyone applauded at the end.

Fourth grade, although I didn't realize it then, was a transition for me. Mrs. Porter did more than tell me I was smart. "You need to go to a different school—a school where you can get the challenges you need from other students," she said.

It's hard to remember how I felt about that—probably more scared than anything else. I liked Pratt-Arnold School and I had a lot of friends there, so I didn't have much interest in changing schools.

When Mrs. Porter gave written assignments, I finished before anyone else. I understood the material easily and sometimes I got a little bored and irritated when some of the kids didn't understand or she'd have to explain the same problem two or three times.

"You have something a lot of other people in our community don't have," Mrs. Porter said to me. "I don't want to see that wasted."

So I listened. I liked believing I was smart, but I wasn't sure about another school.

"You belong at the Julia R. Masterman School—a demonstration school."

Sure, I'd heard of Masterman School, but that didn't mean anything to me. "What's a demonstration school?" I asked.

"It's a school for people who have demonstrated unique ability—for those who are mentally gifted. Smart. Like you. You see, Salome, if you go to Masterman, you'll meet other students who are as bright as you and they'll challenge you. You won't always be the first one finished or have the best grade."

She wanted me to start there in fifth grade. Then she explained what I had to do—something about tests and getting recommended from her and from the principal. She wanted me to get the application in so that I could start fifth grade there.

"The first thing for you to do is to go home and speak with your mother about this."

I knew Mom would want me to go if it was an opportunity for me, but I wasn't sure what I wanted to do. "Will my brothers and sisters be attending this school?"

"No, they will not," she said. "This is a school for people with special skills. You have outstanding ability, and that is why I believe you need to attend. You'll get the opportunities and challenges you need."

"Yes, ma'am," I said, but I wasn't interested in attending a school that my other brothers and sisters couldn't attend.

Instead of going home and telling Mom, I talked about it to my friends. They gave me the kind of answers I wanted to hear.

"You don't want to go to a different school," one said.

"Those kids carry weapons right into the classroom. They're all white and they don't like black kids," said another.

"Man, they don't want you to go out of your neighborhood," someone said. "Don't you know they think you're not good enough?"

It didn't occur to me to ask Mrs. Porter if those stories were true. It also didn't occur to me to ask my friends how they knew all about Masterman School and I didn't know any of that.

As far as I was concerned, I'd stay at Pratt-Arnold for fifth grade. But I didn't know how to deal with the persistence of Mrs. Porter.

One afternoon I had hardly walked inside the door when my mother called out, "Salome! Salome! You come right here!"

From that tone of voice, I knew I had done something wrong. Slowly I walked into the room.

"This thing about Masterman School. Why didn't you tell me about it? How come I had to find out from your teacher? She said she told you to tell me."

"I wasn't interested." I hung my head as I answered her.

"You weren't interested? Salome Thomas-EL, do you have any idea what she is offering you? It is a special opportunity— and you're the only one in the family to get a chance like that—an opportunity to improve yourself—and you're not interested?"

"But—but it means going to a different school in a different neighborhood. I won't have any friends there."

"Then you can make new friends."

"If it's a school that's good enough for me, but it's not good enough for my brothers and sisters—well, I'm just not interested."

"You don't know what you're saying. You have a wonderful opportunity—a chance for a better education. This is a chance for you to go out and learn some new things, meet new people and do different things and this is something you should take advantage of."

I nodded to my mother and promised I'd talk with Mrs. Porter. The next day I told her that I had talked with my mother. "She says it's okay, but I still don't want to go there."

Mrs. Porter wouldn't take no for an answer. When I tried to show indifference, she put her hands on my shoulders. "Now you listen to me, Mr. Thomas-EL. You *are* going to Masterman. This is the best thing that could happen to you. Your mom wants you to go, so you're going to this school."

Our eyes locked and I knew I had lost.

"Okay, then, what's the next step?" I asked, still sure I didn't want to go.

"You have to take what we call the Iowa Test—it's an achievement test. If you show that you are capable of doing work at least two grade levels above what you're doing now, that will get you in."

Then I figured out what to do. If I didn't do well on the test, I wouldn't get into Masterman. So I'd mark a lot of wrong answers and that way I could keep on going to school with my brothers and sisters. Everything would be fine. I had no more worries.

A week later, Mrs. Porter came to me and said, "I've got some news for you. All students in our school are required to take the CAT—the California Achievement Tests."

"I've already taken that."

"Yes, you have and your scores were so high on the CAT that you don't have to take the Iowa test to get into the Masterman School. You're in."

"I—I don't understand—" I stammered. She was interfering with my plan.

"It's quite simple. You don't have to take the test. You're in. I've already contacted them and you've been accepted. Congratulations. In September you will become a student at Masterman Demonstration School."

I honestly don't remember my reaction—whether I was angry or disappointed. Maybe a little of both. I liked Mrs. Porter a lot and didn't want to hurt her feelings, so I suppose I smiled and thanked her.

Part of me felt good because going to Masterman meant that I was going to be different from everybody else in our family or neighborhood. When the kids teased me about knowing everything, this would now validate me. Maybe it made me feel important.

Yet I felt sad because I'd be riding on a bus and going to school in the direction opposite of my brothers and sisters. Coming from a large family and a poor one at that, we had learned to stick together and to share, even though we sometimes fought among ourselves. We were always there for each other when outsiders gave us any trouble.

My siblings were supportive of me and didn't seem to resent my going away. They asked questions about the school before I went. After I enrolled, they'd keep asking me what it was like going to school with white and Asian kids.

Even at that time they were very supportive. They kept asking me questions about my new school, my new friends, because now I was going to school with people from different parts of the city.

Home, neighborhood, Bethel Church, and Pratt-Arnold School were my world. I didn't know that a larger world existed.

Because this was the only life I knew, I was scared to leave and go to Masterman.

3

The Thrill of Teaching

"What am I doing here at Masterman Demonstration School?" I asked myself that question every day for at least the first week. At my old school I had been top kid in the class and everyone told me how smart I was.

I didn't feel smart at Masterman. A few times when the teachers asked questions, I didn't know the answer—that had rarely happened to me before. Or now when I did know the answer, instead of being the only kid who raised his hand, I'd see six or seven other hands go up.

No longer did I get singled out and praised every day. No teacher ever said, "Now, Salome, you sit still and let someone else answer." In fact, most of the kids knew more than I did. Everyone had been a top kid in his or her class or school. Every one of us was bright. For the first time, I sat in a classroom where several students were smarter than I was. That was all new to me.

Kids in our neighborhood attended one of three different elementary schools. From our entire neighborhood I met four other kids—only four—who also went to Masterman. Three of us were in the same grade. I suppose they had it as hard as I did to go from being the smartest kid in the class to just another student.

The day would come when I'd appreciate the fact that I wasn't much different from a lot of others, but it was still a hard adjustment then. For several weeks, I felt totally alone in the class and ignored by everyone. They probably didn't ignore me, but I would have magnified even the most unintentional slight.

I never felt I was as good as many of my peers, or that I belonged there, and I never felt that I was part of the school. A lot of those feelings may have come because I couldn't leave behind my inner-city thinking and friendships. The kids I knew and liked the most were still back in the inner city.

Each school day, as they went in one direction, I took the bus and went a different way. By my second year at Masterman, I felt strange. I didn't feel comfortable at Masterman, and yet I no longer belonged with my old friends.

In the neighborhood, we didn't talk about it. I was getting a better education at Masterman—I realized that—although that wasn't important to me then.

Yes, I had a tough adjustment, but I made it. Some days, I'd beg God to let me go back to Pratt-Arnold, but I knew I'd disappoint Mom and Mrs. Porter. So I'd keep on trying.

I stayed at Masterman from fifth through ninth grades, and those five years of trying paid off. (Masterman now graduates students from high school, but they added those grades the year I left.)

I wasn't ever the top kid in the school. No matter what subject I studied, someone was better or quicker or brighter. Once I had accepted that, I did fine. In fact, I became popular by becoming the class clown, and that worked for me. I'd get the others laughing. When I did that, no one else could compete with me. I was also a natural athlete and popular in the gym, and that helped ease my loneliness.

Some may not understand, but coming from a family of eight kids and being thrust into a school where most of the students were "only" children or had only one or two siblings, I felt different. They obviously came from better neighborhoods and nicer houses. They didn't live in the projects or in low-income housing like I did.

Not that I resented that they had better clothes or a nicer house, because I didn't. It was more that I felt different, sometimes isolated. When they'd talk about where they went or activities they had participated in, I remained silent. Those weren't things our family could have afforded, and not the kind of places I would have been interested in going to.

Because I felt inferior—and it was my own hang-up—I think that affected my grades and study habits. Convinced I wasn't as good as the others, I didn't try as hard, and consequently, I didn't achieve what I was capable of achieving. That was no one's fault but my own.

My world expanded at Masterman. Eventually I was able to see that I was quite intelligent—I was gifted—but I wasn't special. God had given me a good mind the same way we get any of our abilities. As I increasingly would learn, being gifted also carries responsibilities.

Another new experience for me was Mr. Grillet. He had this thing about learning the capitals of all fifty states. No student passed his class without being able to recite them. I'm not sure why, but I thought that was a great idea. Maybe it was because it took concerted effort for anyone to learn them. Not only did I memorize the capitals—and I can recite them today—but after I began to teach, I held my students to the same standard.

When I first went to Masterman, I wasn't glad Grillet was my teacher and I resented the way he pushed me so hard. Of course, I needed that kind of pushing, but I still didn't like it. No one had demanded more of me before. I mean, until then I had been the best in the class. Then I had a teacher who kept saying, "You can do better." It was a new experience for me.

It wasn't all academics with Mr. Grillet either. He cared about me—and I suppose he cared about all the students. I can't speak for any of them, but after I had been there maybe a month, I knew I could talk to him about anything that bothered me. He listened. He told me what I needed to know and advised me when I needed guidance.

I'll tell you the best memory I have of Mr. Grillet. My first year as a teacher in the inner city, he visited me. He smiled, held out his hand, and shook mine. "Salome, I'm proud of you and I'm pleased you became a teacher."

Those were simple words, and yet they remain one of the highest compliments I've ever received.

He died shortly after that and I've thought many times what a sad loss it was for the children in Philadelphia. I'm sure he touched many other lives besides mine.

Despite my adjustment problems, Masterman was a good experience for me. The teachers and administrators probably considered me a discipline problem. I didn't conform easily, and I was physically active. I couldn't seem to sit around and work in silence. I had to be doing something all the time.

Masterman wasn't used to kids like me. They had an outstanding reputation for preparing their students to go on to high school and into top-quality colleges. Most of them had parents who pushed them toward scholastic excellence and constantly reminded them that they wouldn't get into the top universities unless they applied themselves.

Over the years, I've wondered if they shook their heads and

questioned if they'd made a mistake in admitting me. Maybe I was too hard on myself back then, but I still wonder if any of them would have predicted that I'd make the dean's list in college.

School wasn't that important to me then. My awareness would come later.

In 1979, I graduated from ninth grade. Masterman was what we call a feeder school for the top high schools in Philadelphia. My last year at Masterman was the first year they had a high school class. For the new class, they accepted only the students with the best grades. My grades weren't very high—so obviously I wasn't the type of student who would qualify for their high school.

Maybe I felt some disappointment, but I was glad not to be chosen. The main reason is that I was an athlete and they didn't have much of a sports program. They had swimming and gymnastics, and although I participated, I never enjoyed either the way I did basketball.

Before going there I had played basketball and still played in the neighborhood recreation leagues. Masterman, being an academic school, had only an intramural basketball program.

With no basketball team, I sure missed the competition. I really wanted to play basketball. I was at that age when the top basketball stars such as Kareem Abdul Jabbar and Julius Erving had emerged, and they inspired me to dream of becoming a big-name basketball player like them. But then, most of the other guys who played basketball with me had the same dreams. For many of us, it would be our only way out of the inner city.

While I attended Masterman, my twin, Eli, and my younger brother Ray went to Edward Gillespie Junior High, where they had several interscholastic sports teams. They played on the basketball team and constantly told me about all their games. I hated it that I couldn't play, especially when they competed against our friends at other schools.

Although I was one of the smart kids in my neighborhood, my real sense of success had come on the playground and in recreation leagues. I was considered one of the best basketball players in the neighborhood. I played on several championship teams but never had that opportunity in school.

I learned a lot at Masterman and benefited more than anything from the social atmosphere—the expanded world. In the inner city I had lived inside a vacuum. Except for our summer trips to New York City, I hadn't traveled out of state, and neither had any of my friends. We lived in such an insular society, and being at Masterman opened my eyes to a bigger community.

By going to school there, I realized not only that I had entered another world, but I saw people who looked and spoke differently. My world had been almost exclusively black except for a few white teachers. Now my horizons expanded. White kids got into trouble just like we did. I met Hispanics and Asians at school. All the white students were not brighter than I was. Quite a few black, Asian, and Hispanic kids stood right at the top of the class.

I saw that the outside world wasn't paradise or trouble free. Those kids came from less-than-perfect families and some of them had terrible problems—different from ours in the inner city, but problems just the same.

Racial prejudice? Sure, there was some of that. A few students didn't speak to me when I entered fifth grade; they still didn't speak to me when I finished ninth. They made it clear that as far as they were concerned, I didn't belong there. And they weren't prejudiced against me as an individual. They were opposed to any minorities being at Masterman. Those of us who were the minorities knew that.

Not that we talked about it, because we didn't. It was simply one of the things we accepted. At one time, the school had been all white and I'm sure that as they transitioned, a lot of parents objected and their kids picked up the prejudicial attitudes. But I also want to say that there were only a few who snubbed us. Most of them seemed to accept us, and to them I was Salome, just another classmate. One of my best friends from Masterman, Robert Powlen, teaches at Bartram High School, one of the toughest in our district.

I did get a good education at Masterman, even though I didn't stand out academically. I don't think I realized how good the education had been until after I entered college. Masterman had given me a lot of preparation in many ways. I was a little slow to appreciate it.

In ninth grade we began what we called our high school selection process. That is, we had to make decisions on which high school we wanted to attend. One thing all of us knew was that all the high schools wanted Masterman graduates. Most of my classmates chose Central, one of the best high schools in the state, or they went to the equally competitive Girls High. The Philadelphia Magnet Programs all wanted us. All of this meant we had choices we could make and we didn't automatically go to our neighborhood school.

One school did interest me—and it was the only one. In Philadelphia, we had a creative and performing arts high school. That's where I wanted to go and it was the only school to which I applied. It seemed a natural to me. Ever since those plays I had done in Mrs. Porter's classroom, I had acted or been involved in drama. I was in all the Masterman plays.

"What if they don't accept you?" Mr. Grillet asked. He wanted me to go to Central High School and told me so. "You'll do well there."

"No! I want to go to the High School for the Creative and Performing Arts (CAPA)."

"If they don't accept you—then what?"

"I'll go to Gratz with my brothers." What I didn't say was, "Then I'll become a big basketball star." It would be the idyllic life. So, whichever school I attended, I'd be fine.

CAPA contacted me to come in for an audition. They didn't have an athletic program either, but I was willing to sacrifice that part if I could get into a school where I could major in drama and acting.

During my audition I read a monologue provided by the school. I felt I had done well in the audition. "I'm going to Performing Arts School," I said to myself over and over.

I felt absolutely confident that I'd get selected.

Three weeks after my audition I received a letter. "You are on our waiting list because of racial balance," were the actual words. They were set up so that they could accept only a certain number of African Americans. ". . . We will notify you as soon as there is an opening . . ."

That hurt. Maybe it wasn't a rejection, but I had been so sure I would be accepted. No one had told me about racial balance.

"I thought it depended on talent alone," I said to Mr. Grillet.

He sympathized, but both of us knew there was nothing to do. I could apply to Central or I could go to Simon Gratz High School.

"I'm not going to be on any waiting list," I told him. That was my anger speaking, but I had made up my mind. Gratz is in North Philadelphia. William, my older brother by two years, was a senior; I'd be in the same classes with Eli, and my baby brother. Ravanna would follow me in a year. By the time I was in eleventh grade, four of us would have been there. I liked that idea a lot.

As far as my mother and Mr. Grillet were concerned, I was

still on the waiting list at Performing Arts. I never did receive a letter officially removing me from the waiting list.

In the fall of 1979, I enrolled at Simon Gratz. I didn't tell anyone that I had been at Masterman. I wasn't ashamed of it, but I knew it wouldn't be cool to mention it to the kids I would now be going to school with. In my first four years of school I'd had enough teasing and mean remarks about the news reporter and knowing everything. I didn't want that to happen again.

Despite my disappointment at not getting into Performing Arts School, I was glad to go to Gratz. I remember thinking that this was a chance to start over. I didn't care if anyone knew where I'd attended junior high school. Sure, the information was on my records, but as I realized, no one paid any attention.

How did I know that? They placed me in classes that were extremely easy. In algebra class the teacher would assign us a set of problems to do in class. I'd be finished in five minutes and the other kids would spend at least twice that long. It was the same story for me in biology, English, and any other subject. The classes were easy—too easy, because I'd already had most of the same material at least a year earlier at Masterman. Obviously, I was getting the best grades in the class—and I did like that.

But I got bored sitting in the classroom, listening to teachers going over material I already knew. Too often it felt like Pratt-Arnold School revisited—my hand went up for just about every question and I'd have the right answer.

William and I had some of the same teachers. In the middle of the second week, he punched me. "You've got to stop answering all those questions in class."

"Hey, I know the answers, so—"

"Some of the other guys hate you. They're jealous and they're saying to me all the time, 'That Salome thinks he's pretty smart, doesn't he? Thinks he's better than the rest of us.' I've gotten word that some of the kids are going to beat you up after school because you're too smart and you're answering too many questions."

That scared me and I didn't know what to do. I stopped volunteering all the time. If a teacher called on me, I'd have the answer, but I tried to look bored or uncaring. In reality, I felt miserable.

I wanted to fit in—I wanted to belong at Gratz in a way that I hadn't belonged at any other school. Sometimes I wouldn't do my homework and I'd get reprimanded for it. Then I'd see guys snickering over that. It took a while but I soon developed a reputation as a guy who didn't care about school.

That must have worked. No one ever beat me up.

If it hadn't been for Mrs. Smithey, I would have spent all three years that way at Gratz.

4

A Teacher Emerges

About six weeks after school started in tenth grade, Mrs. Smithey asked me to stay for a minute after class. Like all kids who get asked to stay after school, I wondered what I had done wrong. Or maybe I was wondering what I had gotten caught at.

"You're an extremely bright boy," she said. She was a stern, no-nonsense teacher who had taught for many years. She told me how she appreciated me and my quick responses.

"Thank you," I said, relieved to know I wasn't in trouble.

She talked several minutes about my grades and what a fine student I was. "I hope you'll apply yourself a little more, Salome. You could do better, couldn't you?

"Yes, ma'am," I said.

Just as I got up and started to leave the classroom, she asked, "By the way, what school did you come from?"

"I came from Masterman."

"*From Masterman?* No wonder! But I don't think anyone here at Gratz knows that—"

"It was in my records and—"

"You don't belong in these classes. If you came from Masterman, you should be in a special program that we have in this school—the Star Program. Do you know about it?"

I shook my head. No one had ever mentioned that to me.

"It's for bright students like you. The classes are taught by the best teachers at Gratz and the curriculum is far more challenging."

I liked that idea. I was bored in the classes and I didn't like putting on the act all the time. And frankly, I enjoyed having people know I was smart.

"The students in the Star Program are definitely planning to go on to college. I assume you are as well."

Before I could reply, Miss Smithey said, "It would be a terrible shame, Salome, if you didn't. You are the kind of student we need to encourage and you're the kind who would benefit the most."

"Oh, yes, ma'am, I'm definitely going to college." That wasn't true, but I could see from her eyes and her interest that was the answer she wanted to hear.

At Masterman we talked about college all the time. There they *assume* every student will go on to college. No one ever said it, but they left the impression that we would be wasting our lives if we didn't go to college—it wasn't ever the question of "Will you go?" The question was "Which college are you going to apply to?"

I smiled as I thought about it. That question came up all the time when I'd talk to the kids at Masterman. I got so tired of hearing names like Yale, Harvard, and Princeton, so I began to play a game. Whenever anyone asked, I'd mention whatever college basketball team name popped into my head.

Part of me certainly wanted to go on, but I didn't have any plans. No one in my family had ever gone to college—or even talked about it. I had wanted to be an actor. Or an athlete. They didn't have to attend college.

"It's settled then," Miss Smithy said. "I'll recommend you for the Star Program." She smiled and I smiled back.

It felt good to be recognized for being smart. It also felt good to know that she wanted to help me.

The next day, I received word to report to the office. One of the secretaries talked to me about which classes I wanted to take. Before ten o'clock that morning I had enrolled in the Star Program.

Within minutes of sitting in my first class, I knew I belonged, and this was where I should be. These were kids from the inner city like me. We had the same kind of backgrounds and similar values. They were smart too and they knew what it was like to stand out and be hated for being smart.

For the first time since I had left Pratt-Arnold School, I felt at home. I liked the classes—in fact, I could hardly wait to get to school every morning. The teachers challenged me. I didn't feel inferior or unwanted. Immediately, my grades went up because now I had something to work for. I was at the top of the class, but that didn't seem quite as important as it had before. I was learning, and I loved being in a classroom.

During my sophomore year at Gratz, I took the PSAT—the pre-SAT test. It was just a test and I didn't think much about it before or afterward.

A few weeks later, one of the teachers stopped me in the hall-way. "Congratulations," she said.

"For what?"

"Your score on the PSAT test."

I didn't know what she was talking about.

"You don't know? Most of the teachers have been talking about it. You made the highest score we've ever had at Gratz!"

"Is that right?" I said, trying to downplay it as though it was no big deal. But it was. My heart beat rapidly and I felt such a sense of elation. This was a level of success I hadn't experienced before. And I didn't have to compete with anyone or try to prove how smart I was. I felt good that day. I had brought honor to myself and to my family. And I had done it in my own neighborhood.

It wasn't a thing that anyone ever talked about—and most of the kids I hung out with wouldn't have cared. In fact, I don't think any of the other students knew about my score.

I told my mother and my brothers, of course. Although my brothers never scored high academically, they didn't seem to resent me. I think they were happy for me. Of course, they wouldn't tell their friends. They didn't want that bad image hung on them for having a smart brother.

I had talked to Mrs. Smithey and thanked her for getting me into the Star Program.

"You have the potential to be a great student," she said. "You can also be an outstanding leader in your community."

Her words never failed to encourage me. We talked often because she lived in the same condominium building with Julius Erving, and I was a big 76ers fan. I liked asking her if she had seen him and every detail I could find out about him.

Miss Smithey wasn't the only one who had called me bright at Gratz. Once I got into the Star Program, other teachers began to call me smart and intelligent. At Masterman, I was always conscious that I sat next to kids who were smarter than I was. If I hadn't known it, most of them were ready to tell me—often. Later I realized they studied and applied themselves more. This was a great lesson for me.

I personally saw some obsessing about grades or achievement there, and maybe that's inevitable in that kind of school. Or maybe it was because I felt self-conscious and was never sure I belonged. In my mind, I may have exaggerated the quest for grades to justify my not working harder.

At times, I felt I wasn't smart enough to be there among all those bright students. In the regular classes at Gratz, I faced resentment for being smart. But now—at last—I was with inner-city kids who were on my level. They accepted me and I didn't feel an intense rivalry among us. Yes, I liked being at Gratz.

I outshone a lot of them, and when I did, I got attention from teachers. Yes, I liked getting that attention. I also got approval from other students—something new to me—and something I needed.

I did make the varsity basketball team as a tenth grader. And then I realized that sports weren't the most important things in my life anymore. School had become fun and I felt challenged to read, to think, to explore new ideas.

The best part of being in the Star Program was tenth-grade English, and the teacher was Marsha Pincus. A young, energetic teacher, she believed we all could learn. She frequently asked about our families and home life. It was clear that she was smart and well respected, and she cared for her students. She taught two students about playwriting who later became NBA All-Star millionaires. One of them, Aaron McKie, was a student at Gratz when I began my teaching career. Later in college, he majored in education.

Immediately, I realized Mrs. Pincus was the kind of teacher that liked kids who would think and not throw back standardized answers. She often asked hard questions and encouraged us not to give simplistic responses. She forced me to think deeply and not repeat the rote answers. As much as I learned at Masterman—and I did learn a great deal there—I had never connected with any teacher before the way I did with her. I loved Mr. Grillet, but Mrs. Pincus challenged me even more than he did. I didn't think that was possible.

I'll always be grateful to God for Mrs. Pincus because she opened up the world of literature to me. She made learning fun, and I wanted to understand more and to read classic literature. We'd had a little Shakespeare and Chaucer at Masterman, but not the way she taught it. Before I had learned information;

now I understood what those writers were saying. It began to make sense why they were the great classic writers. S. E. Hinton, Richard Wright, J. D. Salinger, and Maya Angelou were all names I now knew and had read.

There was more than her teaching. I don't remember most of the specific conversations, but I knew she had high hopes for me. On several occasions, she talked to me about going to college.

"Yes, ma'am, I'll think about it," I often said. But she wouldn't let me get away with an evasive answer like that.

"Think what a difference you can make," she said once. "And this isn't just to make a difference for yourself, Salome. You could do so much for your community. You have a *gift*. Use that gift. You can help to make the inner city a better place."

There's someone else who influenced me at Gratz. I must mention Dr. Deidre Farmbry. Today she is our district's chief academic officer, but I remember her vividly from my days at Gratz. Although she was my teacher only a short while during my days, she was head of the English Department. She was the one who approved my moving into the Star Program.

During the period I knew her at the school, she encouraged me as a student and mentored me as a teacher. Later, she was one of the first people to urge me to pursue my doctoral degree. Because I respected her so highly, her influence became a significant factor in my enrolling in the doctoral program at Lehigh University, where she had once been a professor.

Looking back, I'd have to say that, next to my mother, Mrs. Pincus helped to shape me. I don't know if it was the words she spoke or the way she said them or the love she showed me—I know only that her influence more than anyone else's eventually enabled me to make a decision. That's when I determined to stay in the inner city and to make it a better place. I had no awareness of it then, but I do think she planted the first seeds. I say that because I haven't forgotten those conversations, those words of encouragement, and most of all, I have never forgotten her faith in me. In time those seeds would bear fruit. Serving the community would become, for me, almost a holy calling.

Something else came out of Mrs. Pincus recognizing my ability and encouraging me. Her brother, Larry Rosen, worked for KYW, a news radio station in Philadelphia. (He has since become Senior Director of Broadcast and Production for the Baltimore Ravens.)

"I want you to meet Larry," she said to me in my junior year. "I've told him about you and I think you need to get involved with the intern program they have. I know you'd fit in it."

"You really think so?" No one had ever shown that kind of faith in my ability before.

"Yes, I absolutely think so. You're articulate, and even more important, you can think."

With that kind of encouragement, how could I not be excited? She sent me to Larry, and he took me on as an intern. They normally work with high school seniors. It was a big station and I didn't receive any money, but I learned a lot.

The six-month news-writing program taught me to speak clearly and to write brief and accurate news copy. Larry helped me and coached me so that I learned good diction and proper interviewing techniques. One rule I remember was that we could not be late. Late once and we were gone. "The show must go on," I heard him say several times.

Of course, I was never late.

I liked being involved with reporting the news. After I had been there a few weeks, Larry even let me do a few voiceovers to introduce news items. It worked this way: News stories would come in on audiotape. Larry showed me how to edit them and cut out unimportant information.

Sometimes we had only forty-five seconds for a news item that came to us at ninety seconds. That meant we had to summarize before or after the audio portion. He taught me to do that kind of voiceover and we aired everything live.

Once I started to do those news voiceovers, I began to enjoy a kind of celebrity status in my neighborhood—and the guys who once had wanted to beat me up now regarded me with admiration.

"Hey, you're the one on the radio, aren't you?" one of them asked me one day.

"Yes, I am," I said and swelled with pride.

"You are the man. Don't forget us when you get on television." Little did he know, I could never forget the neighborhood.

I loved working for KYW, because it gave me a chance to see the professional world and be part of it. Another thing—and this may have been part of Mrs. Pincus's strategy, I saw the importance of education. For the first time, I realized that in the professional world talent alone wasn't enough. Without a college degree, many jobs weren't open to me or to anyone.

I appreciated that opportunity, and I did the best I knew how. The risks that Mrs. Pincus took to expose me to a large world made me realize how much she cared about me. She had gone out on a limb by asking Larry to take me on at the station. I could very well have embarrassed her by doing a terrible job.

When I began to work on this book, Mrs. Pincus had reminded me of an incident in my sophomore year—something I had long forgotten. She had taken maternity leave and the school brought in a substitute for her English classes. The new teacher, Ms. Smoot, didn't know much about Shakespeare—which was obvious. Mrs. Pincus had left lesson plans for every day of classes, and Ms. Smoot tried to teach what she was supposed to.

I felt sorry for the teacher because she lost control the first day of class. In fact, she never had control. That was typical of how kids behaved with a substitute if they could get away with it. As I listened and watched some of the kids cutting up, I got really mad. This had been my favorite class and Mrs. Pincus was my favorite teacher. I knew the substitute would talk to her and she would be disappointed in us.

"Yo, we need to stop this!" I said and stood up.

That got the class's attention.

"Listen, our teacher is out. She's having a baby. We have goals and we're supposed to learn so we can prepare ourselves for college. We can't stop what we're doing just because the teacher's not here."

They looked at me, surprised at my response, because I was usually the one clowning around.

"We don't want to embarrass this teacher, and we don't want to embarrass Mrs. Pincus by having her report that we're such bad students. We know what we need to learn, so let's go ahead and make sure we stay on track. We can't lose all these weeks just because Mrs. Pincus isn't here."

Honestly, I don't remember much after that. Not only did I restore order to class, but apparently, I started them talking about Shakespeare. We were studying *Julius Caesar* and I had done the assigned reading. I must have asked a question about Brutus or Mark Antony because we were soon in serious discussion.

Mrs. Pincus learned what happened because the substitute called her and told her about the chaos. "Then one boy stood up and brought the class under control. And then he taught the entire lesson from *Julius Caesar*."

"Which boy?" Mrs. Pincus asked.

"His name is Thomas-EL. I can't tell you how much he helped. As a matter of fact, he taught the entire lesson."

I didn't realize what an impact I had made. After all, I was doing what I thought was the right thing, and I wanted Mrs. Pincus to be proud of us when she returned.

The classes stayed under control for the rest of the semester while Mrs. Pincus was gone. (When I was writing this book, I ran into Ms. Smoot at a district meeting. She is now a full-time teacher, and she remembered the incident quite clearly and thanked me for "teaching the class.")

Looking back, I think that was where the teacher in me began to emerge. Teaching hadn't been anything I thought seriously about, even after Mr. Grillet's encouragement.

The one thing I do remember is that I enjoyed teaching. If I had been more reflective, I might have realized I belonged in the classroom.

5

A Higher Level

I could never have imagined that standing up in English class in 1980 would have started my teaching career. It did begin at Simon Gratz High School. Even stranger, perhaps, is that later, when I started to teach as a professional, I went to Gratz.

Another important person that pushed me forward was Mrs. Thompson, the guidance counselor at Gratz. I met with her dozens of times and she always encouraged me to go on to college.

When I was a junior, I started applying to colleges and getting ready for my SAT. I didn't think about going outside of Philadelphia. I liked my family and my neighborhood and didn't consider going away. Anytime I thought of college, I had dreamed of how nice it would be to attend Howard University in Washington, D.C., or Morgan State in Baltimore, Maryland. I had visited both of them as well as several others that high school kids from my community were attending. I still told Mrs. Thompson that it would be better to stay close to home near my family and friends.

"I really, really think that you should go to a college that's different from the area you're living in now."

"Why? I could live at home." I didn't understand why she would make such a suggestion.

"Based on your background—your attendance at Masterman and your career goals—I think you will do much better if you go away from home. You have had a good exposure to the world that's bigger than the inner city. I believe you need an even wider exposure."

"I'll think about that."

Not fooled by my evasive answers, the counselor said, "Look at it this way. You know how to fit in. You adjust much better than many of your peers would."

"Yeah, maybe, but—"

"You're an excellent student, Salome. You can do better even than you're doing right now."

She had my number. On the surface, I kept trying to fit in with the crowd and tried not to stand out too much, even in the Star Program. But inside, I couldn't be just average. I had to be better. No, I had to be the best student I could be.

It was tough growing up in the inner city. Maybe this sounds strange to some, but those of us who were serious about our education faced a lot of conflict. A lot of people looked at us with suspicion, as if we thought we were superior to them.

"You go to that kind of school, man, and you are a sellout!" one of my friends said when I mentioned college.

It's a strange mind-set. Maybe it's because so many children in the inner city didn't have a chance or encouragement and they resented those who tried to raise themselves to a higher level of education and income.

The accusation that hurt the most was that whenever any of us in the Star Program talked to our friends not in the program, they accused us of acting white. Even then, I thought, isn't acting black good enough? Does being black mean I can't be intelligent or know Shakespeare?

That was one side. We had to make our friends think we weren't interested in education.

There was another side too, which made it a difficult and narrow road to walk. Inside I wanted so much to go to college and to learn. Mrs. Thompson, Dr. Farmbry, and Mrs. Pincus—as well as my mother—had just about persuaded me that I could do anything or be anything I wanted.

That's part of what the guidance counselor was trying to say to me. She saw tremendous potential in me and wanted me to study in an environment where I could be proud of myself and feel positive about my achievements. She sensed that I couldn't do that if I were around my friends.

"You're bright enough that you can be successful at any school you choose. Most colleges are good. If you can avoid the bad influence from those around you, you'll do well."

She was right. I knew that, and I finally admitted it.

"I'd like you to think about attending East Stroudsburg University. It's in upstate Pennsylvania. It's still in Pennsylvania and you could ride the bus home on weekends. But it's far enough away from your friends that they won't have a negative influence on you." She also mentioned that it was a state-funded university and that would cut down the cost. "They have an excellent reputation as a teachers' college."

She understood my situation and I knew she wouldn't let me go in the wrong direction. And even more, she had faith in me. I wondered why she emphasized it being a good teachers' college. That wasn't the direction I thought of going. While working with Larry Rosen at KYW radio, I decided that I wanted to go into radio or TV.

I took her advice and without even going to visit the campus, I applied to East Stroudsburg when I was a junior. I received an acceptance that year. They were interested in me and didn't even wait until I was in my senior year.

Later I learned that was rather amazing. Most colleges and universities didn't accept students until they were in their senior year. The only thing I got from East Stroudsburg in my senior year was a letter that reminded me that I had already been accepted.

Being accepted at a college took a lot of pressure off me. I knew where I was going after school. It also took pressure off the family because one of the discussions we regularly had was, "But what if no college will accept you?"

No one in my family had ever graduated from college. My older brother William started, but he dropped out before he earned his degree. No one from the families of any of my friends had college degrees either.

One question nagged at me. When I read catalogs from various colleges, they all stressed the need for strong math courses. I wondered if I had taken the right courses for me to be successful in college because I had not taken any high-level courses in mathematics. And yet, I always felt I was an excellent math student.

One day I discovered how to find out. Every year at Gratz they have a contest sponsored by the Math Association of America. Any student can enter and take the exam. It's a difficult, demanding test. If I remember correctly, they compare scores all over the city, the state, and the nation, so that anyone could see how he or she ranked on any three levels in terms of achievement.

I had only one problem.

A math teacher at Gratz didn't want me to enter the contest. "He does not have the courses behind him," the teacher insisted.

"I've always felt like math was second nature to me," I said.

"I just didn't take many math courses because I was sure I didn't need them."

"And what happens if you end up at the bottom? You embarrass the school in the process." Even as he spoke, I didn't feel he was against me personally. He was more concerned about the reputation of the school, and I think he was concerned about what it would do to me. If I took the test and did badly—as he was sure I would—then he felt it would make me feel terrible or depressed.

"I want to take the test," I said.

He tried to talk me out of it, but I was firm. He couldn't stop me—too many teachers spoke up in my defense. Even more important, I had encouragement from Mrs. Pincus and Mrs. Thompson to take the test.

"You can do well," Mrs. Pincus said to me several times. As I gazed into her light brown eyes, I believed it. Just knowing she had faith in me boosted my lagging self-confidence.

I took the test.

I finished third in the entire Simon Gratz High School—far ahead of several students who were older and supposed to be math whizzes.

The school even presented me with a prize along with the other two winners. I burst with pride because I had competed against students who were taking calculus and elementary functions. The only math I had studied was algebra and geometry.

By finishing third in the school, it gave me the confidence to know that I could go to college and succeed.

That experience alone made me realize that I honestly did have God-given ability to succeed. I *was* smart.

The guidance counselor also pointed out, however, that wasn't enough. Being a bright kid gave me an advantage, but it wasn't everything. I still had to study.

There had been some hesitation about whether I should go to college. Do I want to go to college and sacrifice four more years without making any money and trying to help out at home? Our family now numbered thirteen (both of my teenage sisters had two children before I graduated high school), and Mom was still our sole support. Even though my older siblings were on their own, no one was able to make much of a contribution.

"Go to college," my mother said many times. "You deserve the chance."

"But that means that I'll be four years in school—four years when I won't be making any money to help support the family. And even when I get out, I'm not sure what I'll be able to earn."

"I want you to go to college," she said. She needed all the financial help she could get, but my going to college was more important.

My family didn't have any money to pay my tuition. I had raised that question very early with Mrs. Thompson.

"You can get grants and scholarships," she said and told me how to apply.

Before I graduated, I received the Ruth Hayre scholarship because I was one of the top students in the school district. Ruth Hayre had been a well-known educator in the Philadelphia school system. Every year the city awarded top students in the city money to help them with college.

I received a check for $500 in the summer. It would be a big help in starting college. Without that money I would have left for college without sufficient funds to pay for my books.

My family not only had no money to help, but we were considered below the poverty level. My mom had been on and off welfare through the years of my growing up. The one advantage it gave me was that I qualified for full financial aid grants because of my need.

*   *   *

Graduation came from high school and I knew it was only the beginning for me. I was on track for a career and quite excited.

Then I visited East Stroudsburg University in upstate Pennsylvania, in the Poconos, about a two-hour drive from Scranton. I had already heard that it was a predominantly white institution—and I had heard the same things about the university as I had about Masterman.

Within days after starting college, I had what some call the moment of rude awakening. Just as I had learned before, some people would never like me because they saw only the color of my skin. There was nothing I could do that would make them change their minds, because they didn't want me or other African-Americans there. It was as if they said to us, "We don't want you here and you will never be part of this university."

Yes, it was Masterman revisited, because all my insecurities came to the top again. I compared myself to other students and that meant I saw myself critically. Just as I had asked myself during my time at Masterman, I asked myself now, "What am I doing here? Do I belong here?"

Not only did all the insecurities come to the top again, but I encountered prejudice on a level I had never known before.

6

Difficult Days

In 1982, right after I graduated from high school, I went for a weekend freshman orientation at East Stroudsburg University. I had quite an eye-opening experience, and many old issues opened up for me again.

At the orientation, it disappointed me to see few minorities—half a dozen of us at most—and I never talked to any of them, so I felt as if I were the only African-American on the entire campus. When I asked a faculty member, I learned that most of the minority students who attended East Stroudsburg or other Pennsylvania state colleges didn't come under the regular admissions policy, because most of the minority students couldn't compete academically without remedial classes.

To increase their admission of minority students, the university held an intensive summer study program. Those students attend for six weeks of fairly concentrated study. I didn't fit into that category because of my grades and standardized test results. I had been accepted under the regular admissions policy.

Another thing bothered me all weekend at freshmen orientation: I was alone. The invitation to the orientation had encouraged parents to attend the weekend event with their children. Because I knew I would have to go by myself, it didn't occur to me that the other new students wouldn't come without parents. I was so naive.

During my three-hour bus ride through the mountains of Pennsylvania I thought about how nice it would be to socialize with the other students whose parents didn't have a car or couldn't make the trip.

As far as I could tell, every other student had a parent or a family member attending. The two-day program provided an opportunity for parents and students to get to know the university, their surroundings, and the university's expectations of them. Although no one said anything, I felt uncomfortable. Even worse, I had no one to talk to. I'd look around and all the other students were sitting with someone or talking to a small group.

Not only am I a racial minority, I thought, but no one even wants to talk to me. I smiled at people and they always smiled in return, but that wasn't conversation. I had hoped some student would invite me to join his group. No one did.

My mom was home. She had seven other kids, but she also cared for the children of my two sisters, both of whom were single parents. I hadn't expected Mom to go to East Stroudsburg with me.

When I arrived, I learned that the university assigned us dorm rooms with roommates for the weekend. Oh, good, I thought. At least I'll have someone else to talk to. On Saturday afternoon, I walked into the dorm and met my roommate, who was white.

"Hi there," I said and introduced myself and told him I was from Philadelphia.

He didn't say much, just something like "Hello." I'm not even sure he told me his name.

He sat down on his bed and began going through the things in his suitcase. I asked him a couple of questions—they were attempts at conversation. He gave me one- or two-word answers. I gave up trying to talk to him.

Not knowing what else to do before our first meeting, which was more than an hour later, I left my things in the room and went out and explored the campus.

When I returned about forty-five minutes later, he was gone. Then I saw that his large, brown suitcase was also gone. He had obviously moved out.

No one ever explained, but I assumed he didn't want a black roommate.

No one ever came in to take his place, so I had a room all to myself for the entire orientation weekend.

I felt even lonelier.

He won't stay here with me because I'm black. No matter how much I tried not to think like that, deep inside I knew that had to be the reason.

It hurt. I felt rejected—and I had done nothing except try to be friendly.

Having lived all my life in the inner city, I didn't know how to respond to that kind of treatment. Most of it was silence and they did it by ignoring me. After the dorm incident, it did seem that most of the parents and students looked away when I came around. But I may have been so paranoid that I read unkindness and prejudice into just about everything. This much I did realize—and it wasn't imagination—the others there ignored me.

This was 1982, not the pre–civil rights days, so I had assumed that those kinds of prejudices had died. I had felt alone at times at Masterman, and sometimes like an intellectual inferior because of all the bright classmates. But until then I had never experienced rejection because of my skin. Maybe that's why it hurt so much at orientation.

I didn't realize it, but once classes started, racial prejudice would confront me every day I lived in the dorm, often in the classroom, and some of it was the harshest, unkindest treatment I ever experienced in my life.

That weekend, in my misery and rejection, I kept asking myself, What am I doing here? Is this the way it's always going to be? Do I want to spend four years at a place like this and with people like these? At least twice that weekend I felt tempted to leave.

I'm an outgoing person and I make friends easily. Generally, people like me because I like them. Even at Masterman, I made quite a few friends and could always find someone to talk to. I wasn't mature enough to know how to respond. I had grown up with people around me all the time.

I called my mom and talked to her about the situation. "I don't like it here. I'm coming home and I'm not going to stay—"

"You listen to me, Salome. You are going to stay!"

"But Mom, the people here are—"

"You're going to face a lot of obstacles. You have to learn to overcome them."

"No one talks to me. I'm alone here and—"

"You're not alone. You're the first, but you're not alone. It's not only you, Salome—you have to continue because you're doing this for the entire family."

"All right," I said, knowing she wasn't going to let me give up.

"You are going to stay, so just get that in your head," were her final words before she told me she loved me.

That weekend was the first time I called her from East Stroudsburg. Over the next two years, I called several times and always with the same complaints. Each time she persuaded me to stay.

*   *   *

My orientation weekend introduced me to my freshman year at East Stroudsburg.

A month later I was an excited college student, and I did feel a sense of pride in being able to say that I had been accepted into college. One of the reasons for going to East Stroudsburg was that I wanted to breathe fresh air, to be away from pollution, constant noise, and the intense city traffic. Just walking around in the small town of Stroudsburg made me feel as if I were in a different country. Buildings were cleaner and I didn't see a single graffiti-sprayed wall. I could walk down the street and not hear a police siren or be startled by the flashing red light of an ambulance. There was no crime, and people walked casually and freely down the streets. I saw many women walking alone after dark and they didn't peer over their shoulders.

It should have been an ideal time for me. Maybe I didn't have all of those inner-city problems. One evening I made up my mind that I would forget about the lack of friendliness and the indifference to me.

I had made up my mind not to let those things offend me. Then I walked inside the building and headed toward my room. At first I couldn't believe what I saw. Slowly, I walked up to my door. For several seconds I stood there and blinked back tears. My fists balled in anger. The hallway was deadly silent and every other door was closed.

Someone had spray-painted a swastika on my door.

Ray Hamlin, another African American lived in the same dorm and on the same floor as I did. He was a nice fellow, very bright, and a serious student, and we got to be good friends. He was from New Jersey, and he later became a successful attorney.

Ray suffered as much from the jokes and racial attacks as I did, but he seemed able to handle them a little better. Or maybe he had had more experience.

For instance, I came back to my room one time to find I couldn't get my key to fit into the lock. I tried several times unsuccessfully. At first I wondered if I had done something to the lock. It took me a dozen tries and several minutes to realize that the problem was the lock itself. Someone had put some kind of waxy material inside that prevented me from inserting my key.

I had to call the RA—the resident assistant—to get it fixed.

"Who would do something like that? That's about as mean a trick as anything I've ever heard of!" I complained.

He shrugged. "Happens every year," he said. "Someone's just playing a practical joke."

"Practical joke?" I repeated, wondering how he could take it so lightly.

I didn't take it as a joke, but I didn't say anything more. If that had been the only incident, I probably would have agreed.

I had no idea who had done it, of course. The perpetrator had to have lived in one of the other rooms in the dorm, but I had no way to prove it or any idea who to accuse.

I'm sure the person responsible thought it was funny.

There was another little trick they tried several times. Very late at night, maybe even two o'clock in the morning, the dorm would be quiet. Someone would bang hard on my door and yell. By the time I opened it, no one was in the hallway and all the other doors were closed.

Finally, I had had enough harassment and I got on the phone.

"Mom, I'm coming home." I had made up my mind that I wouldn't stay whether she agreed or not, I was leaving. "I can't take this anymore."

"You have to stay. You can handle it. Just don't give in. Don't hate because others do."

"I can't stay. This is too much, Mom. Every day there's something to—"

"And every day you stay shows you're stronger than they are. Just don't give up now." She said a lot of other things, but each time it was enough. After she calmed me down, I was ready to go back and face the hardships again.

"Will this harassment never end?" I asked Ray.

He didn't know either.

Another time I came back to the room and saw a sign stuck to my door with three words on it: "Go home, Nigger!"

Every door was closed so no one saw me, but I stood there and tore the paper into tiny little pieces and threw it in the hallway. Then I went into my room and slammed the door as loudly as I could. I cried for a while and then slept until my next class. I was hoping sleep would help me forget. It didn't.

One morning, I got up, dressed, and hurried to leave the room for my first class. A large tree branch had been lodged against my door, and as soon as I had thrown open the door, the large branch fell into the room and made a loud bang as it hit the floor.

It was the proverbial last straw. Ray and I had quietly endured, hoping maybe they'd get tired of harassing us.

"Just let them play their little tricks," Ray said once. "They'll get tired of it. We can wear them down."

But there was no more silence for me. "That's it!" I yelled at Ray. "I'm not going to take any more of this." I raced down the hall and screamed, "Come out, you cowards!"

Ray ran down the other direction. "We're going to fight back," he said to me and yelled, "This is the last time! No more of this from you guys!"

For perhaps ten minutes, Ray and I raced up and down the hallway. We banged on every door, striking each one as hard as we could. My anger had built up so much, I wouldn't have been surprised if I had knocked a door off its hinges.

"Hey, you coward! Come on out and show yourself!" I yelled. "Be a man! Don't hide behind those sheets you guys wear. If you're so tough, why are you afraid to show your face?"

We must have hit every door four or five times. I don't remember when I'd felt so angry before.

Perspiration covered our faces and drained our anger. It was time for us to take action.

"Listen, we don't know who did this, but if anything—*anything*—like this happens again, we're going to start making people pay." I yelled. I felt a joyful freedom in screaming, even if no one came into the hallway. "It's time for this stuff to stop. You can't keep hiding behind your doors."

"Yeah, and if these kinds of things happen again—even once more—we're going to start making people pay," Ray cried out. "And if it's not you that did it and you get hurt, then your friend will be sorry because he'll be responsible for your getting whatever you get."

I'm not sure what we would have done, but I think they realized that we had reached the limit. We would retaliate—if we had to.

The message must have gotten across, because no more incidents took place in the dorm. I don't know if the guys were tired of harassing us or maybe they saw that we were guys that were willing to fight back. Maybe they even felt ashamed of their actions.

By the end of my freshman year, I had had enough of dorm life. I moved off campus, but Ray stayed. "I'm not going to let them chase me out of here," he said.

Maybe he did the right thing. I admired him for staying. But I couldn't stay in a building with people all around me and none of them willing to talk to me.

I had another reason to move off campus. I had grown up in a house with eight kids and people around all the time. It was time for me to get out of the multi-individual dwellings. I moved to an apartment in town in Stroudsburg. I lived with one roommate who went home every weekend. For the first time in my life I felt as if I were living alone. And about half the time, I was. My roommate and I usually saw each other for a few minutes before classes, and often he'd be in bed before I came in at night. It was strange, but also good to know that I didn't have to listen to music, arguing, and loud voices all the time. It made me feel secure and at peace to know that I didn't have to worry about someone pounding on my door in the middle of the night.

I received financial aid—grant money and loans—that paid for my tuition, room, and board. Although they covered those things, there wasn't much money left. I had to work, and within a couple of days, I found a job as a telemarketer for a ski resort. I did well enough to pay my bills.

I never went back to the dorm. I stayed for a year in my own apartment and then during my third year at East Stroudsburg I moved into the frat house—Kappa Alpha Psi—one of the largest fraternities in the world. I had become a full-pledged member in 1984. Other than my frat brothers wearing my clothes and eating my food—all of that taking place without their bothering to ask—which happened a lot, I didn't have any trouble. Nothing big and certainly nothing mean-spirited took place. We were like one big family. My older fraternity brothers were role models for me.

Just before they graduated, Smiley Shackleford and Earle Greer, both successful businessmen today, encouraged me to persevere. They told me their experiences of encountering prejudice—some similar to mine, but most of them far worse. They also said that the younger students were observing and listening to me, so I needed to set the right example for them.

My greatest honor was that my brothers elected me pole-march (president) of our fraternity chapter, although I was the newest and youngest member.

I lived at the frat house for my entire junior year, but at the beginning of my senior year I rented a house with a graduate student named Rick Philbin, a white kid from almost all-white Williamsport. Eventually he became one of my best friends.

The one bad moment that could have separated us took place when his grandparents came to visit. They didn't like the idea of his living with a black kid. They didn't say anything to me—they didn't have to. They were polite but cold. It hurt to see the way they avoided me and wouldn't even shake my hand. But I understood. They were quite elderly and had not been exposed to many African Americans.

I also felt sorry for Rick because their attitude embarrassed him. By then, I was getting used to such treatment. Funny, but I comforted him for being embarrassed. I explained that their kind of response wasn't new to me, and I realized he respected me for who I was. "Real friends stick together and help each other through tough times," I said.

As much as anything, that incident with his prejudiced grandparents sealed our deep friendship. Many times since then I have visited Rick and his family, and he remains one of my best friends.

At East Stroudsburg I majored in speech communications. As it turned out, in every class in that area, I was the only black student. Already self-conscious and insecure, being the only black made it tough to deal with. One of the hardest things was that every time an issue came up about minorities, everyone turned toward me and stared. By being the token black, they expected me not only to answer but also to defend a position. It happened regularly that whenever an issue came up that involved minorities in any way, they expected me to answer and defend "my" position.

Sometimes I'd say, "I don't know," rather than get into it. I often wondered if the situation had been reversed, would any of the white students have been ready to speak for all Caucasians.

Despite the things I've already mentioned, I received a good education at East Stroudsburg. I also had several good professors. One professor, however, actually told me outside of his classroom, "You aren't college material. You need to drop out now and save yourself all the pain that will come later."

Instead of discouraging me, he made me determined to prove him wrong. Maybe Mom's encouragement was finally getting through to me. I would not surrender to prejudice and discrimination.

I needed to hold on to that commitment, because that professor stayed right on me. At times I wondered if he was on a personal crusade to get rid of me.

I had worked at KYW radio and had done some writing. I'd always considered myself a fairly good writer and good speaker. Until I studied under that professor, everyone had told me that I was an excellent communicator. When I made presentations, the comments from other students assured me that I had done well.

That same professor, however, refused to give me a good grade on any of my presentations. I was objective enough to realize that many of those he graded much higher didn't do well and came off much worse than I did. I would have failed a couple of those that he graded as average or above average.

Even worse, he made one pejorative remark after another about me. Most of them were snide statements and none of them were big things. He'd comment on my "inner-city accent" or the way I pronounced a particular word—something he didn't do with any of the other students.

Later that school year I talked to several other African-American students who had studied under him. All of them had faced the same problems and the constant verbal putdowns, and all of them had ended up with barely passing grades. That information convinced me that his was a racial issue.

No matter how hard I tried or how much I determined that I wouldn't let his sarcastic remarks hurt, they did. I'd tell myself that he was stupid, that he had no idea who I was, that I was as smart as he was, that my race had nothing to do with my mental abilities, and that he was stupid for not realizing those facts.

He would still get to me. I think one reason is that teachers had always been important and influential in my life. I craved their appreciation and assumed that if I studied hard and behaved well, I'd do all right. No matter what I did in that man's classroom, my work would never be acceptable because I would never be acceptable to him.

After one particularly bad situation in class one day, I called my mom. "I'm ready to come home. I can't deal with this ignorant man anymore." I had already packed my bags and planned to leave the next morning. This time I knew she wouldn't be able to talk me into staying.

"You can deal with it, Salome. You're bigger than he is."

"Don't try to talk me out of it. I can't stand any more of the terrible things he does and says and—"

"You listen to me, Salome Thomas-EL. You won't give up! You can't. Don't let him prove that he was right."

Maybe I needed to hear Mom's encouragement. Maybe I needed encouragement from anyone before I could go back into his classroom again.

"You have to do this for the family," she reminded me before she hung up.

Her words soothed me once again, although the professor's treatment didn't get any better.

One day during my second year of college, he called me

aside after another class. "You might want to reconsider pursuing your education elsewhere."

"Sir, I strongly disagree with you." I glared at him. I could feel the anger rising inside me. I forced myself to calm down before I said, "I belong here, and I'm going to find a way to prove to you that I am a good student and that I can be successful—even *in your* class."

He smirked as if to dismiss everything I had said. I think it was his way of saying, "You will never change my mind." Then he made another crude remark about my lack of ability.

"If you give me one more bad grade, I'm going to see the dean," I said, surprised that I had the courage to speak up. "You're unfair and prejudiced. And you know it! All you can see is my race and nothing else." Before he could interrupt, I yelled, "This is not just my opinion. Even the white students in the class know how prejudiced you are."

Once started, I decided to push him to the wall. "Half a dozen students have told me that they're willing to go to the dean with me. They'll stand right with me and tell him how prejudiced you are." That part wasn't true. In my anger and frustration I grabbed for anything I could think of.

Without giving him a chance to say another word, I turned and walked away.

His words had hurt, and I felt totally powerless against his ingrained prejudice. It made me think of all these years that I had worked for nothing. All the things that I had done and the barriers I had broken and the stereotypes I had shattered at Masterman meant nothing.

To calm myself and to diffuse my anger, I did a one-hour workout in the gym with some friends. Just to think that one man—one stupidly prejudiced man—had the power to determine my future was too much. He was judging me based on my skin color and where I had come from, not on who I was or the work I turned in.

*   *   *

I don't know how seriously that professor listened, but that semester he gave me a grade of B for the course. Later when I talked with other black students, they were amazed.

"That's the highest grade he's ever given to any minority student," one of them said and others confirmed it.

If my work had been mediocre, I wouldn't have been so enraged, but my work had been good, and I knew it. I had shown it to the Caucasians in the class. They never said anything in class to him or defended me, but many of them began to feel sorry for me. They kept encouraging me and urging me not to give up.

One time we even considered having a white student turn in my assignment under his name—one of the students to whom he normally gave high grades and then we'd see how fair he was.

We never did that, but I was ready to pursue anything to get a good grade—a deserved good grade. Fortunately it didn't get to that point. I did talk to my advisor, Dr. Francois, about it and he admitted that they had had other reports about that professor. I don't know if maybe he got wind of the fact that I talked to higher-ups or if there were other students who were now a part of this movement to right some of these wrongs. I do know that he began to treat me a lot better.

And even more surprising, that same professor actually began to say encouraging things to me, such as, "That was a fine presentation."

That response surprised me. I don't know if he was trying to save his job, but he became a lot friendlier toward me. He even asked me to take another class with him.

"So I wasn't college material?" I said. "Looks as if you've changed your mind on that."

I never took another course with him, however.

One thing that professor did for me—exactly what he had not intended—he pushed me to do my best. With the encouragement of my mom and a few friends on campus, I determined that he wasn't going to make me feel inferior or discourage me.

I worked hard at the university, but in a lot of ways, I was naive and didn't know much about how the educational system works.

For instance, one morning I was walking across campus and saw a couple of my friends, Junn and Larry Bias, who were cousins. I waved at them.

"Hey, man, you made the dean's list!" Junn yelled as he passed.

Until that moment, I had never heard of the dean's list, and thought, Oh, I must be in trouble. I had been around the girls' dorm after hours. *Had someone reported me?*

When Larry pointed it out, he grinned and added, "Congratulations!"

"What—how did you find out?" I asked, not quite willing to show my ignorance.

"See for yourself." He pointed to a list posted on the wall just inside the one of the dorm buildings.

I rushed inside and stared at it. Then I read the words: Salome Thomas-EL— 4.0 grade average.

What a great feeling that gave me. I hurried to the nearest pay phone and called my mom. I explained the dean's list as if I had known all along what it was. It was one of her happiest moments during my college days. This time I wasn't calling to come home or complaining about East Stroudsburg. I was proud of myself. She cried and laughed and kept telling me how proud she was of me.

The black students were also very proud because there were not many students who could accomplish that, but for a black to do it seemed like a victory for the entire African-American community.

Although I didn't do it, I wanted to burst into the office of that prejudiced professor and show him the printed dean's list with my name circled in red and say, "Read that!"

The one good piece of news about him is that about a year after I graduated from East Stroudsburg, he lost his teaching job. When I heard that news through a friend still there, I said, "What took them so long to get rid of him?"

After my name appeared on the dean's list, occasionally I'd see some of the guys from the old dorm. By now, I guess they figured, "He's still here so he must belong." They greeted me when we passed each other. Two years earlier they had turned their faces to look away so they didn't have to acknowledge my presence.

Maybe now that I had proven myself, they were willing to accept me. And yet, what a shame. I thought of the students who never made the dean's list, or who had gotten discouraged and left because they didn't have the emotional support or the persistence to stay. If it hadn't been for my mother, I would have been one of the hundreds of students who dropped out.

I realized a valuable principle then—and one that I've held onto through the years: Everyone needs a strong support system to survive in a hostile environment. As I would realize years later when I began to teach, I had to help my students by providing that kind of strong network for them. I didn't want them to suffer the way I had—and the way others did who had it much worse than I did.

How would I have made it through my college years without Mom? She sacrificed a lot. Aside from her constant encouragement, and as poor as she was every month, I'd get a letter from her and she'd enclose a five-dollar bill. I made that money last a full month because I knew that was all she had. Her sacrifice spoke to me as much as her words. To keep her son in college, she was going without things she needed. Because of that, every time I accomplish anything—no matter how small—I make sure I include my thanks to her, because I'm doing it for her. And that means for the family.

I also had a number of kind and compassionate instructors. For instance, in my senior year, Dr. Richard Leland was my teacher. Within the first month, he became one of my favorite professors. At that time I had been thinking about going to law school. I've always been articulate and quick thinking, so it seemed to me that I would make a good lawyer.

"I want to be honest and open with you," he said after he had listened to me and my thoughts about the future. "There are already so many lawyers."

"But there's always room for a few more good ones."

He nodded in agreement and then stared at me before he said softly, "I think you would be an excellent lawyer, but we need teachers—*good* teachers."

"That's true. I had some great teachers. That's a big reason I'm here."

He smiled and leaned forward. "And I think you'd be a good teacher."

"Really?" At the time, his words didn't mean much to me, but I listened anyway.

He talked to me about the overabundance of lawyers in the state of Pennsylvania and the growing numbers of lawyers in the United States. "I think you should pursue, if not teaching, at least a profession where you can help your community."

"I thought being a lawyer would help."

"Maybe. But teaching could help even more."

I promised I would think seriously about his words. I did think about his words a lot over the next years. For one thing, teaching had not seemed to be the direction I wanted to go.

Looking back, however, Dr. Leland's advice was the best I ever received during my college years. He forced me to look at myself and think about the service that I could provide for my community.

After our talk, I walked across campus pondering what he had said. He was right. I paused to consider the blessing that I had received in my life. It was my duty to do what I could. And I also realized that, aside from my mother, the most important and influential people in my life had been teachers—such as Mrs. Porter, Mrs. Petit, and at Masterman, Mr. Grillet. In high school there had been Mrs. Pincus, Mrs. Smithey, and Mrs. Thompson, and then in college Dr. Leland and Dr. Francois had become powerful influences.

That afternoon was the first time in my life that I had seriously considered becoming a teacher.

I had been a speech communications major and I had dreamed of working in the electronic media. At that time not many blacks appeared on TV unless they were comedians or athletes, and especially not in the news division. I also wanted to make a lot of money, which was why I had thought seriously about law school. By then, I realized I didn't want to go to medical school, the other lucrative profession I had contemplated.

"I'll think seriously about this," I had promised Dr. Leland, and I did. *Is this the way for me? Would I be happy as a teacher? Could I live on the low salaries teaching pays?* For at least the next two days, those thoughts filled my mind. I didn't know what to do.

I never applied to law school. What I said I would do was

pursue some of my dreams of working in television. If that didn't work out, I would investigate what it would take for me to become a teacher. I had already taken a few minor courses in education to satisfy my graduation requirements for college.

It was a mistake not to take more, but at the time, I had no plans to teach.

7

On the Job

In May 1986, two weeks before graduation, I still had no job lined up. I had received one offer to become a claims adjuster for Liberty Mutual Insurance Company. To take the position, I would have had to move to Williamsport, and I didn't want to do that, so I turned them down.

I had just spent four years at East Stroudsburg; I was ready to go back home to Philadelphia. I wasn't ready to go home without having a job, however. During the four years I had been in college, getting a good job had been important. Whenever I returned to Philadelphia during the vacation periods, my friends and people in the neighborhood would say things that hurt me.

"Sure hope you're not going to get all that education and not be able to get a job," one friend said.

"You're going to be so educated you can't do nothing to earn a living," another said.

Almost always I heard of a cousin or a friend or a relative of a friend who had gone to college for four years and now drove a taxi, worked as a receptionist, or never found a decent-paying job.

Those words affected me, and I would have been ashamed for anyone to think that I had studied for four years and that they had been a waste of time. But what could I do? Except for the insurance job offer, no doors had opened to me. I couldn't afford to go on to graduate school even if I had known what I wanted to study.

Most college students feel that they don't want to be out of the job market for four years and then graduate from college and not have anything ready to start earning money. To go home without a job was a way of admitting failure.

Several of my college friends took jobs they didn't want only because they didn't want to come out of college and be unemployed. "I can take this while I'm looking around," one of my classmates said.

Although I understood, I knew I couldn't do it that way. I'm a person who puts energy and passion into everything I do. If I got into a job that I didn't like, I wouldn't be able to do my best.

So what do I do after graduation? That was the question I asked myself a hundred times every day. I knew I wanted to work in the field of communications. Not only had it been my college major, but it was something I loved to do.

In desperation, I called Mrs. Pincus, my former high school English teacher. When I was still in high school, she had gotten me the opportunity to work with her brother Larry Rosen at station KYW. I told her my situation and asked if she had any information that would help me find a job. "I want to work in communications," I said.

"My brother is now working at PRISM Sports," she said. PRISM was an acronym for Philadelphia Regional In-home Sports and Movie Channel, "Why don't you give him a call and see what he can do for you?"

PRISM was one of the largest cable sports channels in the

East and they televised all of the Sixers, Flyers, and Phillies home games. It's an affiliate of the Sports Channel Network and was one of the original cable sports channels.

When I called Larry, he seemed pleased to hear from me. After we talked a few minutes, I asked him for a job. They had no job openings, but he wanted to help. "Tell you what. We can put you on as an intern. You wouldn't get paid, but you'll gain invaluable experience working in a TV environment."

"That's fine," I said. "What I'll do is give you a call as soon as I graduate and return to Philadelphia."

At least I had something to go home to. No money, but I could tell my friends that I'd be working for PRISM. That information would not only shut them up, but I knew it would also impress them. My next thing would be to find a job that would support me while I learned the business at PRISM.

I wasn't sure what kind of paying job I could get, but now that I had something to go back to Philadelphia for, I felt calm and at peace. Something would turn up. Most of all, I had something to tell my friends: "I'm going to be an intern for PRISM Sports." I wouldn't have to mention that I wasn't going to get any money.

Then came graduation and I wanted my biggest supporter to see me walk across that platform. In four years, Mom had never been able to visit East Stroudsburg. I wanted her to come, but I didn't press it. We didn't have a car and she had no money and I didn't want to create an even bigger financial burden for her. I knew she wanted to be there, which was important to me.

When I invited her, she had said, "We'll have to see. Maybe the good Lord will help me work it out."

When the graduation ceremony began, I kept looking around, but I didn't see her. There weren't many black faces in the crowd. In fact, there had been only four blacks in our grad-uating class, so she would be easy to spot. A wave of disap-pointment swept over me.

I stood in line with my classmates. Because of my position, I couldn't see any of the guests. Just as I took my first step up to the stage, I spotted her in the audience and I know I gave her my biggest grin. Feelings of joy flowed through me. It was the proudest moment of my life. My mother waved at me—as if she didn't realize I had seen her. She didn't care who saw her. She had eyes only for me in those moments.

I felt proud as I took the diploma and started to walk on. Then I turned toward her, held it up, and waved back. That simple gesture was my way to say, "This is your victory as well as mine."

I had finally come to the end of a long journey—a long, hard one.

As I walked off the platform, I realized she wasn't alone. I learned later that some of the guys in the neighborhood had rented a van and they all drove up together. There were eleven of them. It seemed as if the entire inner city of Philadelphia had turned out to see me get my college diploma. All of my broth-ers, Jonathan, George, William, Eli, and Ray, were there, along with some of my friends, Quentin (Ice), Derek, Stewart, and Sean (Doozie). That made the day even more special.

I graduated on Saturday, May 17, 1986. The next week I was home in Philadelphia and called Larry Rosen.

"As soon as you get settled in, you can start your intern-ship," he said.

I may have shouted into the phone, I don't remember. I know I was so excited I could hardly contain myself. "I prom-ise you that I'll be the best intern you ever had in your life. I want to learn from you, Larry, and I'll do anything you ask of me."

"I know you will," he said and chuckled. "I'm not worried. If I had been, I wouldn't have offered you this internship."

On my first day, the Philadelphia 76ers traded Moses Malone to the Washington Bullets—one of the biggest trades in NBA history. The 76ers had won the NBA championship a few years before that. That same day I got to meet Moses Malone, who was one of my sports heroes, and I also shook hands with other members of the team. Working at PRISM gave me many opportunities to talk to the athletes. Two of them, Julius Erving and Maurice Cheeks, impressed me as being highly intelligent as well as totally professional basketball players. Both were members of the 76ers and college graduates. A number of times we talked in the locker room or at practice about education and young people. When I decided to pursue a career in teaching, they encouraged me.

Even years later whenever I saw either of them, they'd always ask, "Are you still teaching?" or "How are the kids?"

PRISM was a great start for me.

But in another way, I felt as if I were back in East Strouds-burg—it was again an all-white environment. I began to see that this was probably what the rest of my life was going to look like. Not quite the token black, but still I felt as if I were the only minority trying to break through. I had gone from Masterman to East Stroudsburg and now PRISM. I wondered if it would always be like this.

There was this one other black employee in that whole organization, named Tony Irving. He became my mentor as well as my friend. I loved him like a brother and he often told me the same. His goal had been to become an on-air personality for PRISM. Like me, Tony had started out as a production assistant. He had stayed, proven his worth, begun to get paid, and had worked his way up.

Maybe about five years older than I am, he also had attended Masterman, although we hadn't known each other then. In many ways our lives were similar. Both of us grew up in North Philly in a single-parent home. The difference is that I had gone to college but he hadn't. Despite being extremely talented at what he did, not having a college degree hurt Tony's chances for advancement.

His inability to move ahead faster because of not having a college education would be one more thing I would remember when I began to teach. It was one more example to use in pushing my students to get all the education they could.

Tony never said anything about my degree or acted jealous. Had he been a different type of person, he could have resented me or ignored me. Instead, he shared his expertise and helped me every chance he could. Tony and I became good friends and I learned a lot from him. He often encouraged me to go on to graduate school.

It was sad that because he had come from the bottom with only a high school diploma, even though it was from Masterman, he had to work harder than many people of lesser ability who had more education.

Tony died with an aneurysm in 1999 at the age of forty-one. But before he died, I saw him on TV interviewing Michael Jordan. "There's Tony," I said aloud. "He's still following his dream." And he stayed with that dream until he died.

Working at PRISM made me realize what limited access we minorities had. I didn't see it as purely a racial issue, because it wasn't. Most minorities—at least back in the early 1980s—didn't have the education they needed to get into those fields.

Working with Tony and at PRISM gave me the opportunity to see how the job market worked from the inside. Especially, I realized the importance of getting a good education. I knew then, and have been even more convinced since, that kids in the inner city need to get a good education just to compete. As I continued working at the station, I also sensed that they needed more than education. They also needed someone who could motivate them and get them involved in their own success.

By then I was in a heady environment where I rode on the same elevator with Julius Erving and Michael Jordan. One time I went to Red Auerbach's house, the famous Boston Celtics coach, for an interview. While there I gazed at all the famous people and the millionaires—the icons in the sports world.

It was exciting to be around these high-achievers of all races. I also realized something else. I was able to be there in the same room with them because of my education and my affiliation with the people at PRISM. Even though I wasn't earning money, if I had not had the educational connection, I would not be in the same company as these people.

For days I thought about that experience and others like it when I was in the presence of gifted athletes. I wouldn't have articulated it quite that early, but inside my heart, I knew that something was stirring me. I had to find ways to improve the educational situation in my community. I had been helped and now it was my turn to pay back my community by providing opportunities for young people to have that same exposure.

I spent more than four years at PRISM as a production assistant, which meant I assisted Marc Zumoff, our on-air sports anchor, in producing television sports shows and doing interviews. Marc, Tony, and I traveled up and down the East Coast together, from Boston to Miami. We became brothers.

More than once Marc asked me, "How did you make it out

of the inner city when so many other young black males have not?"

I didn't know the answer then, and I'd throw out a number of reasons. But the more I thought about it, the more I realized that the single, most significant fact was that I had chosen to get an education. Just that college degree alone opened doors to move beyond the inner city itself. Even more, it opened the doors for me to move beyond the inner-city mentality.

Eventually, PRISM did start paying me, and that was a great experience to get a regular paycheck. Just getting paid made me aware that they did like my work and valued me as part of the team. Larry and the others always admired the fact that we interns started out as unpaid trainees. Although some left, for those of us who stayed, it showed our dedication. They liked the fact that I stuck around.

While I interned, I began to do volunteer work by visiting various schools and speaking in their assemblies about my work at PRISM. Because most of my work was at night, I went to inner-city schools whenever I was invited and talked to kids about the opportunities. I never left without encouraging them to do their best in school and go on to college. I knew I wasn't anything big at PRISM, but in their minds I was a minor celebrity. I used that to encourage them.

My mom worked in a school, and she was the one who had started my speaking to classes. One day she invited me to come to the school where she worked as a classroom assistant. "This is your chance to encourage them. Tell them to get educated and to set goals for themselves."

I went and I spoke for about half an hour. Everyone responded and the kids and teachers loved my presentation. My communication skills were paying off and that first speaking opportunity opened the door for other invitations. Teachers and principals from other schools heard about me and also asked me to speak to their students.

I would toss out names like Julius Erving and Michael Jordan, and I could do that because not only had I met those important players, but I knew them and they knew me by name. I could honestly tell the kids what outstanding athletes they were and then I'd say. "They're also really smart. And you know why they're so smart? They went to college." Then I'd pause and say, "You need to go to college."

As soon as that sank in, someone would usually ask, "What did you have to do to get into college? How hard was it?"

Those were the questions I loved to answer.

When I was growing up, it also seemed to be that going to college was impossible for any of us. I didn't know anyone in our neighborhood that had gone beyond high school—and many of them dropped out before they got their diploma. Because no one had done it, it didn't seem like any of us could either. Now I wanted those kids to be exposed to an inner-city kid who had grown up and graduated from college. If nothing else, I hoped my example would inspire them.

One thing happened every time I went to a school. Without exception, after I finished speaking, I'd stand around and talk to any of the kids who had questions. At least one kid would say, "You should be a teacher."

Or I'd hear, "I wish you were my teacher."

"We've had so much fun, and we learned so much," another would say, "why aren't you a teacher?"

"Why can't you be a teacher?"

It didn't matter which school I visited, every time I heard essentially the same words. I wasn't listening at first, but I think God was giving me a message. Maybe I needed to hear it a hundred times before it got through to me.

The message finally sank in, and I thought a lot about what those kids said to me. Then it dawned on me that I could be a teacher.

As I looked at my work with PRISM and my own goals to stay in TV, I decided that I could do that and become a substitute teacher when I wasn't working. Because I usually only worked evenings, my days were free. On those rare days I wasn't free, I didn't have to be available to teach.

I applied to be a substitute teacher in Philadelphia and didn't hear anything right away. I was ready to teach, so I put in more applications as a substitute in the other school districts outside of Philadelphia, and even to some of the private schools.

When I had applied to substitute, I listed some of my strengths, such as writing and drama, but most schools looking for substitutes will grab anyone, regardless of their areas of expertise. Frankly, they usually need a warm body for a day or maybe a week. I knew that, but I also knew I could make use of the opportunity to motivate and encourage kids.

I put in those additional applications on a Monday. The next day, the principal of a private elementary and high school, Abington Friends, called me.

"Can you come in starting Wednesday?" the principal asked. "Our drama teacher is on maternity leave and we need a substitute immediately."

"I can do that," I said, "but I don't know about staying for the whole semester. My intention is to substitute in the inner city."

He wanted me to come anyway, and I said I would. Abington Friends was practically an all-white school and a place where just about everyone drove a Mercedes Benz or a BMW. I caught the bus to work. Oh, well, I thought, I ought to be used to this by now.

I went, fully prepared for the worst experience. Kids always make it hard on substitutes and being a black sub in a white school made me prepare for the worst day of my life.

Instead, I received a pleasant surprise. Everyone I met received me warmly. One teacher gave me her only coffee mug so I would have something from which to drink tea. Others offered information without my having to ask. Without exception, they made me feel absolutely welcomed as a teacher.

I remember thinking, at Stroudsburg, I couldn't even get people to shake hands with me. These people shook my hand and gave me tea. They also showed me respect and they smiled. No one turned away when I came around.

Although I loved the students and got along well with everyone, I substituted for only two weeks before I realized that I couldn't finish out the semester. "I like it here, but I want to teach in the inner city," I said.

During those two weeks, something kept pulling at me. The inner city. I knew then that I belonged there. Those kids needed me. Even if they didn't know it, I did. I had never felt such a strong pull toward anything before in my life. I was in a situation where it wasn't a matter of choosing, but a matter of taking the next step forward.

The principal and the staff understood. In fact, they seemed to respect me for wanting to go back into the inner city.

One day, I had the opportunity to substitute in the inner city at Strawberry Mansion High School. The principal at Abington understood, and every one on the staff supported my decision. In fact, they seemed appreciative of the time that I could give them. I loved the atmosphere.

I couldn't stay. My heart was in teaching, but not teaching outside the inner city. After I told the principal, I announced to my classes that I was leaving.

"Can't you stay?" the kids at Abington asked.

"Can't you come back?"

"Probably not," I'd had to say truthfully. "I love it here, but I need to teach in the inner city."

It had now become clear—I wanted to teach in the inner city. I looked back over the past few months of going to schools to talk to them about my work at PRISM. Even then I saw their faces and I was already thinking that I wanted to help them become the best, to overcome the odds of the inner city, and to be living examples to the community.

In late January 1987, I reported to Strawberry Mansion High School, which is an all-black middle and high school. Not only were all the students black, but the school is located in the middle of one of Philadelphia's toughest neighborhoods.

This is where I belong, I remember telling myself. Now I'll find out if I can make it.

At Strawberry Mansion I received a one-day assignment to teach English. I suppose it sounds odd that I turned down a semester's worth of teaching at the Friends school to teach only one day in the inner city. I knew I had made the right choice and I felt good about doing that. At that time, I still wasn't getting paid at PRISM, so it was also a financial risk for me.

Still, it was the right thing for me to do.

Although it was only a one-day assignment, I knew that no matter how bad it was, I'd survive.

Despite all the stories I had heard, I saw no evidence of violence, drugs, or crime. Not only did I survive, but I liked it and even teaching that one day, I felt attached to those kids. I loved Strawberry Mansion and the kids. I had not been inside an hour when I felt as if this was the kind of place I belonged. Maybe it was because I loved those kids even before I met them. Maybe they sensed that I cared when I walked into the classroom the first time.

I wasn't normally a praying person, but I did pray for God to help me stay there.

At the end of the day, I said goodbye to the kids and started to leave. A wave of sadness came over me. I had loved the entire day, and now it was over. I didn't know if I'd ever get another chance to teach there.

God, please help me, I asked. I'm not much at this praying, but I want to help these kids.

One thing had become clear to me: teaching was where I belonged. This was home to me. And for me to become a teacher, I would have to enroll in graduate school and earn the certification so I could be a full-time teacher.

"Come back again, Mr. Thomas-EL," yelled one of the kids who was standing in front of the building.

Two others shouted out how much they had enjoyed the day. "Can't you come back tomorrow?" one of them yelled.

I smiled and kept walking.

"Mr. Thomas! Mr. Thomas!" I heard an adult voice behind me.

I turned around. "Yes, ma'am."

"Wait a minute, please." She introduced herself as Marian Martin, the roster chairperson. She was responsible for rostering teachers and substitutes. "Several children, as well as one of the teachers, came to my office and talked about you. They also told me how thoroughly the children enjoyed your class today—"

"I was happy—really happy—to be here. Great kids to teach and—"

"Would you be interested in staying in this school for the rest of the year?"

"Excuse me?" I answered. I couldn't believe that God would answer me like that.

"Would you be interested in staying in this school for the rest of this school year?" she repeated.

"Yes, yes, I would."

"We have an available position. A teacher is out and she's seriously ill and facing major surgery. That means she'll be out for several months. We'd like you to fill in the rest of the year. Starting tomorrow."

"I'll be here."

She gave me the details and I was back the next day teaching reading in high school at Strawberry Mansion.

Even more firmly, I knew I had to go back to school. Not only did I need to get my certification, I needed a master's degree to get anywhere in the school system.

I was there the next morning. And the next. I stayed at Strawberry Mansion from late January until early June when school closed for the summer. I had a summer job at a camp and they asked me to return to Strawberry Mansion in September for another long-term substitute assignment.

You've got to go back and you've got to earn your master's degree. That thought plagued me and I couldn't get away from it. I started the application process and enrolled in a master's degree program at Antioch University in January 1988. (The school is in Yellow Springs, Ohio, but in those days they had an adjunct campus in Philadelphia.)

In my first semester as a teacher, I broke my arm as a passenger in a car accident. The accident was at night, and the car was totally destroyed. The next morning, with a cast on my arm, I left the emergency room. One of my brothers drove me home, where I changed clothes, grabbed a quick breakfast, and reported to school on time.

I overheard one teacher say to another, "He must really be dedicated to teaching."

Obviously, I liked hearing that. For me, *dedication* wasn't the way I thought about it. Even though I was in a lot of pain, I went to school because I didn't want to disappoint the kids. So if *dedication* was the word, it wasn't dedication to teaching as much as it was commitment to the kids.

In September 1987, I went back to Strawberry Mansion and filled in as a math teacher until the Christmas holidays. I loved going to school. I couldn't remember when I had been so eager to get up and get to school as I was in those days. I would have worked for no pay, but I made sure my principal didn't know that.

In January, the teacher returned to teach her class. For almost a week I received no calls. Then I received a call from my former high school, Simon Gratz.

"We understand you're a substitute teacher," the principal, Dr. Reeves, said. "We have a vacancy and we'd like you to teach for the rest of the school year. We'd be honored to have one of our former students as part of our faculty."

I felt thrilled to teach alongside Mrs. Pincus. I had already started classes at Antioch University toward a master's degree in education with certification, so I was also excited about getting certified to teach.

It was a busy time for me. I was still working two nights a week for PRISM, and getting paid. Most of the events were still on weekends and I arranged my TV work schedule around my school nights. At Antioch I had signed up for three nights of classes from four to seven each of those nights. I was teaching full-time at Gratz, so my life was full.

My plan was to keep getting substitute jobs in the school district until I had my graduate degree and teaching certificate. This plan would give me a lot of experience. Also as a single man who lived at home, I didn't have any money problems.

My goal was to earn my certification and my master's degree

as soon as possible. Finally, I decided a part-time plan was moving too slowly—it would take me several years of going part-time to Antioch. I had to get a permanent school assignment as soon as possible. The answer was simple: I acquired a student loan to speed things up.

I decided to cut back on my hours for PRISM so I could go to school full-time at night. The guys at PRISM understood fully and supported my decision one hundred percent.

Not only was I speeding up my education, but I felt as if I was living out a dream. I was teaching at Gratz. It seemed so unreal and yet so stimulating to be able to return to the high school from which I had graduated and stand up as a teacher.

In June 1988, I finished the assignment at Gratz, and I was still in graduate school. They invited me back to Strawberry Mansion in September to fill a one-year vacancy as an eighth-grade math teacher.

By June 1989, I had earned my master's degree, which I did in a year and a half. With an M.Ed. and a major in special education, I was ready to take the certification exam. In those days we had to take the Pennsylvania Certification Exam as well as the National Teachers' Exam (NTE). I passed both tests.

I had completed the steps for my state certification.

All I had to do now was to get hired by the Philadelphia School District as a full-time teacher.

I had started down the career path.

I knew the direction I wanted to go.

8

I Chose Vaux

My goal was to work in Philadelphia, although I hadn't contacted any schools about teaching that fall. First, however, I had to pass the oral and written exam that the city school district required of all applicants.

I took the exam and had one problem—I didn't finish the written portion. Not aware that they had a time limit, I wrote a rough draft and then started to recopy it on their paper. I ran out of time before I completed the copying.

"May I turn in the rough draft then?" I asked when told I couldn't finish copying my draft.

"No, it has to be on our paper," the examiner said.

Immediately, I requested a retest, because I knew I wouldn't have a problem with the writing. I also knew I wouldn't have a problem with the verbal portion because my whole life had been a verbal parade. The examiner did allow me to take the written portion again a month later, and I passed without any difficulty.

When I began my oral exam, I sat down in front of three district administrators. The speaker said, "This is our first question. What is your philosophy about teaching?"

"My philosophy is that students are there to be educated, and it's my job to educate them. I have a right to teach and every child has a right to be educated. I want every child to believe in that philosophy." I knew what I wanted to say and I was excited to have a chance to lay out my way of thinking. "The children also need to understand that I'm the only one in that room that's capable of educating each child in that room. None of them is capable of it. They need me to educate them and they need to understand that."

Then they asked other questions such as, "How would you handle a disruptive student?"

"I would talk to the student, maybe call the parents and let them know. I'd also find out about the child's background and that would give me insight on the problem area."

They asked me a few of what I call "courtesy questions," such as: "Why do you want to be a teacher?" "What makes you think you'll make a good teacher?" "Tell us about your experiences in school as a child."

I told them I had grown up in the inner city. I also stated that I wanted to be able to give back to my community and that had been one of my goals. Giving back was something my mom had taught me a long time ago and I told them, "I received so much from my mom and others, but especially from teachers who cared about me. When I started college, I was there to prepare myself to do something for my family and for my community." They seemed impressed with my statements about wanting to give something back.

I felt nervous, although I'm sure it didn't show. I wasn't sure how I had done on the interview. When it was over, one of them asked, "Do you have any questions?"

"I have one question. How did I do on this interview?"

That evoked smiles and one of them on the interview panel said, "We're not allowed to tell you. I can say this, however,

I'm a principal at one of the Philadelphia schools. Would you be interested in working at my school?"

I knew I must have done a good job.

I received a temporary assignment to teach in an elementary school in the Roxborough section of Philadelphia, at that time a predominately white section. They needed a teacher to fill a vacancy immediately so they sent me right away to this school. I was being paid as a full-time teacher but was listed as a temporary replacement. My starting salary was $24,000—I had never made that much money in my life. *Total.*

It was fine and I liked teaching there, but I still wanted to be in the inner city, and this wasn't the inner city. The school bused in many minority kids, but I felt that they looked at me as an outsider. I taught all subjects for fifth graders and they responded well. But it still wasn't where I wanted to be.

I told everybody I could where I wanted to teach. "I want to work in the area where I grew up," I said to a lot of people. I didn't understand why no one assigned me there right away. There are always openings in the inner city and most teachers didn't want to go into such situations. I was volunteering! I couldn't understand why they didn't jump at the opportunity to have me.

"Just be patient," was the message I kept getting from the human resources department.

I wasn't patient, but I waited. I had to wait—there was nothing else to do.

After four weeks, I received a phone call, followed by a letter, from the school district asking me to come down to the education office; they would allow me to pick whatever school I wanted to teach in.

At the education office, I studied the list and one of the many openings in the inner city was at Vaux Middle School.

"Before I choose, tell me the story on Vaux," I said.

"I'll put it to you this way," said the clerk. "They haven't been in the news lately, and with Vaux that's good news." Even her voice made it clear that it wasn't the place she thought I ought to go.

"Then that's where I want to be. Send me to Vaux."

"Are you sure?"

"Yes I am. Please send me there."

They did. That's how my teaching career actually began.

I started at Vaux in October 1989 as the special education teacher. I was responsible for all subjects, because I taught fifteen kids, mostly boys, and all of them with reading problems. Black boys make up less than 50 percent of the school system, but they're almost three-fourths of all special education classes.

The other kids called them the losers or the slow kids.

Immediately, I became a father figure for those boys and gave them a sense of direction. They had been recognized as the tough kids in the neighborhood and got into a lot of fights. They hadn't been able to fill the position because nobody wanted to work with those tough kids. I became the third teacher they had had in that class since September.

Almost immediately, I felt that I had bonded with those kids. Even now, after all those years, I'm still in contact with several of them. In fact, I'm working with the children of some of them. It was a great experience to be able to guide those "slow learners" and lead them in the right direction.

I loved seeing kids achieve, but it always hurt—like a personal failure—when one of them turned in the wrong direction. Some kids didn't make it, and despite everything I did, they chose the street life.

"Instead of feeling so bad over those who don't make it," another teacher asked, "why don't you rejoice over those who do?"

One of the members of that class is now a school district employee in the facilities department, and he's begun to talk about going to a community college. He did his best, and I felt I helped to pull him off the streets. Even today, it gives me a good feeling to be able to see a kid who was in a classroom with me who's gone on to make something out of his life.

That, of course, came later.

The first day was scary.

On that first day I felt intimidated. Although they were thirteen- and fourteen-year-old boys, they were also the school's troublemakers. They were large—some larger than my own six feet height—and they were broad shouldered and looked a little mean at times, but they also responded to my smiles and greetings. I had made up my mind that I was going to get to know them as much as possible and I was going to help them stay out of trouble.

Before and after school, I made sure they didn't start any problems in the hallways—one of their big trouble spots. I did everything I could to convince them to think positively about education, to behave properly, and to respect authority. I convinced my kids to come to school early and to leave late. This gave me more time to help them catch up on their work. Many of them made extremely fine progress.

One day I received a summons to the assistant principal's office. An older teacher, Bobbie Dixon, was nearing retirement, but until then she was teaching and filling in as an assistant principal.

Man, I've done something wrong here, I thought, as I walked up the stairs and down the hallway to her office. Maybe parents were complaining about the hours their children were keeping at school.

"I want to talk to you, Mr. Thomas," she said in a no-nonsense voice. (During my first year at Vaux most people called me Mr. Thomas.)

"Yes, ma'am," I said, trying to figure out what I'd done wrong.

"I've seen a lot of teachers come through here, Mr. Thomas. They come, they leave. They use Vaux Middle School as their starting place until they can find a better situation. You seem to be different."

"Thank you for saying that."

"You seem to be really, really involved with the children. You're active and you show a lot of initiative. You don't wait for anybody to tell you what to do and you're motivated. I would like to see you go far. I think you can go far in the school district."

"Thank you—"

"But you need to keep your mind focused on your work. I've seen others like you. They come here, determined to make a difference and eager to change the whole system." She paused and stared into space. "Yes, I've seen them. They start well and have such high ideals. They try, oh, yes, they try. But then things don't move fast enough, or they become discouraged, or sometimes they get involved with other things, and then they move on."

"I won't move on—"

"You seem to have something special," she continued as if I had said nothing. "I hope you'll keep that."

I've always remembered those words. Recalling what she said helped me on those days when things didn't go well.

During my first year at Vaux, I still worked at the TV station and got paid. On many weekends, the crew would pick me up at Vaux on Friday afternoon and we'd drive the van to New York to see the 76ers play the Knicks, or watch New York against Chicago, or drive in the van down to Washington. We went to the games so we could interview the players. Afterward, we'd put together feature packages for televised home games. Then PRISM would air those packages during home games. That meant I got to talk to the star players while they were on the road and attend many all-star games. That gave me even more prestige with the kids.

"I can't believe you're still working here at the school," more than one student said. "You should quit teaching and only work in TV."

They saw only the glamour and my being with millionaire athletes. They didn't know that many of those athletes valued education for themselves and their own children. They couldn't understand why I wanted to stay and teach in a school that didn't pay much; they didn't know that I was a low-paid PRISM employee. I felt that by staying, I was teaching these kids invaluable lessons. One of them was that money isn't the most important thing.

The members of my PRISM crew knew I was doing the TV work for good experience, and they understood where my heart was. The people at PRISM allowed me to hang on anyway.

One experience made me realize the level of rapport I had developed with those kids after having taught less than two months in the school. One day there had been an early dismissal from school. The kids hung around outside with some older boys, as they normally do. Like any other group of kids left alone and unsupervised, they decided to invent their own fun.

They went out to the street and began to jump on cars. They pushed, rocked them, and actually turned one teacher's car over.

"Mr. Thomas! Mr. Thomas! They're out there jumping on cars," one of my boys rushed back inside to tell me.

"Oh, no," I groaned. I had just gotten my first real car. It was a Honda Accord, and it was still new. It had been the kind of car I had wanted to buy for years. My heart sank, because I was sure they'd damaged it. They must have seen the distress on my face.

"Hey, no sweat about your car," came the word from a student named Isaac.

I didn't understand. I could only envision my car with dents and bruises. How could I not be sweating?

He laughed. "We stopped them when they got to your car, sir."

By then another boy had rushed inside. "We sure stopped them. 'You don't mess with that car!' We told them. *That car* belongs to Mr. Thomas, and if you touch that, then you got to deal with us!'"

By the time I got to the street, the excitement and chaos was over. No one had touched my car. I felt bad for the other teachers who had had their cars vandalized, scratched, or dented. At the same time, it meant a lot to me that even though I was a new teacher, the kids had cared enough to make sure that their friends didn't damage my car. None of the cars suffered any serious damage and the car they turned over was a small sports car. I helped the teacher turn his car upright. Even now, years later, whenever we see each other, we laugh about how the kids were strong enough to turn his small car over.

Right then I knew I had been accepted by my kids as part of their family.

That evening as I walked out of school I realized how destructive kids could be, without being mature enough to realize what they were doing. At the same time, I also saw how caring they could be. Those kids—maybe eight or nine against a large group—had stood up for me, and they wanted to make sure *their* teacher's car didn't get damaged.

My first year at Vaux went smoothly enough, and I didn't have any serious problems with students. The longer I taught, the more I saw the need for extracurricular activities. The only way I knew to bring that about was either to extend the school day or to extend the school year.

Mom and I talked about the need several different times. I spent a lot of time at home, so while we ate dinner, we'd talk about it. She was even more committed to the community than I was. This became even more apparent when we realized that the summer vacation was almost there. For three months the kids had nothing to do and too often no place to go.

"We have to find a way to help them," was Mom's answer every time the subject came up.

After thinking of a number of different possibilities, she and I decided to start a voluntary program on Saturdays for kids who wanted to go to school for an extra day in the week. Mom opened her home so we wouldn't have any problem with getting permission from the school.

In the fall of 1990, we opened the Saturday academy. We tried to get permission to use the school and couldn't get it. That was such a shame, but the rules wouldn't allow us, even though we were offering classes to help the children.

We met for three hours, beginning at 10:00 A.M., and sometimes we went as late as 2:00 in the afternoon. Some Saturdays we had as few as three, but we figured they were three kids who wouldn't have had extra help otherwise. Eight was the largest number we ever had on any Saturday. Most of the children came for extra help in reading and math. Some showed up a few times to catch up with the rest of the class. No matter who was there or what subjects they needed help in, Mom and I also made sure they learned black history.

Some weekends, of course, I had to be away because of my work at sporting events, and we didn't have Saturday academy then, but we always told them beforehand.

We were beginning to reach those who wanted to beat the system and become successful. They inspired us because it helped us know that there were children in our community who wouldn't allow things to stay as they were. They were going to improve themselves. In so doing, they were also going to raise the spirits of the community. The regulars were fairly good students anyway, but we wanted to enrich their training and inspire them to keep learning. We wanted them to see learning as a lifelong achievement.

Even though the numbers remained small, years later, Mom and I rejoiced because seven of those kids who came to our Saturday academy went on to college. For instance, I think immediately of Samirah Lawson, who graduated from Morgan State in Baltimore, and Blair Biggs, a graduate of Lincoln University in Pennsylvania. Those are the human results that inspire me to continue to work with young people the way I did during their early years at Vaux.

Another student, Shawn Murphy, graduated from college in June 2001. He was then, and has remained, an inspiration to me. Maybe I especially remember him because he started at Vaux during my first year. He was one of those kids the school system considered below average, who couldn't keep up with his peers. He lived in a house with twenty different people and in a lot of poverty. Despite all that chaos, Shawn never gave up. Individuals like Shawn have helped me realize I can make a difference.

Shawn became a vital part of that Saturday program. I had also started an after-school program where I taught algebra for those whom the school labeled as low functioning in math. I didn't care about the labels because I believed I could teach any kid to do high-level math. Some of those who came had been discipline problems. I realized that part of their problem in school was that they hadn't achieved any success in their classroom. We wanted to change that.

I'll never forget that on one of his first days in my class, Shawn said he wasn't able to achieve because "there's a conspiracy against me."

He was too young to understand what a conspiracy was, and I knew it was something he had picked up from adults. I told him, "If you can use a big word like *conspiracy* in a sentence, you can achieve anything."

He believed me. He learned. In fact, he did so well in math that in high school they assigned him to tutor his peers in algebra.

The others also learned. Even the worst discipline problems became model students. The Saturday academy may have been small and in some ways others didn't think it was important. But it was a beginning.

I began my second year of the Saturday academy in 1991, which was my third year at Vaux. That fall, I started an alternative learning program at the school called the Second Chance Program. We started this because my principal, Harold Adams, had used this concept at his previous school, so he brought it to Vaux. I did this during school hours and it was for students who got in trouble or misbehaved badly enough to be sent out of their regular classroom. That meant they were sent to the basement to my special classroom instead of being sent home to do nothing for one or more days. The idea was to separate the kids from the main population while they were in the Second Chance Program so they could feel as if they were in a new environment—a place where they could learn and not be ridiculed. That atmosphere would also help us to convince the students to adopt new attitudes and principles.

Obviously, students who committed serious offenses continued to be suspended from school immediately. But the majority of the students in our school were not serious offenders, just children who were misguided and who needed direction. They stayed in the basement anywhere from one to three days. I told Mr. Adams that I was going to work those kids very hard. He agreed, and reminded me that their coming to the basement was supposed to be a form of punishment.

Instead of toning down the regular curriculum as they had done in Mr. Adams's other school, I *increased* the level of the curriculum. I didn't want it to be a program of babysitting or a situation in which the kids merely maintained what they had learned. Especially I wanted them to grasp the fundamentals they hadn't learned in the regular classroom. Also, I wanted them to gain knowledge and to be challenged to learn even more. I started teaching high-level mathematics, binary systems, and then we did base two and not just base ten calculations. They were sixth-, seventh-, and eighth-grade kids who had been failing math. Soon, however, they not only learned algebra but began to pull down top grades.

We also taught them ancient African history, including the building of the pyramids. It amazed the kids to learn how those people of the centuries earlier had figured out how to make them. Then I could again stress the importance of algebra and higher-level mathematics.

To that we added geography, especially about Africa, Europe, and America. My students had to learn the names of the countries on every continent. They even learned the names of the provinces in Canada and the states in Australia—things they had never been challenged to learn before.

Additionally, I asked students to talk about themselves and their heritage as African Americans. They needed to learn about specific black people before them who had made it through struggles. That way they could grasp the contributions that blacks had made to science, literature, and society. I believed they needed to know that blacks in the past had been more than slaves, and that would enable them to hold up their heads as equals in society.

"You're not upholding your level of commitment," I said several times. "As black people, you have to learn to give back to society. Your ancestors fought and died to free the slaves." I talked about some of their specific accomplishments. "They helped to design the city of Washington, D.C., and you come to this school and say you don't care about education? These people fought and died for you to be educated."

This was something I tried to inject regularly, so that they got the idea.

We also talked about how to develop self-esteem. High self-esteem is essential to young people, and I felt it was even more important to kids who had been taught to believe they were losers. If they didn't feel that they were valuable or useful, what chance would they have to succeed? I wanted every child who got sent down to the basement to go back up feeling important and special.

One thing I saw was that whenever students learned to read, they developed a significant level of self-confidence. More than anything else, I was convinced that the ability to read made the difference in their level of self-confidence.

Another thing, I tried to build them up by raising my level of expectation for them. I have always believed that children will rise to whatever level we expect them to reach. Children are very good at meeting our expectations as long as we're clear and convincing about our goals for them. I didn't want to make it easier for them; I challenged them always to do better. I wanted them to believe that they could achieve more than they had thought possible. At first, most of them were skeptical, but

I kept insisting they could do better. I was there to encourage or to lift them up when they couldn't achieve, but I never let them rest by saying, "Oh, that's all right." It wasn't all right unless it was the absolute best they could do.

As they began to realize that I kept raising my expectations of their performance, they changed. They reached higher. They made higher scores, read better, and solved problems more easily.

In those days, I began with a principle that would become extremely important during our chess competition. I wouldn't allow them to think they couldn't do anything. "You're smart. You can do it," I said often. I meant those words.

Those weren't slow minds I was dealing with. Those were kids who hadn't been challenged, who hadn't been told they could reach the top.

"If your mind can conceive and your heart can believe, you can achieve," I often said to them. "There is only one person capable of preventing you from reaching your goals—that person is *you*."

Initially they responded because I told them they could do it. Eventually they responded even more because they told themselves that they could do it. We were both right.

The Second Chance Program developed those kids, and their lives changed. They talked about the program in their regular classes, in the hallways, and away from school. Not only did they improve academically, but they also began to realize that their behavior needed to change. It amazed me to see how they slowly began to accept the reality that rudeness and bad behavior hurt *them* and inflicted pain on others. Once they grasped that, I didn't have to talk to them very much about their behavior.

It was a miracle in many ways.

And yet, not every kid changed. I wish I could report 100 percent success. We had dropouts and a few kids who started out hostile and left indifferent. It always hurt me when someone didn't respond, as if I had failed. No matter how much my head said otherwise, my heart said I had failed.

We did have more successes than failures and that kept me motivated.

Another thing I did was to push them to face themselves and their own mistakes.

When a new student came to the class, I'd ask, "Why are you here?"

"I don't know," was the usual answer. But I kept pushing.

"They blamed me for—" the child would say and then start a litany of things for which he (or she, but mostly they were boys) had been blamed but were innocent of.

It took a while, but I kept asking and talking, and most of all, I tried to listen to them and their problems.

"What did you do? What did you actually do?" I'd say and finally the boy would admit what he had done wrong.

"Now, tell me, who benefited from what you did? Who was hurt by what you did?"

That started them thinking and talking. It wasn't easy for them to be self-reflective, and it wasn't anything they had done before. They'd always blamed someone or some rule. Now they were facing the fact that they *chose* to do mischievous and wrong things.

About that time, I became the basketball coach at Vaux because the coach moved on to another school. Basketball is the most popular sport in the inner city because every kid dreams of being another Michael Jordan. To be on the team, I required every player to come to my after-school enrichment program.

"I want to play basketball," one kid argued. "I don't want no studying."

"You aren't going to be a basketball player for me if you can't read," I said.

Most of the kids cooperated. I did have to kick two kids off the team that year because they wouldn't participate. The word got around—especially because one of them was a good player.

Actually, most kids wanted to be a part of the enrichment program.

It was also a hard struggle. I wanted to be a good role model for those kids, and I wasn't sure how to do it. I wasn't the kind of role model they had seen, because their eyes had been filled with dreams of becoming multimillionaire athletes. Some said they didn't need an education in order to be successful. I had to help them see how narrow their thinking was—and I couldn't do that by telling them. My goal was to get them to strive for an MBA instead of the NBA. They had to figure it out for themselves. And the best way I knew to do that was to be myself and to show them love. I determined that no child would leave my classes without knowing he or she was loved. I wanted to be a father figure to them. Deep inside, I wanted to be for them the kind of father I never had myself.

That's when I decided I had to find something else to challenge them. I had to find something to get them to expand their minds. I wanted sharp minds so they would be at their best to compete.

Then I figured out what to do.

The answer was simple. It just took me a little while to figure it out.

9

Second Chances

"I'm going down to the basement," was the way the kids said it, or they called themselves the "basement kids." They had their lunch brought to them, because going to the basement meant they couldn't eat in the lunchroom or participate in any activities.

This program also gave many students the opportunity to eat free lunches and get seconds without being teased by classmates. Although the entire student body was eligible for free lunches, there was a stigma attached to accepting them. Some kids would go without lunch so that their friends wouldn't tease them about eating "freebies." Among the children, free lunches were thought to be only for poor people and it was disgraceful to accept such handouts. Every day, I tried to convince the children that in some way, all of us are poor and added, "Yes, even Mr. Thomas-EL."

Those statements and my encouragements made children feel more comfortable about eating free lunches.

Teachers sent students downstairs to the Second Chance Program as a disciplinary action and to get them focused educationally—and some had never been focused. We had tremendous success with the program, although the kids stayed only a few days at a time.

Early in the second month of school, a parent came to me with a request. It was one I would hear often for the rest of the year. "Can my child stay in Second Chance all year long? He's been with you for three days and this is the longest time between phones calls from the school about his bad behavior."

"The goal is for your child to be here for three days, ma'am, and then he has to go back to class. I want him to go back and to be successful."

She looked doubtfully at me. "He's never been successful in class before."

"Maybe all of that will change now."

I felt touched by her request. I knew her son fairly well—he had been with me already on four occasions in two months. She wasn't exaggerating. I also saw the gratefulness in her eyes for what we had achieved with him, and it made me want to do even more to stimulate the kids.

The following week her son got into trouble again. He grinned when he walked into the room. This time I knew he had misbehaved on purpose.

I smiled back, but this incident threw me into a strange predicament. The boy wanted to learn, and I knew I could help him. But the only way he could get the kind of help he needed was to misbehave. Something was wrong with an educational system that worked with that set of values.

As the program continued, I kept getting many of the same kids back again. I had expected that before we started the program. What no one had anticipated was that they would intentionally mess up. They wouldn't do anything serious enough to get expelled, but just enough to get reassigned to Second Chance. Shoving another kid or talking back to a teacher was about all it took, and a few of them became experts at minor infractions.

When I asked them the reason for their misbehavior, they wouldn't say they wanted to be down there. But I knew, and I think they also knew that I understood. In the basement those kids felt important. They could achieve and they knew I cared about them.

I don't want to give the impression that I was the only compassionate teacher in the school, because that wasn't true. Vaux had a lot of good teachers and caring adults, and many of them stayed year after year because they cared and they wanted the kids to learn and to be successful.

I'm not sure why I connected with them so readily. Maybe it was my own background of the absent father. I like to think it was a God-given gift. A talent. It was something I could do, and it felt natural for me.

I do know that those so-called losers kept finding ways to become labeled as basement kids. I could see they loved being there. They even walked differently after they had been in the Second Chance Program. Because I could—and I could never explain how—I enabled them to feel important, they then raised their own level of self-esteem. They were learning, of course, but the major reason was because I helped them feel better about themselves.

Then came the backlash from other teachers. "What kind of punishment is Second Chance if kids want to go to the basement?" That one came from a teacher who only lasted at Vaux one year. She wasn't a very effective teacher and probably shouldn't have been in the inner city to begin with. In fact, I got more kids from her class than any other.

"That program's not working," was what one other teacher insisted. "It's the same kids almost every day. As soon as they get to class, they misbehave and I have to send them back downstairs."

In her case, I assumed it was jealousy. She did admit reluctantly that they were doing better on their tests and homework than they had before. Eventually, she volunteered to help us during her free periods.

I know only this much: The kids themselves loved to come down to the basement; their parents loved it when they came down.

More than one child begged the principal, "Please don't suspend me, Mr. Adams. Send me to 'in-house.' If you do that, I'll be good." In-house suspension was the term the kids used for the Second Chance Program.

Another thing is that many of the students who had been sent to Second Chance began to stay after school for what I referred to as the enrichment program. It was an extension of the Second Chance Program. I found such joy in seeing the kids respond, that I told any of them who wanted extra study time to come on down. They wouldn't show if I called it remediation.

One parent said it was like watching a flower slowly blossom.

"Hey, I can read this book!" I heard a boy say one afternoon in the enrichment program. Tears came to my eyes: He had been labeled a slow learner.

"Now I understand what the teacher's been trying to show me," said a sixth grader who had finally understood how to do math problems.

It amazed me as well as my classroom assistant, Mrs. Scott, to see their increased vocabulary and their reading skills. I did everything I could to challenge the children. I made it clear that I expected more of them and they fulfilled my expectations for them. For instance, I made them learn the names and capitals of all fifty states, just as I had done in fifth grade, and just as I had done in the Saturday academy. Maybe it wasn't such vast knowledge, but I saw it as a way of disciplining their minds. As their reading and math skills improved, so did their writing.

"School is lots of fun," said a seventh-grader. He was one that his previous teachers had labeled as incorrigible.

I can still remember many incidents because those kids struggled. It wasn't easy for many of them. They had been in school five, six, or even seven years, and were now learning the basics. But every time a child took a leap forward, I felt as if I shared in that victory.

By 1994, we had the full support of the parents and community. We made tremendous demands on the children, but they were making progress.

The majority of the teachers were supportive. And bless them, a few came down to the basement after school and volunteered. Some of them regularly gave their free ("prep") periods. *They cared.*

The kids soon began to know who cared. A number of staff people volunteered their time. They smiled and did simple little things and the kids knew. I felt so encouraged to realize that I wasn't alone and that other teachers wanted to give our children positive experiences.

More than one teacher came and said, "I want to see if I can replicate that in my classroom." That always gave me a good feeling.

Then came the bad news.

At the end of our fourth year, the school decided that in one more year they would stop the program. They called it phasing it out. Strange as it may seem, they got rid of the program because kids wanted to come to the Second Chance Program. Because they had to misbehave to get there, school officials decided the program wasn't effective. They did not replace it with any enrichment or alternative program.

My heart broke the day I heard the news. How could they take this away from the kids and me? We had worked hard to build this program into something we were proud of. So many of the children had found themselves and become model students through the program.

For several days, bitterness raged inside me. I couldn't let the kids know how I felt, so I didn't say much. But inwardly, I fumed. I tried everything I could to get the program reinstated, but no one listened.

Someday I will find a way to help kids to believe in themselves, I vowed to myself, *someday*. That vow to myself enabled me to keep going.

I could mention a number of success stories that came out of Second Chance, but one of the most inspiring was Thomas Allen. He had gotten into a fight with another boy, and his teacher sent him down to the basement. When I began to talk to him, he responded immediately. A few days later, he became a regular at the enrichment sessions. He wasn't very good in math and his teacher rightfully complained about his writing. He needed help—a lot of it—but Thomas was also willing to work. His schoolwork improved almost overnight.

Thomas began telling all his friends and they figured out ways to become part of the program as well.

As I tell later on, Thomas Allen, the kid who hadn't done well in math, became one of our national champion chess players and *Chess Life* magazine wrote an article about him. He competed in a national championship chess tournament and did not lose one game. This is a feat rarely achieved by professional chess players, let alone school-aged players. Even more important in my opinion, Thomas went on to make the honor roll.

In those early days of teaching, it was the Thomas Allens that made me know I was doing the right thing. Despite the failures I would have through the years, there will always be kids like Thomas Allen.

10

A Woman Named Shawnna

Graduation day for Vaux Middle School in June 1991 turned out to be a special day for me. We held the graduation ceremony every year at Bright Hope Baptist Church, where Bill Gray was the pastor. (A former U.S. congressman, he is now executive director of the United Negro College Fund and was the man to whom Bill Gates gave a billion dollars for the Fund in 2000.)

As the day approached, I eagerly looked forward to it. Our kids—many of whom I had helped and worked with—were graduating from the eighth grade. They were not dropping out but going on to high school. I loved seeing the kids go on for more education. I felt proud of every one of them.

In that sense, every graduation is special to me. But there's another reason why the graduation of 1991 stands out so clearly—far brighter than any at Vaux.

The one thing that was different was that I spotted a stunning young woman immediately before the graduation ceremony. Obviously, I'd seen attractive women before, but this one caught my attention and momentarily diverted me from focusing on the kids. That in itself was unusual.

I knew then that I wanted to meet her. However, I didn't get a chance to talk to her because I was too heavily involved in getting the kids ready. Maybe I behaved like a nervous, fussy parent, but I wanted everything to be perfect for those kids. This was a big moment in their lives. I went around the graduating class and spoke to every child. Whenever necessary, I adjusted the cap or the gown. My preoccupation with the kids meant I didn't have time to talk to anyone socially.

That didn't stop me from glancing at her several times. She was tall, athletic-looking, and wore a nicely tailored business suit. I'm not altogether sure what it was, but she arrested my attention like no other woman I had seen in a long time. Because of my involvement with the kids, I couldn't focus on anything else. Otherwise, I'm not shy, and I would have gone over and introduced myself.

The graduation started and demanded my full attention. Even so, I stared at her off and on during the ceremony.

At Vaux, the tradition has been that after graduation, we have a dinner and dance for the graduates. In 1991, we held it at the Cornucopia Reception Hall on Parkside Avenue in West Philadelphia.

As soon as graduation was over and I had taken a few pictures with the kids and their families, I rushed over to the Cornucopia Reception Hall to help them finish setting up.

As soon as I walked into the reception, I spotted that same young woman. Apparently she was related to one of the kids who graduated. I smiled, hoping that I would have a chance to talk to her. Those expected free minutes didn't materialize because one of the graduates called me and introduced me to her family and then someone else demanded my attention.

Then came the dinner and I still hadn't spoken to her. As I ate, I saw where she was sitting. I tried not to let her catch me looking her way but it was difficult. I thought I saw her staring at me several times, but I wasn't sure. This was a strange situation because I didn't want her to see me looking at her every minute, but I also did not want her to think that I was not interested in her. She sat at the same table as graduate Shirelle Erving, one of our star athletes, so I guessed that was who she was related to.

Once the dinner was over, it was time for the dance to begin. The DJ started playing records, but no one moved to the floor. Slowly, a few girls found their way to the dance floor. I watched until one entire song finished, and still none of the boys had gone out on the floor.

I walked up to the podium and picked up the microphone. "This is a dance, and you're not dancing with each other. Come on! Let's dance, or we'll turn off the music!" I knew they were shy and waiting for someone else to start. "You're here to have a good time. It's the last time many of you are going to see each other. You can't stand around and watch everybody. Okay?"

Finally, a few boys moved out on the floor. That encouraged others to join them. By the end of the second song, at least two dozen graduates filled the floor.

"Why are you telling these young people to dance with each other, but you're not asking anybody to dance?"

I whirled around and stared at her. It was the woman I had seen at graduation. Up close, she looked even better than she had from a distance.

"I didn't know anybody here wanted to dance with me."

"I want to dance," she said.

That's how I met Shawnna Key.

She told me she was Shirelle Erving's cousin. "I know Shirelle very well, but she never told me she had such a beautiful cousin."

She laughed, and we danced for a few minutes without talking. Oddly enough, I wanted to know everything about her, but didn't know where to begin. Was she college educated? Did she like children? Was her family close? Would she be interested in a poor kid from the projects who wasn't from a close-knit family? That kind of family was something I had always longed for.

"Why did you come to the dance?" I finally asked.

"My grandmother came up from Georgia for Shirelle's graduation. My uncle is also getting married this weekend. That makes it a very special time for our family, and my grandmother can take in both events."

I knew right then that I wanted to know more about her.

What I didn't know until much later is that Shawnna had spotted me at the graduation. When she saw me, she watched the way I interacted with the children. She observed how readily they listened and followed my orders without question. That interaction immediately impressed her.

She turned to her grandmother. "I'm going to marry that man," she had said.

I loved dancing with Shawnna and felt attracted to her. I knew I had to see her again and I told her so.

She offered to give me her phone number, but I felt embarrassed. I didn't want the kids to see me writing it down. This may sound a bit silly, but I felt very self-conscious. I wanted to be a good role model for the kids, and I didn't want them to think that outside the classroom, I was some guy that went around and picked up women and got their phone numbers.

"I don't want the kids to see me writing it down," I said and explained my reason.

To my relief she understood. "Would you mind calling me at school one day? Just ask for me and then you can give me your number and I'll call you later."

"No, I'm not going to do that," she said.

I had really messed up, and I started to apologize.

I think she enjoyed my discomfort, so she laughed and then

said, "You give me your home number and I'll memorize it. That way the kids won't have to see you give me anything."

I told her the number and she memorized it.

We danced maybe five songs together. Again, I felt too embarrassed to stay out on the floor any longer with the same woman. But several times I smiled at her from across the room.

I kept hoping she'd call. All the next day, I went over everything that had happened and kept punishing myself for all the wrong and stupid things I'd said. I told myself I should have memorized *her* phone number. What if she didn't call? How would I get in touch with her? I didn't like having to call Shirelle's mom and ask for Shawnna's phone number.

My worrying and obsessing were for nothing. The graduation had been on Friday. Saturday night Shawnna called me.

We talked for nearly three hours—the longest and most interesting phone call I had ever had in my life. In fact, I was amazed when I hung up and realized how long we had talked.

I learned that Shawnna had gotten her degree from Philadelphia's Drexel University. She had taken a position at the university to recruit students. We talked about our other interests.

Before we hung up, I invited her to dinner the next evening. She accepted.

She went out to dinner with me the night after that.

Shawnna traveled often for Drexel, and sometimes she'd have to be gone for three or four days at a time. But almost every evening when she was in Philadelphia, we found a way to get together.

One of the concerns I had about dating any woman was that it might cause a problem by my spending too much time with school kids. I figured most women would get jealous or possessive and find ways to sabotage all the time and energy I spent with them.

It's difficult for someone to be in a relationship with a dedicated teacher. It takes a tremendous amount of sacrifice on that person's part. Many of my friends and colleagues who were educators told me that they had gone through troubled relationships because of the time they spent in school or with kids. Was she ready to get into a relationship with me when she saw how much time I spent with students? Would she get upset like the other women I had heard about?

Not Shawnna. In fact, it impressed her that I wanted to work with young people so much. She encouraged me, and I felt she fully supported my involvement with them.

Shawnna came from a family of four girls. Her older sister, Karen, was a graduate of the University of Pennsylvania and a college administrator. Shawnna's younger sister, Delores, was a student at Messiah College in Harrisburg, Pennsylvania. Delores went on to become a teacher, but died at the age of twenty-four. Shawnna's baby sister was finishing high school.

Those girls didn't grow up in the projects, but they had lived in a poor neighborhood in West Philadelphia. Shawnna also had grown up in a two-parent household, which I envied. She was bright and articulate and did well in school, and even had the opportunity to attend a private high school. Eventually we would find out she attended high school with my friend from Masterman, Robbie, who is now a teacher at Bartram High School.

We dated for two years. During that time, we had only one serious difference—our religious backgrounds. Shawnna was a deeply committed Christian and an active member of Resurrection Community Methodist Church.

I had been in and out of church most of my life. At one time my mother had become a Muslim. That's when she added EL to our name, which is Arabic and Hebrew for *God*. Although I went to the mosque many times, I never lost my faith in the

Church. I wasn't a born-again Christian, but I did respect the faith.

Here's Shawnna's version of our story:

Salome and I had been seeing each other for a couple of weeks when we decided one night to have a conversation about religion. We talked about how we were out at dinner recently when I noticed Salome signed his name Thomas-EL. I asked him what *EL* meant.

"I was wondering when you were going to ask me about that," he said, and explained about his mom's involvement with the Islamic religion when he was a young boy.

I told him I had recently ended a relationship because the man was not interested in going to church with me and especially that he wasn't open to becoming a Christian. "My faith is very important to me, and I don't want to get seriously involved with anyone who can't share that commitment." I also made it clear that my next serious relationship would be a move toward marriage. I wasn't interested in playing the dating game.

"You know I am not a Christian, right?" Salome asked.

"Yes, I—I guess I did know that."

"If that's the way things are, what does that mean?"

"It means we can't see each other." Those were hard words to say, but my faith in Jesus Christ and my commitment to my church were the most important things in my life.

Salome went on to explain that he had spent a large part of his childhood in the church, studying the Bible, and learning about Jesus Christ.

"But are you a believer?"

"I've never been confronted with that question before."

As I watched his face, he seemed confused. I don't think he

realized then that when I said the word *Christian,* I meant more than a strong religious preference. For me, it was a lifestyle and an experience that many refer to as being born again.

We had a long discussion. He didn't believe as I did and he wasn't going to become a believer to please me. I respected that, of course. In the end, we agreed that we would not have a relationship. I had to hold back tears when he left, because I was already falling in love with him. But I had made my decision and I knew it was the right one.

For a week neither of us made contact.

I missed him, I really did. From the time I had first seen him at the graduation, I believed that God had planned for us to be together. I didn't want to compromise my values—and I wouldn't—but I didn't want to give up so easily.

I wrote him a letter and said, "When I first saw you with those kids, I told my grandmother that I was gong to marry you . . . I feel that God has presented me with a challenge."

Salome called me. "We need to talk," he said.

We went to dinner later that week. As we talked, I discovered that Salome actually did believe in Christ. It had not been put to him that pointedly. We talked about his joining a church and resuming our relationship. (Later, when we visited a friend's church in Atlanta, he made a public commitment of his faith.)

That major issue now settled, we continued to date over the next two years.

On election night in 1992, I had just gotten the news that Bill Clinton had been elected President of the United States. I was in College Park, Maryland, where I had been recruiting students for Drexel University.

The hour was quite late and someone knocked on my door. I didn't know anyone in the hotel, and that knock scared me.

"Yes, who is it?" I asked without opening the door.

"Did you call hotel security?"

I laughed. I would have recognized that voice anywhere.

When I opened the door, Salome took my left hand and placed a half-carat diamond engagement ring on my finger.

Then he asked me to marry him. I had no idea Salome wanted to get married so soon.

How could I refuse?

We set the date for July 2, 1993, and we were married in a candlelight ceremony. It was very special because four of Salome's students from Vaux—Victor, Rodger, Lasheena, and Lovesha—were ushers at our wedding. We spent a week in St. Thomas, Virgin Islands, to relax and honeymoon.

This is Salome again.

Shortly after I married Shawnna, we moved to the Atlanta area and I found a teaching job. Shawnna would start working as a recruiter for Georgia Tech. This would be a great opportunity for both of us to pursue graduate degrees.

Immediately I landed a teaching job, and I loved the kids, but we both missed Philadelphia. It shouldn't have made any difference where we lived, I kept saying, as long as we were both doing the things we loved.

We might have stayed except that several kids from Vaux wrote me letters. "We miss you Mr. Thomas-EL." (By then, everyone was calling me Mr. Thomas-EL instead of Mr. Thomas.) "When are you coming back to Vaux?"

"School isn't much fun since you left," one letter said. I reread that letter half a dozen times and couldn't hold back the tears. I felt as if I had let them down. I had gone there to be their role model, to show them that there were honorable men in this world who would come and be there for them. I called a teacher at Vaux, Mrs. Octavia Lewis, and asked her to stop the students from sending me letters. "They're beginning to depress me."

"Maybe you need to think about that some more," she said.

"Yeah, maybe," I said.

So many of those inner-city kids had no significant male figure in their lives. It wasn't unusual to have two or three children in a family, all with different fathers. I heard countless stories of men who came, stayed a short time, and left.

"I'm like the others," my conscience kept saying. "You loved those kids, but even more important, they loved you. They believed in you. Then you deserted them."

I had been with some of those kids four years and had known them when they entered fifth grade. I had watched and worried over them every year.

"We have to go back," I said to Shawnna. "I miss those kids too much. They depended on me." I started explaining all my reasons, but I didn't need to. Shawnna understood. She liked Atlanta, but she was ready to return.

Once we had agreed, I called Rotan Lee, the school board president in Philadelphia, with whom I had developed a good relationship. He had been part of a program I had set up in the community where men came on Friday evenings and Saturdays and played basketball with neighborhood kids. It was another way for wholesome adult black males to interact with kids from the projects. We did something else as well. Occasionally, we took the children to see New York or visit the Guggenheim Museum. At other times we went to dinner in center city Philadelphia. We also made it a point to ask the kids to read for us or to name a few colleges they had thought about attending.

"When you get back to Philly," he said, "call me. I'm sure I can help you find another teaching position."

As soon as the Christmas vacation rolled around, I resigned my teaching job. We packed up and returned to Philadelphia.

The day after we returned, I called and Rotan referred me to a woman in Human Resources. She invited me to come to her office and assured me that she would have no trouble finding a teaching position for me.

Excitement raced through me all morning. I was going home—to Vaux Middle School. I would be with my kids again.

That didn't happen.

"I'm sorry, but we have a more pressing need at University City High School," she said. University City is in the area where the University of Pennsylvania is located as well as Drexel University and the University of Sciences, so they call it University City.

"Isn't there any way for me to go back to Vaux?"

"We need you at University City High School for the rest of this school year. If you'll finish out the year, I'll talk to you about you going to Vaux in September."

I didn't argue. She was doing the best she could for me.

"If you're willing, you can start teaching right away."

I pushed aside my disappointment, smiled, and said, "Okay, yes, I'll go to University City." I became a special education teacher again and taught science and social studies.

The school was about fifteen minutes' drive from Vaux. I don't know how many afternoons I drove past Vaux school, wishing I were back there. And each time I prayed, "Please, God, let me go back."

I began to go by Vaux after school to play ball with the kids in the afternoon and evenings. I didn't create any problems and was careful not to undermine anything going on at Vaux. I wanted to be around those kids again.

At that time, University City High School, predominately black with a growing Asian population, had a lot of discipline problems. For instance, students seemed always to be standing around in the hallways. There was no period during the day when groups of kids were not standing around talking, making noise, and sometimes scuffling. I didn't have any real authority, but I wouldn't let them stand outside my classroom.

"Can you help me, Mr. EL?" the principal asked me after I had been there about three weeks. She was new and this was a big challenge to her. "I've talked to other teachers and they say you're a good disciplinarian. You're what I need."

"Count on me to do anything I can."

"Can you help me keep the hallways clear during the lunch period?" She knew it meant giving up my own lunch period. "We need to start somewhere and I think that's the worst time and place."

"Sure, I can help you," I said. "I don't know how well I'll do in high school because most of my work has been in middle school, but I'll do what I can."

Students who had been assigned to the first lunch period finished before the bell rang. So they walked up and down hallways or anywhere else they wanted. They disrupted other classes and the teachers didn't know how to stop them.

Together, she and I mapped out a plan to keep students inside the lunchroom. We decided that once they came in for lunch, they would not be allowed to leave. I would enforce that rule. Also, once the lunch period started and the bell rang, no student would be allowed to go into the lunchroom. That way, no student could wait somewhere and go up and down the hallways and then come into lunch late.

That meant we had to have somebody who was brave enough to confront students who tried to leave and who would stop latecomers from entering. She asked me to take on that task.

It was difficult, and I had a lot of complaining at first, but they complied. I've always believed that children want discipline, even if they deny it or fight against it.

The real test came the third day. I'm six feet tall, muscular, and in good physical shape. A group of four large boys—three of them larger than I am—got up and headed toward the door. Obviously, they planned to leave the lunchroom.

The leader must have been about six-three and weighed at least 225 pounds. For the two previous days, he had come up to me by himself and wanted to go out. "You can't leave the lunchroom," I said matter-of-factly. Both times he turned around, went back, and sat down.

On the third day, he brought his friends with him. As they came toward me, he said in a loud voice to his friends, "The first person that says anything to me is going to get punched in his face."

This kid knew I would be the first person to say something to him. My eyes focused on them, and even though I felt afraid, I knew I couldn't back down, regardless of what they did.

"I mean it!" he said even louder. "If anybody says *anything* to me, I'm going to drop him."

I figured I might as well face this. Instead of waiting until they swaggered to the door, I walked right up to him and stood with my face about four inches from his. "I heard everything you said just now," I said in a calm voice. "But you have to go back in that lunchroom." I didn't blink.

"I knew you were going to tell me to go back." He turned around, the others followed him, and they all sat down.

That was the end of it. I think that he wanted to know how dedicated I was. That could have been the end of my career, but instead it was the beginning of serious discipline. Once the students saw that this was now the policy, and we would strictly enforce it, they didn't trouble me. No one ever tried to leave the lunchroom early after that.

At times the students got out of hand, but the principal and I sensed they were looking for direction. Once we adults started to assert ourselves, the school began to turn itself around. It's in good shape now. Many of the students are going to college, and they have a dedicated, committed administration. The children wanted to see that adults were committed to their goals and to make sure that they stood up for what they believed in.

I stayed at University City until the end of the year. I loved teaching there, but my heart was with the kids at Vaux School. I was determined to get back to them.

Just before school ended in June, I returned to Human Resources and spoke to the woman who had sent me to University City. She started to put me through the whole process of selecting a school when I reminded her, "You told me that if I went to University City for the rest of the year, you'd make sure I went back to Vaux."

She remembered her promise. "Very well. You can go back to Vaux."

I was home again at Vaux and began to teach there in the fall of 1994. They assigned me to work in the alternative learning center—the Second Chance Program. This was its final year. Mrs. Lewis, a dedicated teacher at Vaux, had kept the program running in my absence. In addition to teaching in the Second Chance Program, I was assigned the additional duty of coordinating a small learning community.

The small learning community idea is that of a school within a school. At Vaux, we had three small learning communities; each had about three hundred students in it with ten or eleven teachers in each small community. Members of each community met weekly, and we set up programs and expectations for three hundred kids. Of course, we also had other programs where the entire school worked together.

In working with these communities, we all ate lunch together with the smaller community and had all our classes together in a teaming model. Each small learning community had a coordinator and they covered all the grades five through eight.

As far as I'm concerned, it was a rather uneventful year except for one thing: That's the year we began to rebuild the official Vaux Chess Team.

11

Resurrection

When I returned to Vaux in 1994, I became involved with the basketball team. I wasn't the coach because Mr. Edwards, a new physical education teacher, took on that responsibility. I served more as a mentor and tutor for kids who were interested in the sport. That was fine, because basketball is the sport I love the most. One thing, however, bothered me. I got fed up with the students who attended school only so they could play basketball. They all had fantasies of becoming big-time members of the 76ers.

I wanted them to play, and they were good players too, maybe not star-quality, but better than most of the others at Vaux. Yet as much as I love basketball, education had to take precedence. I wanted them to get involved in something more academic—something to help them in their life after they left school.

After the start of the basketball season, I laid down an iron-clad policy, and the basketball coach fully supported my policy. To stay eligible for basketball, every player had to have a passing grade in every subject. We lost two players, and I hated that, but I had made the rule and I would not allow any exceptions. It saddened me to talk to kids who envisioned themselves becoming athletes as their ticket out of the projects. They weren't willing to work hard and use their brains. They only wanted to play basketball. I had to show them there was a better way. I had to find something to stir their minds.

I wanted to do something to challenge the kids to strive for academic achievement. Sports were fine, but so few ever made it big time. And what about the kids who weren't physically large or strong?

"A mind is a terrible thing to waste," is the motto of the United Negro College Fund. I knew—and had known for a long time—that it was the minds of the children I wanted to reach.

But how?

Shortly after the 1994–95 school year began, I started thinking about the rich chess history at Vaux. No one could be involved very long in the Vaux community without knowing of the school's past glory with their chess team. A PBS station had made a video about them called *The Mighty Pawns* that highlighted the national titles those inner-city kids had won. The library contained almost fifty trophies—they were old, but they were there to remind everyone of their great past.

When I moved to Atlanta and mentioned I had taught at Vaux Middle School, many educators knew about the school's history.

"That's where they had the terrific chess team, wasn't it?" It amazed me that I heard that kind of response from many, even when I lived in Georgia.

After I returned to Vaux, I checked out the video and watched it several times. As I watched, I mentally compared the various sports they could get involved in. As I did so, I thought, this is a mental sport where they can gain fame, and they can be one at Vaux and one from Frederick Douglass Elementary School, which was then a feeder school for Vaux. They started a chess program at Frederick Douglass that fed into the Vaux program. The Douglass and Vaux programs were the first in the country to feed chess players from an elementary school into a junior high school. There are hundreds of programs like that now in the United States. I proudly point out to my students that the first one started in the inner city.

The Vaux chess team won their first national junior high championship in 1976. They competed, of course, only with their own age group, and won against the best junior high schools in the nation. Subsequently, they won six more national championships for a total of seven consecutive national titles from 1976 to 1982. No other school has come close to matching that record.

In the mid-1980s the original coaches moved to other schools and cities, and the program eventually died.

My biggest challenge will be to get the kids to buy into chess, I thought. It won't be the same because this is now a totally different culture.

Chess is a game of algebraic concepts because the board has sixty-four squares and each square is a coordinate on a plane. Each square has its own name. In algebra, we talk about variables (a, x, y), letters that represent unknown numbers. Each square on the chessboard has a letter and a number like a1 and b4. So it would be easy for the students to transfer those skills right over into the algebra classroom.

That's it, I thought. If they could grasp those concepts, not only would they play excellent chess, but it would teach them to think, to analyze, and to broaden their knowledge.

That's when I knew chess was the answer.

popular in the school for achieving. Kids—like everybody else—want to be noticed, to be accepted and valued for themselve This would make them athletes of the highest caliber. The could get attention, just like athletes, and be known and a firmed all over the community. Most of all, there would be th educational benefit.

I lay on the sofa as the video played again. This time I watched the faces of those junior high school students. They glowed. Their eyes revealed pride and excitement.

Yes, this could work.

But how would I start it?

The Vaux chess program had been dead for years. The more I pondered what to do to help these kids, the more I sensed that learning to play chess and competing in tournaments was the answer. I'm only slightly above average as a player, so I knew that my skills weren't enough to take the kids where they needed to go. I had to have help. I also figured that if I could teach the kids the basics—and get a little coaching help from someone else—they could learn and they could be better players than I was.

Right from the beginning, I worked on a single principle. These students would never know they couldn't be successful—I would inspire them to believe they could win.

I had no idea how well that simple philosophy would pay off.

The Vaux chess team had been formed somewhere around 1975. In those days, Vaux had been an integrated school that gradually made the transition into an all-black school. I've spoken with alumni members who told me they were a part of a chess club even in the sixties. In those days, they had a Russian club and a chess club. The *competing* chess team—so far as I know—dates back to the early seventies. They had two coaches,

I needed to restart the chess program. It was a natural.
It was time for a resurrection.

Because I knew he was an excellent chess player, I met with one of our parents, Ishmael Al-Islam, who was also one of our school volunteers and a man heavily involved in the community. He often volunteered to help in the Second Chance Program. Many of the boys looked forward to his mentoring and words of wisdom on a daily basis. In the past, he had tried to keep the children involved in chess but had never received enough support. He was exactly the man I needed.

"Would you like to help start up the team again?" I asked. "Here's my goal. I want these kids to play chess well enough to compete on the national level. That's my goal for them, but I need help."

Ishmael could have been shocked at my dream for the kids— even before we had a team—and I didn't know if we could motivate and teach the children to play.

He smiled. "I'm willing to help."

"That's all I need to hear," I said. I'm a high-energy person; I love organizing and promoting exciting activities. I was in my element.

During the old days at Vaux, they had what I'd call a chess culture. Students pulled out the boards during their lunch periods. Some kids stayed after school to work on their game. For a few years after the national chess tournaments ended and the coaches had moved on, some of them continued to play. Each year, I was told, the number of players had decreased because no one led them or challenged them. With no encouragement, how could they have continued to grow?

By 1994, no one played chess at the school. I heard that a few of the kids played at home with their parents. As I would learn later, a few were actually good because of that opportunity to play at home.

I had to figure out a strategy to make kids *want* to play, even to get them to beg to be on the team. If I announced we were starting again, I figured I'd get a few takers, but that wasn't what I wanted. I wanted kids who saw this as an exciting opportunity to have fun and to improve their minds.

In the advertising industry and in public relations they talk about creating a need. That's what Ishmael and I decided to do. We would create a need for the kids. Then they would come to us.

One day Ishmael and I walked into the lunchroom carrying five chess sets. We had maybe a dozen sets left from the old days, but I didn't want to bring them all out at one time. I placed four of the boards on a nearby table and opened the fifth board. Without saying a word, I set up the pieces.

All the kids were watching and the room had gone silent. Someone asked, "Are you going to play chess?"

Ishmael sat across from me and neither of us said a word, as we had agreed, because this was part of our ploy. We began to play and intentionally ignored the kids. By now, half a dozen had grouped around us.

They watched and one or two began to tell us how to move. We continued to play as if we were the only ones in the room.

"I can beat you, Mr. Ishmael," one student boasted.

"I can beat Mr. EL. I can. My dad taught me."

"You're supposed to be quiet while they're playing," one boy said.

We didn't say anything or acknowledge their presence, but we kept playing.

"I know how to play. I play with my dad," someone said.

"You aren't very good, Mr. EL," another said. She was right, but I ignored her. "I play with my grandfather and he's better than you are."

Someone giggled. "Mr. EL ain't very good. Even I can beat him."

"Why can't we play?" someone finally asked.

"Can I play? Will you teach me to play?"

That was what I had waited to hear. Until then, they had watched out of curiosity, but now they were interested. They *wanted* to play.

"Step right up and show me what you have," I said. I couldn't help it. I grinned and wanted to jump up and shout. This was working better than I had expected.

Within two minutes the other four boards had been set up and those who knew how to play had started their own games. I smiled to myself because some didn't know how to play but acted as if they did. That was okay with me. It was interest in the game I had wanted.

Soon we had four kids playing against Ishmael and me. Between forty and fifty kids had circled the tables and watched. They cheered on the kids, of course, and trashed my playing. I loved it. This was even better than I had hoped for. A few probably would have rooted for me, but their friends were there and they wouldn't have dared to encourage me. That was exactly what I wanted to happen.

Ishmael and I easily won the games—he more easily than I. I knew that if these kids began to play seriously, it wouldn't be long before they would beat me. To beat their teacher would make them feel good about themselves.

We had the perfect setup, and we had created a need. The kids competed against two men in the community. They respected Ishmael and I knew they responded to me.

The resurrection had already begun to take place, but only Ishmael and I knew it.

"You want to learn to play?" I looked around and asked. I tried to make my face look as if I didn't think they would be interested.

The kids were almost wild in shouting yes to us.

"We can teach you if you want to learn. These kids that played today can get better. So, okay, here's what we'll do. Mr. Ishmael and I are going to start a chess team and you can sign up. You don't have to know how to play to join."

"When? When are you going to start a team?"

"I want to sign up."

"Where do we sign up?"

"Soon. Real soon," was all I would say. I wasn't quite ready to start the team. I needed to fan the flames of desire a little more first.

For another three or four days, every lunch period we set up the boards and played for forty-five minutes—that's the most time they had while they ate.

The kids who knew how to play would be ready and grabbed the chessboards. They played and others watched.

"This isn't enough time," they grumbled when the bell rang. "We just got started."

"Wait! I didn't have time to eat," one boy said. He had played chess the entire lunch period and forgot to get in line for lunch. Luckily, the cafeteria manager gave him a boxed lunch. I knew that boy would go on to use the same determination to become an excellent chess player.

"There's no time to learn," another boy said. "They keep playing and they won't take time to teach me."

I then took the next step. "You can practice after school. If you're willing to stay an hour or so."

"If I come, will you teach me to play?" another child asked.

"Absolutely," I said. I was grinning and ready to shout. They were responding exactly as I had hoped they would.

That afternoon when they came down to the basement, I set up the boards for those who already knew how to play. I gave them only a few words of instruction. "Now, here's what you need to do. When you lose, I want you to go back and think about the mistakes you made. Figure out what you could have done better. If you'll do that, you can be champion players."

They believed me.

Now we were ready for serious playing. I had made up posters and placed them in the hallways:

> **DO YOU WANT TO PLAY CHESS?**
> **DO YOU WANT TO BE ON TV, RADIO, AND IN NEWSPAPERS?**
> **DO YOU WANT YOUR GRADES TO IMPROVE?**

At the bottom of the posters it said that this was for beginners as well as those who knew how to play. I listed the times and indicated they had to sign their names in order to join the team.

Ishmael had already taught a few of them to play, and he was willing to teach others. In fact, that was his job: He would teach; I would motivate.

My job was also to get them more chessboards. If we were going to compete—and I made it clear from the beginning that not only would we compete, but we would be better and tougher and meaner than the Mighty Pawns—it involved money. They would have to travel. They would have to have transportation just to be able to compete on the state level, let alone on a national level. It was up to me to raise the funds.

I could buy a chessboard and set for about fifteen dollars. We already had twelve old sets with only one or two pieces missing. That was enough for the start, but eventually we would need more.

From the first meeting, we had a large turnout—actually better than I had expected. I had hoped for at least ten. We had about twice that many. These kids were the important ones. If we got them excited, they would become our best advertisements.

The kids also needed chessboards so they could practice at home. At first, we let them check out the boards overnight or on weekends. That didn't work well. They would come back with pieces missing or a board damaged. Soon we were down to ten complete boards and sets. We couldn't do that any longer.

I didn't know much about fund-raising, so I began to buy as many boards myself as I could afford. I gave them to the kids. "Take this home. It's yours as long as you're on the team. You practice at home and you'll get better."

I wish I could put words on paper to express the gleam in their eyes. When those kids took a board and knew it was theirs, they glowed. Perhaps for the first time in their lives, they felt important. I told them they could be outstanding players and they believed me.

As I continued to buy and give away chess sets, I remember thinking, fifteen dollars isn't much money to help a kid feel special.

We kept putting up posters. New kids came to almost every practice. The old timers—the first ones—explained the rules to the new ones. I loved watching them assert themselves.

"You can't be bad in here," a sixth-grader would say to an eighth-grader. "You have to keep your grades up. If you're having trouble in any subject, you can get help here." They sounded grown up and so proud of themselves.

We did have tutoring available for any subjects they needed help with. One of the requirements to being on the team was that they had to keep up with their class work. Bad grades meant being dropped from the team. So far as I can remember, that entire first year I never had to drop a child from the team.

I stopped playing chess to work with the kids who needed help with their homework or who had gotten behind in a subject.

We kept hanging up signs and putting up posters. Kids visited us. Not all of them signed up, but most of them did. Some came to watch or support a friend. Not once did we ever have discipline problems down there. That wasn't even an issue. Those kids were motivated.

The students had to keep their grades up, and I reminded them of that almost every session. On any afternoon after school, some kids would be playing chess, while others would be finishing their homework. We always had one or two who needed tutoring.

Once in a while, I'd realize that several of them were having a problem in the same area, so I'd stop all the games and gather all the kids together and spend a few minutes teaching. I would stop the entire chess class and I'd start going over problems on the board. Science and math seemed to be the hardest for them.

We also used chess as the means to enrich the children's minds. When I stopped everyone, I always had one or two complain, "We want to play chess."

"You can. Later. But you need this more. If you stretch your mind with math, you'll be a better player."

No one ever challenged that statement.

As I look back at those first kids who came, it makes me feel good to realize that they've continued to do well in school. Several have gone on and graduated from college. Of course, there were failures, and that hurt when a kid dropped out. But I found consolation in reminding myself of those who had made it.

"You can only be good if you're smart. You have to have good brains," I'd say. "You have to develop those brains." That became a part of my daily pep talk. I meant it and they believed me. The children would often complain about my preaching, but they listened and my plan worked. They didn't know what they couldn't do, so they did what I told them they could accomplish.

"The only way you're going to be able to compete is if you do well in class." I'd pause and look them right in the eyes. "You have to understand that."

They nodded and smiled.

Peer pressure was an important and often negative factor we had to cope with.

"You don't need help," some of their peers would say. "You're smart enough already."

My chess kids stood up for themselves and education. More than once I overheard them say, "I need help and I'm going to get it."

"I'm doing much better in math since I've been coming to chess practice." I heard that often. Some of those same students asked for additional math work so that they could advance.

I had no problem with that either.

An interesting fact is that the previous chess team had been all boys. From the beginning we had a few girls participating. When we started, we actually had three girls. Kenyetta Lucas, who was the first female from Vaux to compete on a national level, also became a straight A student. She is one of my great success stories, which I'll share later in this book.

Sometimes, even now, I get a little down, especially when I hear about one of our inner-city kids being killed or turning to drugs. It hurts . . . it really hurts. Then I think of Kenyetta, Thomas, Demetrius, Denise, and a dozen others, and it lifts my spirits again.

They are the results.

They made the effort worthwhile.

12

Competition Begins

When I returned from Atlanta, my goal was to become a principal. I enrolled in a principal certification program at Cheyney University, which is one of the oldest historical black colleges in the country. Located in Delaware County, near Coatesville, Pennsylvania, they have a graduate urban campus in Philadelphia.

I started that program in the fall of 1994 to earn my administrative elementary principal certification. While studying there, I had the opportunity to take two international courses and stay in England for three weeks. One course, on school finance, was at Cambridge University, and then I participated in a curriculum workshop at the University of London. As part of my studies, I visited many schools in London and Cambridge and observed the way the British financed their schools and developed their curriculum.

Because the late afternoons were free, I spent those hours teaching British children how to play chess. Someone took a photograph of me teaching several of the kids in an elementary school to play chess and sent the photograph back to the Commonwealth of Pennsylvania. The photo was featured in the

State System of Higher Education's 1996 calendar. This gave my students and the rest of the world an opportunity to see my universal philosophy about educating all children regardless of their race or global address.

I loved being in England. At Cambridge, when people found out I was an educator, they paid me a lot of respect for my profession—something I didn't receive much of in the States.

I returned to the States, finished my graduate work at Cheyney, and received my principal certification in 1996.

I had achieved one more goal.

The Vaux chess program went forward even when I was in England. We continued to get in new kids and the interest grew. As soon as they signed up, if they didn't know anything about the game, we put them in our beginning program. If they knew how to play, we let them play with others of their own age to determine their strength level.

As I mentioned earlier, one of our first important female players was Kenyetta Lucas. She didn't know anything about chess when she came into my math class. Actually, she didn't come into my classroom to play chess at all. It's quite interesting how she got involved.

Kenyetta's teacher, a white female, quit the second day on the job because she couldn't take the stress of teaching in the inner city. There had been no discipline, the kids were shouting and making noise, and the principal asked me if I could go in "to stabilize the classroom."

I did that and got to know everyone in the class. Almost immediately Kenyetta stood out because she demonstrated a strong mathematical aptitude and the ability to pick up on combinations and algebraic configurations right away. Ishmael taught her the basics. In addition to being smart, Kenyetta was different from many of her peers. She not only wanted to learn, but also wanted more of a challenge.

I spoke with her parents and the principal, and with their consent, I had her moved into my homeroom classroom so she could spend the majority of the day with me. One of the first challenges she accepted was to enroll in the chess program. In fact, she was one of the first to sign up. Although some of the kids picked up the game faster, she was unquestionably the most dedicated. And that dedication paid off.

Once we started the chess program, I took all the beginning students and worked with them so I could apply my ability as a teacher of mathematics to teaching students the foundation. Once they understood the basics, Ishmael taught them advanced strategies.

It was actually Ishmael's idea to do it that way. He said to me, "When you teach, you talk to the students about geometrics on the chessboard and different combinations. I've never seen it taught that way before. The kids seem to pick up on it." He had seen chess taught primarily as a way to make moves with winning combinations. "I see our kids creating new types of combinations."

I wanted to do two things with the students. I wanted the game to come alive so that they'd have fun and enjoy themselves. This had to be fun learning for them. I also wanted them to learn the principles that they could apply to other subjects in school and, even more important, principles they would use to live fuller lives.

"You need to learn to put yourselves on the chessboard. Think about the decisions you make." I would go on to explain how certain pieces had to be supported by other pieces. Then I'd say that's the way it is in a family—we support each other.

I'd show them that mathematical equations had to be balanced on each side, and it was the same thing on a chessboard—they had to have a balanced attack.

The kids related to what I was saying. Sometimes I made analogies in sports. I'd talk about Michael Jordan, who was everyone's hero. I'd show them that the queen on that chessboard was like Michael Jordan—athletic, powerful, versatile, and most valuable. The students grasped that explanation and the game seemed easier for them.

So that's how we did it. I taught beginner players the basics and the purpose of the game. I taught a lot of simple directions and I kept reinforcing them: Control the center of the board. Develop your pieces. Protect your king. Delay development of your queen. Force your opponent's uncastled king to the center of the board and into hostile territory. Dominate the squares in the center. Mobilize your pieces and make sure each piece is protected and defended. Attack your opponent's pieces more than once.

Once the students picked up on those tactics, I turned them over to Ishmael and he would teach them other principles, defensive tactics, and openings. Right off they learned the Sicilian defense and the French defense. He taught them different openings like the English and the King's Indian, as well as other Italian openings.

When the opponent didn't know the line of attack, it nearly always forced them into submission. Some of those attacks would have ten, perhaps as many as fifteen, different variations, and the kids memorized them all. They also learned that their actions were predicated on what their opponent did.

I almost burst with pride over those kids. I was already thinking ahead to competition. They weren't ready. Not yet, but they would be.

We kept matching them up to play within their strength level. If a student got better, he or she moved up and played against a more advanced student. Sometimes we intentionally asked weaker players to compete with the stronger players. The weaker would learn from the stronger, and that, in turn, would make them stronger.

We had to watch and make sure that the stronger players didn't make fun of the weaker. We had a few incidents, but when I became aware of them, I stepped in and explained, "You're now the teacher. You didn't want to be laughed at when you were learning. Don't laugh at the person you're teaching. He's going to learn from you even while he's losing."

I never had to make that point to a player more than once. They felt quite excited to know that they were actually teaching their peers, and it raised their own self-esteem.

There was something else I said when the better player made fun of the weaker: "When you play your best game, you don't always win. You do your best. You're going to face times in life when you have to lose. It's all right to lose if you've played your best."

Ishmael and I brought in adults to play against our kids. In the beginning, of course, the kids lost every game. But that didn't last long. Soon they were as good—and often better—than the adult opponent. I wanted to prepare them for the time they would play older kids and even adults in competition.

(They did play against adults in 1997. It was a team from Bucknell University, and our kids beat them in an open tournament with college students and adults. They were ready, so playing older players didn't intimidate them.)

We worked with the kids and pushed them to be the best they could be. We let them compete to see who played on what we termed first board. First board was usually reserved for the best player on the team. One important thing was that no one could be first board without having good grades. I wanted them to know that this involved more than being able to play well. It was an honor to be first board on a championship-caliber chess team. Many times that was the most respected and feared player at matches and tournaments. We often had in-school tournaments to determine our first board. The winner was first board and second place winner was second board. The tournament rankings decided who our top five players were.

From week to week the board positions usually stayed the same unless someone won first place in a major tournament. Depending on how much the kids practiced, they could challenge someone ahead of them. The heaviest amount of pressure was always on the first board. That person had to work hard to re-tain the place as best player. He or she was *the* leader who set the stage for everybody else. The kids all recognized this, and who-ever was first board received the utmost respect.

A few kids shied away from trying to move forward. "I don't want to be first board," more than one kid said. "I get too nervous," or "I get scared when I try." They were usually content to be number two or three.

Our first board the first year was a smart kid named Joseph Falligan, who is now a top amateur boxer and trains with Olympic athletes. Willow Briggs, about whom I'll write more in another chapter, was our first board at the national level. Willow's story is also one of the saddest and most painful ones I've ever experienced.

After watching them for a while, I learned that the children behaved essentially the same way on the chessboard as they did when playing on the basketball court or the football field. But in chess, they were using their minds even more. There was more trash talk than on the local playground.

"Your queen is my lady now." "I'm in your house and the door is wide open." I heard such remarks frequently at our in-tense chess sessions. Their voices were sometimes loud, even shrill, but always friendly, and always extremely competitive. I noticed that the students who were passive in nature played chess in a very relaxed manner and the aggressive students were very offensive-minded on the board. Our female players would be very reluctant to trade pieces, treating them almost like siblings or offspring. Our young ladies were notorious for playing games that typically lasted well over two hours. These were children who truly lived their lives and showcased their personalities on the chessboard. I also learned a great deal about them by watching them play.

They teased, boasted, and jabbed at each other most of the time. As long as they were smiling, laughing, having fun, and forgetting about all the troubles there in the community, that was fine. Some of those kids had no home life, and the chess team became their family. They bonded with other players, and they cared for one another. By becoming part of the team, it gave them a chance to escape every day for a time on those sixty-four squares.

Originally, we started by practicing during the forty-five-minute lunch period. After we started the club, we added two afternoons a week after school. Before long, the students started coming every day from three to four.

That still wasn't enough time for them, so I extended the time from three o'clock until five, sometimes six. Even when I called time, most of them didn't want to leave. For some kids, that reluctance made sense. What did they have to go home to?

Most of the kids wanted to keep playing because they were having the time of their lives. This was fun, they were learning, and they wanted more. It was the first time some of these kids had ever excelled at anything in their lives.

"What time are you leaving, Mr. EL? Can I stay till you leave?" That became the usual question. If I stayed beyond five, they wanted to stay and play until I left.

They still wanted more playing time, so I let them come in on Saturdays to play chess. That still wasn't enough. Ishmael and I arranged for them to play chess at the local recreation center at Twenty-Sixth and Master Streets two nights a week and on weekends. Our chess kids would tell their friends in the community that didn't go to Vaux about our program and some of them wanted to learn how to play, so a few showed up after school. I didn't say no to any of them.

I'd get phone calls from parents whose children went to other schools. "May I bring my child to your program?"

I never turned down parents as long as their children were willing to follow our rules. By allowing others to join us, the Vaux kids felt even more important. We were reaching out into our community and sharing. We were helping other schools start chess teams. We weren't able to be much help to other schools during our first year, because our kids were still learning the game themselves. They hadn't played in any competitions, so it was still fairly new to them.

During our second year with the chess team, we were able to join with the people at McMichael Elementary School and start a chess program with them. Like Vaux, that school is also located in the projects and serves low-income families. They started a chess team, and in 1997 we traveled together with some kids from their school to compete in Knoxville, Tennessee, at the Super National Chess Championships.

We began our first season in the fall of 1994, which was our training period. We wanted to prepare the kids to play in competition, so we focused on teaching the basic skills, and as they were able, we taught them whatever moves and tactics they could learn and remember. We played a few matches against other schools in Philadelphia, but we didn't get into any serious competition. I didn't want them to feel pressure until they were ready.

Just before school ended in June 1995, we did a wrap-up with the kids and laid out our goals. "Next year we want to compete on the national level. That means we'll travel to other cities."

Not only did I want to motivate them to think big and dream great dreams, but I also wanted them to keep playing during the summer months and not to lose the skills they had worked so hard to acquire.

To help them with that, I told them, "We will open the school every weekday so you can come in and play during the summer." I didn't know if they'd come or not—and it was a risk to make the offer and then not have any of them come. But they came. It was strictly on a voluntary basis, but they came anyway.

Some would drop in only a couple of days a week. That didn't matter. Others showed up every day that we were there. They were coming, they played, and they were improving.

I was there all summer during the hours the school was open. They could come in anytime during those hours and practice. Almost every person on the team kept to our practice schedule that summer.

By the time school started in September 1995, they were fired up and motivated to start playing in matches and tournaments. Our first goal was to make those kids good enough to compete strongly for the city championship. They had to have a taste of victory before I could take them to the state level and eventually on to the national level.

Originally, I assumed I'd have to keep motivating and pushing them. To my delighted surprise, I didn't have to. No longer would I have to convince the kids they could do it. They had worked hard by competing with each other, with people in the neighborhood, and with a few other schools. They had done fairly well. *They* believed they could do better. Now that they believed it, we were ready to go forward.

As far as I can remember, the second year was the first time they became aware of their possibilities. "You can do it. If we can do well in the city, we can go to the states and the nationals."

At first, they hadn't believed me, but they became increasingly results-oriented. As they learned and won more games, especially when they were able to play older and more experienced players, they began to say among themselves, "Maybe we can."

Once they played with that positive attitude, something powerful changed: They began to see how good they were.

"You know something, Mr. EL? I am good at this," Willow Briggs said once. He was the first. Soon others were assessing their abilities and knew they were good.

Within a short time, they were boasting to each other, "We can beat those other teams." Some of that was empty bragging, but they had begun to believe in themselves. They grasped that they could be successful at playing chess.

I believe it was because that fall when they played against adults in the community and against some of their own teachers, in most of the instances, they won. They no longer occasionally beat them, but they took almost every game. And how they loved it when they beat a teacher!

These were inner-city kids who had thought they couldn't do anything, who saw themselves as having no value. Now they believed in themselves. "We can do it! We are all that!" they chanted.

And I knew they were.

Then they started to beat me. One of them said, "Mr. EL, you're probably the smartest man on the earth, and I can beat you." (They had started to call me Mr. EL instead of Mr. Thomas-EL, and that was fine. Since then, everyone at the school calls me Mr. EL.)

Out of nine hundred students enrolled in Vaux during the 1995–96 school year, we had about twenty kids who played chess competitively. That may not have been many, but these kids became the role models for others. About two hundred kids played chess in the morning before school, in the lunchroom at lunchtime, and in class after school. Their peers respected them. I don't think top athletes at Vaux got any more respect than our chess players did. That had been one of the things I had hoped would happen. These were stars without being athletes. The attitude was beginning to change.

I wanted respect for the mind and not just athletic prowess. That was happening. It was also carrying over into the attitude of the school. I saw fewer discipline problems and the culture changed. It had become all right to learn to be smart, and to achieve.

Another positive thing happened. A few of those students with reputations of being tough characters got interested in chess. No one ever laughed at them for learning and playing the game.

What a wonderful feeling it was for me. No one had ever realized how smart these kids were or how much potential they had. They hadn't known themselves until they became chess players. By the middle of 1996, it was the popular thing to become a chess player.

All of that respect, and our team hadn't become successful. Before long, we had about forty kids playing chess with the team after school. Because of a lack of space and too few chessboards, we had to cut down on playing time. The kids could come to practice only on alternative days. Some came on what we called A days, which were Mondays and Wednesdays; the others could play on B days, Tuesdays and Thursdays. That worked out, although I wished we could have made it possible for every kid to come every day. Tournament players, however, were allowed to come every day.

We practiced every day getting ready to go into local competition. We had started the 1996 school year by competing in chess matches with other schools. There's a league that matches city schools with chess teams against one another.

"We blew them away," one of the kids said, and he was accurate. Except for Masterman, my alma mater, we badly beat all the other schools. That school recruits students from all over the city, and Masterman could attract the brightest and the ablest. Every one of our kids came from the projects or from somewhere in the inner city—all of them were what the media and experts called underprivileged. Parents of some of the kids at Masterman paid for chess lessons. In fact, a few of the parents were chess masters themselves. So, no, we just couldn't beat them.

In the city play-offs, we were one of the four schools remaining to compete for the championship. There were three magnet schools and Vaux. A magnet school is one that does not have to accept neighborhood students, and parents have to apply to be in a lottery. In a nutshell, they get to pick the best. One of the things needed to get into magnet schools is good grades.

Our kids played remarkably well, especially for their first year of competition. We ended up in the city's semifinals—a feat other coaches had told me was impossible for us during our first year.

But we were there as one of four schools in the semis to play against Masterman, Conwell, and AMY. I was so proud of our kids because they were all top-notch schools. Every day I reminded our kids that we didn't have any extra help, but we didn't need it, because they were good enough.

And they believed me.

This was our first year, and the attitude of the other three schools was that our wins had been easy. None of them ever expected to see us in the semifinals. I overheard the other coaches talking about playing each other. They acted as if we were not there.

Although that saddened me, I understood. That's the way they had been for several years—just magnet schools dominating the final games. We hadn't won anything yet.

I was pumped. It was time to change things.

We played a magnet school named Alternative Middle Years but which everyone called AMY. Everyone—other than our own team—assumed they would beat us and then go on to play Masterman. Not one coach or team even seriously considered that our kids could beat AMY.

Although the attitude of the coaches of the magnet schools upset me, I kept smiling and didn't show any negative reaction. Most of all, I didn't want my kids upset. I reasoned that if I stayed upbeat and kept telling them they could win, they would believe me. I went back to my basic philosophy that they didn't know they couldn't win. "You can do it," I said again and again.

They smiled back at me.

"If Mr. EL says we can beat them, we can beat them," Willow said.

The others quietly clapped and agreed.

They believed.

Competition outside of Vaux was still quite new to us. Our kids had competed in the city-wide competition the year before—their first year of playing. They had played against schools that had been participating in such tournaments for years. Most of those other students had coaches who had been on the scene many times.

The three magnet schools assumed it would be a repeat of our previous years. Everyone knew that Masterman would be the eventual winner, but the question was always, which of the magnet schools would hold second place.

"Remember this," I told our kids. "They talk big, but those schools have to come through us. We're not going to let them intimidate us!"

I tried not to let the kids get too excited, and especially, I didn't want them to worry. "Just think about the game when you play. Forget about them. Remember what you were taught." And I always added, "Don't even worry about winning. Just remember that if you play the way you're supposed to, good things will happen for you. If you try to concentrate too much on winning, you lose sight of what you're here for. You're here to compete and represent your school and community."

Most of the time, the kids relaxed. I didn't want them to feel pressured to do anything except play their best. "It's more important for you to be here and you have teammates who support you. You're here to use your brain, and every time you play, you're going to stretch those brains and you're going to get better."

Those kids were wonderful. They were hyped. Unfortunately, they had also heard some of the harsh remarks, and it did upset them that the players and coaches from the other schools didn't think they were on their level.

We had five players against AMY and one of them was Kenyetta Lucas. We beat them four to one—only one of my boys lost a match.

It was one of the happiest moments of my life.

The next week we played the finals, and as everyone had expected, the school to beat was Masterman.

We lost that day.

Our kids cried.

They cried because they were playing a school that they knew was in a different league, but they still wanted to beat them—and they had believed they could. In fact, after the game, they were all down on themselves. "We should have beaten them, Mr. EL," they complained.

As I studied their faces, I thought, here are some of the toughest kids in North Philadelphia, and they've been reduced to tears.

"We have to move on," I said. "You may have lost the finals, but you're still winners in my eyes." I reminded them of the victories they had won. They had already come further than anyone would have expected—especially the magnet schools.

I took all of them to McDonald's to celebrate their victory—and I never let them forget it was a victory for us, even though they lost the finals.

Despite having lost the city championship, we could still go on to the state. Any school can do that as long as they feel they can compete on a state level. Some schools came to the state tournament without even participating in the city tournament, but they didn't usually do well.

"Next we play for the state championship," I told them. "And we're going to win."

It was a moment of great celebration. As they finished their hamburgers and shakes, they were already talking about the victories ahead.

These were my kids and I was proud of them.

13

Bigger Competition

The state championship was on my mind. It's always a two-day event held in March at Bloomsburg University, which is about 150 miles from Philadelphia.

I was determined that the kids would go to the state event in 1996. We had one serious problem—and one that constantly faced us—lack of money. But I had made up my mind. "The team will go to Bloomsburg," I promised. I had no idea how we'd raise the money, but I knew we would. I was prepared to get a personal loan if necessary, but my kids *were* going to compete.

On my own, I wrote letters to people in the community, businesses, and churches. The school secretaries worked on addresses while the kids stuffed and labeled envelopes. I sent a letter to every Vaux school alumnus I could locate and appealed to his or her school loyalty. We wanted them to know about our kids and to enlist their support. Regular updates followed, letting them know how the chess team was doing and our plans, as well as our hopes for the months ahead. Of course, we asked them to make donations to the school for the chess team.

I took a big risk in sending out those letters and knew the

scheme could backfire. It didn't, because people responded generously. Since our first letter in 1996, we've received donations from as far away as California and Minnesota. Sometimes the amount was a dollar or five dollars. Other times we received as much as one hundred dollars. Some contributors saw our kids on TV and others read about us through magazines and newspapers. Anytime we received publicity, the donations increased.

Because people gave so generously, we were able to rent a van for the trip to Bloomsburg. For most of our players, that trip was an immense journey, because they had never been outside the city limits of Philadelphia.

The state tournament takes place on Saturday and Sunday, so we left Friday after school, and they also had the great thrill of staying in a hotel for two nights.

They would play a total of five times in the competition, regardless of their wins or losses. The judges determined the champions by the total score of games won—that is, one point for each win, which meant five was the highest score any of the players could have. On Saturday, they played three rounds and the next day, two. For instance, they might play their first round at 9 A.M. Saturday morning, the second at 1 P.M., and the final around 4 P.M. On Sunday, they would likely begin at 9 A.M. and play their final match in the afternoon at 1 P.M.

With four players to a team, that meant that twenty points was the maximum any team could score. In the first round, our four top players all won, which meant we had a score of four. We were in first place going into the second round. However, we didn't finish well at our first state tournament.

I wasn't discouraged, although some of the students were. I tried to motivate and let them know that they had an opportunity to travel, to be away from home for a full weekend, and they were having an invaluable experience. "You're playing kids far more experienced than you. Think about the moves they made. Remember how they played and how you played, and learn from it."

I soothed a lot of hurt kids and saw tears in a number of eyes.

Willow Briggs cried more than anyone.

We had no way to know that it would be the last time many of us would have a chance to see Willow's tears.

"It's all right," I said. "You played well. We didn't win anything, but you tried. I'm proud of you." Before they could start feeling bad again, I said, "This isn't the end. We're not going to stop now. We're going to the nationals."

"Us? We're going to the nationals?"

"We're going," I promised, and I meant those words. What I didn't tell them was that I didn't know how we could afford to go. After our expenses, we had about a thousand dollars left from this trip. That meant we had to start appealing again to people who cared about the children and the opportunities they had. I didn't want anything for myself, but I was willing to beg to anyone for the kids. When it came to helping them, I said to one of my friends, "I have no shame or pride. They deserve the best and I'm going to give them as much of it as I can."

I wanted to encourage the kids, and yet I wanted them to realize that they had to work hard to be ready for the national championship. We had gone to the state championship in March, and we had a little more than a month before they played in Orlando at the nationals.

"We need to go back to school and work on our game before we go to Florida," I said. "You've all done great, but now you have to do even better."

I don't remember what they said; I do remember the shining eyes and bright smiles. For some of them, it was the first time an adult male had ever believed in them. I knew they wouldn't let me down.

*   *   *

I had promised the kids that somehow I would raise the money. "You get your game together and I'll get the money for us to go to the nationals."

They accepted my challenge. Those kids studied hard—and that was part of it because they had to keep up their grades. But chess dominated their thinking. They showed me that, young as they were, they could focus on goals. A few times when I became discouraged and wondered how I could pull off everything, I'd watch those kids. Their concentration on the game and their enthusiasm in being the best they could be inspired me to try harder.

One day I sat at my desk and figured out the costs for the trip. As the figures grew larger and larger, I kept saying to myself, we can do it. Somehow we can do it.

When I pushed aside all the extras, it came down to this: We would have to take twelve kids, Ishmael, two chaperones, and me. The total amount staggered me—we needed nearly ten thousand dollars for all of us to fly to Orlando, stay in a hotel, eat, and I wanted them to have a day at Disney World.

"We're going to do it," I vowed to myself. "We will do it."

Every day they practiced, and I continued to send out letters asking for donations. "How are we going to get that much money?" I asked myself several times. I didn't know how I could pull this off, and I wouldn't let myself think of the consequences if we didn't have the money. I had to find a way to keep my promise, even if I had to go to a bank and borrow money.

We were able to get an article written about us in the Philadelphia papers, and that article made the difference. Money came in—most of it small amounts.

Right about that time, KYW-TV contacted me about doing a story on the chess team. Much to our surprise when the crew arrived, they sent Ukee Washington, one of the best-known newsmen in the city.

"I want to see how good these kids are," he said.

I smiled, and welcomed him to find out by playing. "Try a game and find out." I knew then that he had no idea how good our kids were.

I knew Ukee's coming to interview us was an answer to many of my prayers. We needed money to travel to Florida, and if our players impressed him, his interview would generate funds for our team.

There was something else involved besides raising money. I believed that our players were outstanding and I wanted the world to know that this was going to be their first return to the nationals since the early 1980s.

Ukee, a fairly good player himself, sat down at a board and challenged one of our kids, Charles Mabine.

In only five moves, Charles beat him.

Nothing could have convinced him more powerfully about how sharp our kids were than that experience.

After the show aired, we received thousands of dollars through the mail and made the trip. A Minnesota foundation sent in a single gift of $3,000. I was so elated I looked up the phone number and called to thank them personally. I spoke to a woman who said that her parents had been students at Vaux years ago.

Ten days before the trip, we had raised over $10,000. No one was more surprised than I was. We made a big event out of it. I wanted the kids to be able to look back and remember that event as a special time in their lives, regardless of the outcome of the chess matches. I also wanted everyone at Vaux school to see this as our celebration—our team—our school. I knew how easily kids identified with sports teams. I wanted the same kind of loyal fanfare for our chess kids. The local Food Workers' Union, along with the Vaux Alumni Association, raised $7,000 for the chess team. The check was presented to the team at City Hall with all the media and city officials present. Listeners to Radio station WHAT-AM sent $4,000 in donations.

We had a big pep rally at school, just the way most schools do for their football and basketball teams. "This rally is for kids who are using their minds," I said. I didn't put down sports, but I wanted them to know this was far more important. The auditorium was full. Not only was every student and teacher present, but we had print, radio, and TV reporters covering this event.

One thing I did for the pep rally was that I made sure the kids had uniforms. Sports teams have them and I wanted this intellectual event to equal or even surpass any physical activity. I used some of the donated money with some of my own because I wanted to send a message that we had our own "uniform" on the chess team and every kid wore that uniform proudly. We had Vaux team sweatshirts, khaki pants, and black sneakers, which a discount store gave us at an even bigger discount. We couldn't afford Michael Jordan sneakers, but at least they looked alike. Later, Arnold Schwarzenegger's foundation, the Inner-City Games, and our sponsor, Cendant Mortgage would provide blazers and travel bags.

The student body was more impressed by the uniform than anyone else—just exactly the group I wanted to be impressed.

A few weeks before we went to Orlando, WDAS-AM talk radio station called us. Someone at the station had read about us in the newspaper and they asked our kids to come and do a question-and-answer session with their listeners. They were impressed with what the children had been doing and they wanted to help us raise money.

Callers asked the children how they felt about being good chess players. A few called to give them tips on how to play chess. Others called and said things such as, "I have a brother I can't beat in chess. Give me inside information on how to win."

The best calls, as far as we were concerned, came from other kids. They asked, "How can we get involved in chess?" "What made you decide to get involved in the game?" "What do you do when kids tease you about using your mind being smart?" "How do you find the strength to keep playing chess when your friends want to hang out and keep begging you to join them?"

This was a high for our chess players. They now understood that they could be outstanding in whatever they chose to do. And they would be outstanding by using their minds!

We chartered a large bus to take our luggage and us to the airport. We could have coordinated this with parents in their vans but someone paid for us to use the bus. This might be the most significant event in the lives of some of these kids. I knew it would also expand their vision of the world—a world beyond the projects and Philadelphia and the state of Pennsylvania. I wanted them to see the possibilities of a bigger, larger world.

As it turned out, this was the last time some of them would ever leave the city.

The police provided an escort for us—and that thrilled everyone. Those kids knew they were going to represent Vaux School, and they wanted everyone to be proud of them. Parents and friends turned up to wave us off when we left the school. We almost had a pep rally at the bus.

One of the big moments for the kids was right after we reached the airport. While we stood in line to check our baggage, people walked up to them and shouted and laughed. Because of the media exposure, many people already knew about them. Several of them asked our kids for autographs.

I watched in utter amazement, thinking how little it took to raise the self-esteem of these kids. They deserved every second of attention they were getting. My chest filled with pride as I watched those inner-city kids smile, laugh, and giggle. This was a great moment.

We flew nonstop to Orlando, and like our bus trip to Bloomsburg, that was a great adventure. So far as I can recall, none of them had ever been on an airplane before.

One of the things I had done was to build in one day for the kids to see the sights of the city. First, we booked a tour for them to see in and around Orlando. They swam in the hotel pool. They were all excited and happy, and I wanted that, but I also wanted them to relax.

The best part was coming after they played, because we were going to visit Disney World. I didn't even tell them, because I wanted them to give their full attention to being ready for the chess tournament.

Once in Orlando, I talked to coaches who had been in previous national tournaments. I received a lot of helpful advice from Steve Shutt, the former chess coach at the Frederick Douglass School, who was now the coach of the Masterman School and director of the Chess in the Schools program in Philadelphia. This program, which is part of their curriculum and is similar to one used in New York, allows children to learn problem-solving skills from playing chess in school and after school.

The program uses chess as a motivating factor to improve attendance, promote higher achievement, and encourage better behavior. Thousands of children have benefited from this program in Philadelphia and New York. He generously told of his experience of working with kids and gave me a number of tips. Despite his school being our rival, he shared information freely, and I admired that. He cared about his kids, and was open to help our kids as well.

Some of the schools had professional coaches. We were a bunch of inner-city kids who were giving their all to the game. When I looked at the other students and some of the coaches, and the way they behaved, a scary part of me would taunt, "What are you doing here? These inner-city kids can't compete with these professionally coached kids." I stopped listening to my doubts.

The secret—if there is any such thing—is that our kids didn't know they were novices. They knew only that they had worked hard, had given everything they had, and believed they were going to come home champions. Not once did I ever tell them they didn't have a chance.

Once the tournament started, we restricted their diets and made them cut back on junk food. Whenever we ate, I made sure they had a variety of fruits and vegetables, plus a lot of complex carbohydrates to boost their energy. Some of these matches would last four or five hours at a time and they couldn't afford to get tired in the middle of one. (I still remember that other coaches and players commented about the kids' stamina and ability to concentrate at tournaments.)

The nationals take place over a three-day period from Friday through Sunday. They played seven rounds—two on Friday, three on Saturday, and two more on Sunday. Approximately 150 schools competed in our division, which was kindergarten through grade eight (K–8). There were two sections in the K–8 division, the "open" section and the "under 1000" section. Each section crowns a national champion every year. In this kind of competition, no one was ever eliminated and each school played all seven rounds. The totals of the seven rounds determined the winners.

We competed in the K–8 "Under 1000" section. The number 1000 indicates the rating category. Players on advanced levels play in sections above 1000 or in open sections. Novices or those not yet advanced play in sections rated 1000 or below. Such a system prevents kids who have recently taken up the game from facing young chess masters. Master players are typically the best in the country if not the world. Usually elementary and middle schools do not have chess masters on their teams. Most of the time, master parents or private coaches train them. The majority of scholastic players are not master-level players.

When we went to Orlando, Kenyetta was one of only two females on the team, and as boys tend to do, they teased her.

"We don't even know why you came down with us."

"You're not a good player." At school, most of the boys were able to beat her and they didn't want her to forget it.

"Why would a girl want to play anyway?"

These were her own teammates and it upset me to hear them trashing her like that. They made her feel bad and I came down hard on them. "You don't talk that way to a teammate! *Not ever.*"

The boys apologized—but I knew it was only because I had forced them to.

Kenyetta had done well against other females, but somehow most of the boys always beat her. But she had stayed in there to play and she tried hard. I encouraged her not to listen to them, and they did stop berating her.

At the competition, our boys didn't do well. They won only one or two games each out of the seven. As I kept running totals, it looked as if we would finish in the twenty-fifth spot in our division. (The top twenty-five teams go home with trophies.) We needed two players to win four games for us to make the top twenty. Before we left for Orlando, I had prayed for God to help us make it among the top ten, and if we could reach that high, I would have been satisfied.

Willow "Fu" Briggs, one of our seventh-grade boys, rushed up to me and said, "I was getting ready to play this kid and he's in a corner and he's crying. What do I do?"

"Why is he crying? What did you do to him?"

"Nothing. I just found out I was going to play him and I wanted to say hello. When I told him who I was, he started to cry. He says he doesn't want to play against me."

Willow took me over to the boy. Sure enough. He was sitting there crying. I don't know where his coach was or why he wasn't around. "Hey, what's wrong?" I asked. I told him I was the coach of the Vaux team.

Then he really started crying. I wrapped my arm around the boy and tried to soothe him.

After he had calmed down, he said, "I'm scared to play you guys."

"Scared to play us?" Willow asked, totally dumbfounded.

"Our coach showed us the *Mighty Pawns* video before we left home to get us motivated." *Mighty Pawns* was made of the old Vaux chess team after their seventh national championship. They had won the first time in 1977 and every year through 1983. It had never been done before or since in America.

"And—and that movie was about you guys. It showed us how good you are and I'm scared to play you."

"These aren't the same kids—"

"Yeah, but if they're as good as the kids on the video, I'm going to lose."

"Don't be scared," I said. "That movie was made a long time ago. And I'll tell you something else. That's nothing but a video and those kids aren't playing anymore. You need to get in there and play and make your own movie. You play well and you can be known as the kid who beat the kid that was in the movie."

His eyes lit up, and he smiled. Yet he still found it hard to believe what I was saying. Eventually, he recovered enough to play.

The kid went inside and played; he played extremely well. But not quite well enough.

Willow Briggs won all but two of his games. In fact, when all the scoring was over, they listed Willow among the top twenty-five players in the nation in our division. That was exciting and thrilling for him and for all of us. He was our first player to win an individual trophy at a national tournament.

It's also interesting that Kenyetta won more than all the boys who teased her. Willow, one of the few who didn't tease her, scored higher than she did. Her four wins gave her second place on the team, which is great for someone accustomed to getting beaten.

Kenyetta did well even though all the boys expected her to fail in her final round. She had already beaten all boys, but they didn't think she could do it in the seventh round. To their amazement, she won. Her win guaranteed us the thirteenth-place finish in our division.

Kenyetta said then and again years later that she felt more pressure on her in Orlando than at any other time. The taunting of the boys didn't bother her as much as the stress of competing against top-quality players. In her final game, Kenyetta was losing. She didn't know the girl she competed with, but she played an outstanding game. In fact, she was so good, Kenyetta was ready to give up.

"I watched her carefully, like you told us to, Mr. EL," she said. "She had more pieces than I did, and I knew I was going to lose. Then she made one bad move—one of those you taught us not to make. That gave me the advantage." Kenyetta smiled.

She won that game.

As a team, we finished number thirteen in our division. The kids felt extremely high after they heard the rankings. This was their first national competition and that meant that they had outscored all but twelve schools in their division.

When I checked the list, the entire top twelve had long histories of tournament experience. We got excited when we realized that our kids beat veterans of several tournaments.

Although I didn't say anything, I felt it was a bit low. I had prayed for us to hit the top ten. I spoke to several coaches and mentioned my disappointment.

"You're *thirteenth* and this is your first time in the nationals?" He shook his head. "We've been to the nationals for five straight years and we have never gotten past the top twenty."

Every coach I spoke with said that we must have an unusual team to rank so high during our first year.

I felt a lot better.

I felt better because Kenyetta finally overcame her fear of beating boys at chess.

I think it was so great because she was teased on the way

down by her male teammates about not being as strong a player as they were but she ended up being one of the strongest in the country. Most of the guys did not do well.

If they had done as well as Kenyetta, we would have finished in the top ten. This would be her last national competition. She was an eighth grader then. That was her last year with us as a team. Having her on the team allowed us to attract other females for the chess program. She was a great spokesperson, and a National Honor Society student.

The boys never picked on Kenyetta again.

14

Summer of 1996

Past victories were not enough. We had to keep pushing forward and not look backward. Now that our team started to win, I wanted to build on that. In May 1996, I decided they needed to compete in another tournament.

"Just keep playing," was my advice to the students. I didn't want them to be idle during the summer and have to start learning all over again. "I want you to work on building a winning tradition."

To make them even more aware of the importance I placed on their skill development, I announced that they would be competing in the Atlantic Open Tournament, which was in Hagerstown, Maryland. The word *open* means that anyone could enter and play, and that included adults.

The tournament officials didn't have high expectations for the Vaux team, but I tried not to communicate that fact to the team. They would have to be ready to play against all levels and against some tough competition. Even though I assumed they wouldn't do well, I also believed they needed to know how difficult it was to become a winning chess team. I never wanted them to believe that winning was everything.

I began to wonder if I was pushing the children too much. I always wanted them to understand that they could learn a lot from losing but that they were not ever losers.

When Ukee Washington aired the story about our winning tradition, his coanchor, Larry Kane, said, "What Salome Thomas-EL is teaching kids about losing is a great message at a time when athletes are saying that winning is everything. They ruin a lot of minds that way."

I didn't want to ruin any minds so I decided to slow down. Eventually, it would be the students who would pick up the pace.

We had already raised enough money to rent a van, and we squeezed everyone into it. It was another all-weekend tournament, so we drove to Maryland on Friday afternoon and returned Sunday after it was finished.

The kids didn't do well. In fact, Hagerstown was their worst showing so far. I had been prepared for the stiff competition, so I wasn't badly disappointed.

Kenyetta Lucas and Chineta Haines played and defeated several male players, but they didn't win enough games. Chineta was one of the finest chess players I had seen, and she had a great future in store for her. Unfortunately for us, she moved to Orange, New Jersey, that summer and it was a great loss to our team.

The one bright spot for us had been a sixth-grader named Demetrius Carroll, who ended up as a top junior scholastic player. He went on to do what many thought was impossible—he defeated not one but several of Masterman's top chess players during his career, and he did it so smoothly and effortlessly—or so it seemed to observers—that the Masterman coach started calling him "Masterman Killer."

One difficult game was when he played against one of their Russian players, a boy who was almost at the master level. (A master is a player who has been rated higher than 2200 by the

U.S. Chess Federation. Less than 10 percent of all scholastic chess players are masters.) The Russian player had years of experience and a staggering number of wins behind him.

Demetrius was winning the game, and then he made one mistake and had to give the Russian a draw, which is a tie. So this kid from the inner city didn't actually lose to the master. Practically everyone I talked to marveled at Demetrius's skill.

The others on the Vaux team, however, played poorly during our competition. Our younger players lacked the experience of their older competitors and it showed. That would soon change.

"You're just beginning. You'll learn and you'll get better," I said. "You will never win every game on the chessboard or every game in life. But you don't quit. You get up and keep going. The more experience you have in competition, the better you'll do and you'll feel less stress."

I couldn't let them lay off competition after this. It's the old idea of getting back on the horse immediately after you fall off. So we went right back on the road. I entered the team in the U.S. Open Chess Championship in Alexandria, Virginia, in August 1996.

This was part of my plan to keep the kids playing chess all year round. Some schools didn't do anything during the summer months, but I knew that if the students kept playing, it would make a tremendous difference. And it did, because they didn't have a chance to forget. Everything was chess.

That defeat in Maryland upset the kids. Of course, it was a learning experience to let them know how cruel life could be. But then, these kids knew that aspect of life, now they needed to know victory.

We raised enough money in the spring so that the kids could play in the U.S. Open in Alexandria. To educate the students even more, we went by train. I wanted these kids to know the big world and to set their sights high.

Money continued to come in and we tried to be frugal with what we received. It constantly encouraged us that the community stood firmly with us.

In August 1996, we went by Amtrak from Philadelphia to Alexandria. As the team watched the countryside of Maryland and Virginia, they could hardly believe that such places actually existed with cows in pastures and crops growing in the fields. Some of them had never seen so much grass and empty lands in their young lives. "Where do all the people live?" one of them asked, amazed at all the empty spaces.

We competed in the U.S. Open, where all the best chess players in the world meet for the championships. The U.S. Open is the championship that child prodigy Bobby Fischer won and that made him an international chess star. Hollywood even made a film about him. That's how prestigious this championship is. Our students were able to see some of the best chess players in the world and compete in the same environment.

We were aware of how few African Americans had come to play. "See, you're opening doors for other black kids! Do your best for yourselves and for Vaux and for African Americans everywhere!"

They didn't know that Maurice Ashley, who had played there, would become the first African-American Chess Grand Master. He is one of 470 grandmasters in the world and the first African American on that list. Grand Master is the highest title in chess, short of World Champion. The grandmaster must score the highest performance ratings known as "norms" in three tournaments against top-rated chess players. Most players spend a lifetime trying to achieve this goal. Ashley reached it at the age of thirty-three, and he was a wonderful role model for my kids.

The Vaux players met a number of chess celebrities and collected a number of autographs. It was as if they had been transported into a different world. In fact, they had been. That was one of the things I wanted them to grasp—that there was a much bigger world than the inner city of Philadelphia.

An interesting note is that when any of our kids mentioned Vaux Middle School, people asked for *their* autographs. Even though the old Bishops team (called the "Bad Bishops") had faded, the memory of seven successive national championships had not. We were no longer known as the Bad Bishops because our student body thought that the word *bad* would bring negative attention to the new team. We asked the students to come up with a name for us. The school hosted a contest and a student came up with the new name and a new logo, which is seen on all of our T-shirts.

Earl Jenkins came home from Alexandria with a trophy and money as the top scholastic player. Since the U.S. Open attracts the best professionals in the world, there are cash prizes awarded to winners in different categories. Some awards total close to five and ten thousand dollars. Several of our students were able to win cash prizes. Of course, the cash prizes for scholastic players were much smaller.

In early September 1996, we set out to "seek new civilizations." We were starting a new academic year at Vaux. We'd lost Kenyetta Lucas and Willow Briggs as they moved into high school. A seventh-grader named Demetrius Carroll had already shown a lot of promise and I watched him closely. I knew we were going to see even bigger wins for him.

We were grooming our youngest students, boys and girls.

Because once Kenyetta had broken the gender barrier, it was never an issue again. Our big problem was in recruiting and teaching the new kids. Those I had started with when they were in fifth and sixth grades were now leaving us and we needed new kids to take their places.

Not only did our chess players do extremely well in the competitions—especially when they won so many awards after having such limited experience—they also became top students. As far as I was concerned, that was only the beginning. I watched their academic careers and most of them went on to high school and became members of the National Honor Society and honor roll students. Some are also excellent musicians. That didn't surprise me because research has shown that students who play chess are also excellent musicians and vice versa.

Now we were ready to start the 1996–97 school year, and I began to plan our trips for the next twelve months. We knew that we wanted to return to New York. That was important because the Vaux chess team had not been invited to participate for the New York championship.

A story had circulated at Vaux that we were not allowed to compete in New York because the team won so many of New York's titles right in their own city. That rumor was already a decade old; we never learned whether it was true, but we decided to register for the competition anyway. Because we didn't receive word not to show up, we assumed our application had been accepted.

I was pumped over this because I felt that in 1997, I had the best students ever. Even the poorest chess players had improved immensely. One girl, Denise Pickard, had shown amazing ability. Although she had not done particularly well over the summer, I knew she had a great year ahead of her.

By now, the kids knew more about chess than I did. I wouldn't have tried to compete against Earl Jenkins or Denise Pickard because they would have beaten me every time. I needed help—someone who could take their games to higher achievement level.

Then Kevin Giles showed up. He came to us and volunteered. A former member of the national champion chess team at Vaux Junior High School, Kevin was now an adult. He visited me and said, "I want to help rebuild the chess team." He became the volunteer assistant coach who helped Ishmael and me to build the team that would become highly successful. Because of school, work, and family responsibilities, Kevin wasn't able to remain with the team very long.

Chess was important, but it wasn't everything. At the same time, we wanted to put a major focus on academics at our school. I tried to make the kids aware that chess was a means of stretching their minds, of helping them overcome the many obstacles they faced. About once a week I'd talk to them about college and start urging them to work hard, to get into the good high schools, which would give them a better chance for the top colleges.

We focused on chess too, of course. Our kids practiced every day from the time school let out at 3:00 until 6:00. They even came by on Saturdays.

More than once, the kids came to our house to practice. I knew that for some of them, chess was the only stable, happy time in their days. Occasionally they spent the night. I wanted to bond with them and for the kids to see themselves as a family—a family within the community. Shawnna understood what I was doing and never complained about the kids being around or the telephone calls or my having to drive them home.

I had a philosophy about this and I'm even more convinced

today that it was correct: The more stable their social environment and their sense of belonging, the better they improved in their chess. That carried over to their studies, and their grades always improved as well.

One obstacle we overcame at Vaux that most of the other chess-competing schools didn't have to struggle with was all of our players were inner-city kids. Some had almost no home life, often living in wretched, abusive situations, and not more than a few had any kind of stable environment with a solid male role model. The more of that I saw, the more it compelled me to do whatever I could to make a difference. I had lived the same type of life.

Other schools with chess teams shared the same problems. I had to find a way to make life better for those children too. I kept thinking that if only I could find a way to encourage good teachers to work with these inner-city youths and *remain* there and become a part of their lives, things would change. They all needed someone who was stable and caring like the teachers that had helped me.

Some days I felt guilty or blamed myself for failing them. My life was already crammed so full I had no idea how to eke out more time for the kids and yet I knew they needed me. I felt guilty for not spending more time with my wife and she deserved more attention. We tried to carve out small periods of time for the two of us and we were also involved in church activities, but I kept trying to figure out how to spend a little more time with her.

I was teaching full-time and working hard at Vaux Middle School, and of course, coaching the chess team demanded a lot of time and energy. On top of that, I had started going to school at night to earn my principal's certification.

As important as my certification as principal was—and I wanted it very much—I also made one other decision. I would study for that certification, but I would not allow it to take precedence over my students. In the few years I had been in the teaching profession, I had seen the idealists who burned out and either left or worked themselves up the supervisory ladder.

I refused to let my kids down. They were the reason I had stayed in the inner city. I had already made up my mind that even if I never became principal, my kids would come first.

I want to be honest about my ambitions. I was trying to build a foundation for my future career. I had already decided that my goal was to become a principal and eventually the superintendent of schools in Philadelphia. If I could show what could be done with a dozen kids in one inner-city school, why couldn't I show what an entire school could do? And why stop there? Why not move toward doing this for the entire Philadelphia educational system? I wanted to see thousands and thousands of kids light up the way some of my students have been able to light up and are able to understand that they can't fail because there's no other way. They have to succeed. And I want all students to believe that. If they believe that, then the majority of the battle is won.

Some may call my ideas grandiose, but those were the goals I set fairly early. But I reminded myself constantly, I will not allow my ambitions to supercede over the needs of the children.

So not only did I work hard, but my kids practiced every day. It took off some of the load that, by now, we were getting outstanding support from most of the parents. Because they trusted me and knew that I loved their kids, they did everything they could to help me so that I could help their children succeed.

Their trust was extremely important for my chess players. Those kids would practice at school for three hours in my care, so they had to have a lot of trust there. That also meant that I'd be responsible to see that they got home. In the winter, it would be dark at least an hour before they left school. Part of my commitment was to make sure their children were taken home safely every day.

Most of the time, I took them home myself. I'd fill up my car with as many as I could take and drive them home while my assistant stayed at the school and worked with the remaining students. Then I'd return to get the rest. Now and then other teachers stayed and helped with the transportation. We didn't want even one child to have to walk home in the dark.

The kids had made their commitment to do something that was going to bring glory to the school. Their hearts were totally involved in being excellent students and in being the best chess players they could. I felt the minimum I could do was to make sure they arrived at their home safely every day.

I've frequently thanked God that we never had a problem. We did have a few incidents when I took the kids home and no one would be there to welcome them. I refused to let them go inside alone.

"Get back inside the car," I'd say. While we sat in the car and waited (or sometimes I took them to my house), I helped the children with their homework. Most of the time a parent arrived within an hour.

They may have been safe to leave without an adult home, but I could not feel right about sending a child into a dark, empty apartment.

In January 1997, we were ready to conquer New York City as the new champions from Vaux Middle School. We had reached thirteenth place in Orlando. We wanted to do better in New York.

I also knew that we would face some of the best chess players in the city of New York. It was a one-day tournament held at the Borough of Manhattan Community College. I wasn't worried; our kids were ready.

Because of the home situations my kids came from, I couldn't depend on their getting to my house on time to leave on an early train for New York. Sometimes those kids stayed awake late. Sometimes they couldn't sleep because of the fights and drugs and even shootings in the neighborhood.

The only way I could be sure they were ready to leave on time was to have them spend the night before the trip at our house. We didn't do this often and I would only allow the male chess players to stay over with Shawnna and me.

Everyone who stayed overnight had to have parental permission. I got them up before 5:00 in the morning, and Shawnna fed them cereal before we left for the train station. It was a one-day Saturday tournament, so we would return later that evening.

Of course, it meant raising money for the entry fees and the travel expenses. Raising money would always be a factor. I felt as if I were a constant beggar, but then I'd remind myself that I wasn't begging for me or even for an organization. I was begging to give kids like Latoria and Nathan a chance.

By then we had a community of people who supported the kids and took pride in seeing our school and our kids come into prominence. Parents who were able to do so wrote checks and they also asked their friends and relatives for help. Our policy then—and it's still that way—is that we would never ask the children themselves for one dime. And we never did. We also vowed not to ask the school system to help finance this. We were doing this for our kids and for our community. "This is the community's responsibility to raise the money," I said again and again. "These are our kids. We need to show our support by giving our dollars." We also wanted to get away from the old idea of begging the system for money.

Money began to come in. Sometimes it was barely a trickle. When the *Philadelphia Daily News* ran an article about the team or a Philadelphia radio or TV station mentioned us, the contributions increased.

As we prepared for New York, we saw that enough money had come in for us to spend Saturday in New York.

Once we arrived in New York, our plan was to take a cab from the train station to the college.

That cab idea turned out not to be so wonderful. I stood on the curb and signaled, and every cab passed me by. I tried not to let my anger show, but it was the worst kind of discrimination I had faced. Drivers of almost every racial group, including African-Americans, zoomed past, but not one of them would stop.

"This isn't going to work," I told the kids. I asked a passerby where the nearest cabstand was. He told me and we walked several blocks until we found it. We got in line, because I knew they could not refuse us. There were eight of us—two adults and six children—so we needed two cabs to get us there.

I said nothing, but obviously the new laws weren't working.

Once we reached the Borough of Manhattan Community College, our kids were ready to play. I had given them all the pep talk and encouragement possible. "Now it's up to you," I said. "Make us proud of you."

Before they played, I discovered they had imposed a new-but-sad rule. No parents or coaches could stay in the room during competition. The officials had imposed this rule because they said that the adults had gotten so emotionally involved in the games, they disturbed the children. Coaches accused others of cheating and parents were calling decisions unfair.

New York was the first tournament I had been to where I wasn't allowed to watch my children play. I didn't like that, of course, but I understood. It also saddened me that immature adults couldn't allow the children to play and have fun without trying to interfere.

Our children did well. As a team, we came in fourth place, which was quite a jump upward. Even more exciting to me was one of our players, Charles Mabine, tied for first place.

I loved the way they announced our fourth-place win. The emcee said something like, "And returning for the first time to New York after a long time away is Vaux Middle School from Philadelphia." Then he outlined the history of the school's seven straight national championships.

That was the big test as far as I was concerned. New Yorkers were always the major competitors for the national titles. Bobby Fischer, who was a child prodigy, came from New York. Most of the top chess players are from New York. That was our first test and we actually didn't do too badly.

Only one thing marred our return to Philadelphia. After the tournament we faced a similar experience with not getting a cab. We couldn't find a cabstand nearby and nobody on the street seemed to know where one was. I stood out in the middle of the street, trying to flag down a cab. It took almost half an hour before someone stopped.

"Thanks for stopping," I told him and then told him that we needed a second cab. He got on his CB and called a driver he knew. As I thanked him for stopping, I also told him how long we had been having cabs pass us by.

"That's illegal now to pass anyone because of their race," he said. He told us that the actor Danny Glover couldn't get picked up and he had made a big issue of it. Since then, police had begun to write tickets for cabs that wouldn't pick up African-Americans.

*　*　*

Despite the problem with getting a cab, I don't think I stopped grinning all the way back to Philadelphia and probably kept it going all through the weekend. On Monday, Charles Mabine and others were superstars at school. And they deserved every bit of attention they received.

Denise Pickard came to my attention during the summer of 1996. She had finished fifth grade at Reynolds Elementary School and was going to enter Vaux that fall. Her grandmother enrolled her in Vaux's summer enrichment program.

Denise was one of those bright students who did well academically and had no problems with reading or spelling. She had never played chess until that summer. Her uncle Jeff had a chessboard and taught her the basic moves. As she said, "It interested me because I found that it occupied my mind."

When Denise first visited the school, she saw me in the hall and we chatted for a few minutes. And one of the first things I asked, as I did of all incoming students that I met personally, was, "Do you want to play chess?"

She said she didn't know much about the game and hadn't played much.

"I understand, but do you want to learn to play chess here at Vaux?"

"Oh, yes," she said.

She worked at learning the game as well as any student I've ever had. In fact, I can't think of anyone who worked harder at the game. She started that summer and by the following spring she had progressed so well, she went to Bloomsburg with us and won second best female in the state.

Right after that in Runnemede, New Jersey, Denise played in an adult tournament. By then she had been playing a total of eleven months. Her opponent was a man in his forties and an excellent player.

There had been a question about the clock expiring and Denise thought she had lost. The flag on her clock dropped, which meant that her time had expired, and because she had not moved, she thought it meant a loss.

"Forget the clock," the man said. "You have dominated this game so much that the clock doesn't even matter. I had no chance to win this game. How long have you been playing, child?"

"About a year."

"I've been playing for more than twenty years and you beat me. And I'm considered a pretty good player."

That's when Denise began to realize she was good at this game. She also started beating her classmates. By the time she entered seventh grade, almost no one on the team could beat her on a regular basis.

Later, when she was in high school, Denise looked back and said to me about her chess experience, "The game taught me how to make good and wise decisions in life. If I know I'm doing something wrong or getting ready to do something wrong, I stop and think about it. That's what chess taught me—to reflect on the consequences of my actions. Now I can think about what an action will lead to and where the next action leads, and then I stop instead of going ahead." She smiled and added, "I learned that it's easier to go and do the right thing. And sometimes when I don't make the right decisions, I've learned to look at my mistakes and I know I won't repeat them."

As of the time of this writing, Denise is in tenth grade and is not only playing chess, but also teaching other children the game.

15

Group Challenges; Personal Struggles

Shawnna finally complained—and justifiably—that I was spending too much time with the kids at school and not enough at home. I knew she was right. I was working full-time at the school with the students. After being with kids all day, I stayed to coach and encourage them three hours a night, five days a week, and then I had to take several of them home. And, as I've mentioned earlier, some evenings we had children with us as late as 8:00 P.M.

"I'd like us to spend this weekend together. It is Valentine's Day," was all Shawnna had said, but I knew it was an important thing for her. Rarely had she asked for a full weekend alone with me. She had known when we married how committed I was to the kids and she remained my biggest supporter. She was also my wife and wanted time alone with me.

Shawnna agreed to allow me to spend Sunday and Monday with her, and in fact, I eagerly looked forward to it.

I had planned to take the kids to Fredericksburg, Virginia, on Friday after school and we would return on Sunday morning. That way I would be home all day, and there was no school on Monday, so we could have most of the two days together.

That would have worked except for one problem.

It had become a ritual that whenever we went on a trip I would forget to pack at least one item, and the kids would try to guess what I'd forgotten. That meant I always had to stop at home to retrieve those items. This time was no different. We were packed, ready to leave the city, and I rushed inside to get my forgotten shaving kit while the twelve kids and two other adults waited in the van. The phone rang seconds after I entered the house.

"Sorry, Mr. Thomas-EL, but we've had to cancel the tournament," Mr. Cornell said on the phone. "We've had a major snowstorm in this area. Nothing is moving in or out of the city."

I understood, of course, but I had promised the kids that they would play in February, so I needed a tournament. They knew we would compete in the state and national championships during the next two months and they needed the experience. Hurriedly I checked the tournament schedule in *Chess Life* magazine. It shocked me to note that the only other tournament in the Eastern United States in February was the U.S. Amateur East Championship in Parsippany, New Jersey.

My heart sank. It was the only one, and we couldn't compete because the tournament was a Saturday, Sunday, and *Monday* event.

I had promised Shawnna that I would be home early on Sunday. If we had gone to Virginia, I would have been back on Sunday. If we went to Parsippany, I wouldn't be home until quite late on Monday night, February 17.

After I hung up the phone, I stared into space for a long time, trying to resolve my own conflict. I wanted to be with my wife, but I didn't want to let down those kids.

Finally, I realized that I was going to have to disappoint the kids. I went outside to the rented van I was driving and said, "They've canceled the Virginia tournament." I explained about the snowstorm.

"Aren't there any tournaments anywhere else?" one of them asked.

"What about Parsippany?" Demetrius asked.

"We can't go there," I said. Earlier in the year we had briefly considered entering that tournament, but I had decided it was too tough a challenge so soon. "We will get creamed."

"We don't want to go back home," one of them said. "I think I'm ready for Parsippany, Mr. EL," Charles said, despite the stern look I gave him.

"We're all ready," another one said. Parsippany, in northern New Jersey, is about an hour's drive from New York.

"We can't go there," I said. "It just won't work."

"Why not? We're ready," said Denise.

"Because I told my wife that I would be here on Sunday." As far as I was concerned, that was the end of it.

"Why don't you ask her?" Earl asked.

I stared at each of the children in the fifteen-passenger van. Then I shook my head.

"Yeah, why don't you? Why don't you ask your wife if she'll let you go?" Thomas Allen asked.

I wish I could describe their faces. It was more than a suggestion; they were begging for the chance to play. If it had been any other weekend in the year, it would have been no problem. I shook my head. "I don't think it will work."

I didn't want to give them too many details about my personal life. The relationship with Shawnna was already strained. I was actually spending more time with the kids after school than I was with her. Good marriages need time together and I knew that.

"Please ask Mrs. EL! Please!" All the kids persisted in begging. In their naiveté, they assumed she'd agree.

I tried twice to explain that it didn't work that way. "Besides I've promised my wife. I gave my word."

"She'll understand. You can spend next weekend with her. Give me the phone and I'll ask her," someone said.

Those faces that only minutes ago had glowed with excitement were now crestfallen. They stared at me, their voices silent. They wouldn't push anymore, and they were ready to go home. When I saw the disappointment etched in their faces, I knew I couldn't let them down like that. "Okay," I said. "I'll go inside and call her."

I called Shawnna at work and explained the situation. Even before I asked, I knew she didn't want me to go. I was calling, hoping she would say, "Don't worry about it. We can have next weekend together. Go with the kids because they need you."

Shawnna didn't say those words.

"I'll let you make the decision," she said before we hung up.

If there had been any question about her attitude, it was clear now.

I stood at the window and stared at the kids grouped around the van in front of the house. "God, help me know what to do. Please help me."

I didn't want to jeopardize my marriage, but I couldn't disappoint those kids either. As I thought about it, I remembered vividly the occasions when my own dad had let me down. As a child, many times I had built up big hopes of doing things with him, and he let me down every time. My heart ached for those kids. I couldn't let this happen to them.

As I walked toward the van, I prayed that God would help me straighten out my marriage. I forced a smile on my face and said, "Okay! We're going!"

I'm sure neighbors a block away heard their excited voices. The eagerness and confidence in their faces temporarily erased any misgivings on my part.

I knew that if we showed up, we could play. That was the

advantage of traveling on the day before a tournament. Not only did it give the kids a chance to relax and breathe some fresh air; we could always register for tournaments the day before.

One of the kids in the van—and an important reason for my decision—was Demetrius Carroll. His family had been evicted only the day before the tournament. The landlord wouldn't let him go into the house and get his clothes, so he had nothing to wear. That Friday morning I had given him the chance to stay in Philadelphia.

"No, Mr. EL, please. I want to go. I've been practicing for this tournament. And I want to go."

"You'll go," I had said.

We picked up a few clothes he had left at his grandmother's house. We keep a few items at the school, so we helped there. But he still didn't have enough. During the lunch break, I asked one of our dedicated teachers and chaperones, Mrs. Frances Thomas, who wasn't related, to take him to a discount store on Girard Avenue to buy him underwear and socks.

"We're part of your family, Demetrius," one of them said— and we all felt the same way. "We'll see that you've got the clothes you need."

The boy didn't say much, but he couldn't hide the anger on his face. He hated having to depend on us to supply clothes for him to wear. I also knew that our kindness touched him and he was thankful for what we were doing for him. I wanted so much for him to turn that anger around and elevate him so that he'd play a good game.

Now as I stared at him, tears filled my eyes, because I realized how much it meant to this kid to play even though he had no idea where he would sleep when we returned to Philadelphia.

*   *   *

Within five minutes after the phone call to Shawnna, our van with kids and luggage squeezed in tightly headed for New Jersey. It was the U.S. Amateur East Championship. On the way, I realized that we not only didn't have tournament reservations, but we had no hotel reservations either. Immediately after our arrival, we registered for the tournament and asked about hotels, but there were no vacancies in the area. We needed three rooms.

For about forty-five minutes we drove around, stopping at every hotel we could find. We finally found a Hampton Inn, and because we agreed to stay for three nights, it turned out to be cheaper than all the others.

In the U.S. Amateur team championship, players on one team competed against those on another team of four players. It was also open, which meant that our kids could end up playing against anyone—students, expert players, as well as master players. *Chess Life* magazine called it "the biggest team versus team event in the world." It was larger than the Olympics. At the end of the weekend, the judges had a number of ways of awarding prizes. For instance, they had winners for the biggest upset when young teams played against older people. There were rating winners—when low-rated players defeated high-rated players, and top teams in a variety of categories.

Before our kids played their first round, I sensed that this would be a special time for us. We had good players, and two of them were outstanding. We had Demetrius Carroll and his cousin Earl Jenkins playing. Both were among the best in their age category.

Latoria Spann played in that tournament. She was the youngest of four sisters who attended Vaux. All of them were good students and each of them became a member of the National Honor Society. Latoria was an excellent chess player and showed an immense amount of stamina.

I had a rule in tournament play that none of us would go out to eat dinner until everyone had finished playing. That way we would support every player, and if we went hungry for an extra half hour, that was our way of showing support.

Saturday evening at Parsippany, Latoria's round didn't start until 6:00 and she was still playing at 10:00. The last player before Latoria had finished his game just before 9:30, so this was becoming a long day for us. Every one of our players was hungry. Naturally, they wanted to eat. I was hungry too, but I reminded them of our rule. "If you were in there playing, wouldn't you want to know that the rest of the kids were out here cheering for you?"

Latoria was playing a much stronger player, but she didn't buckle or lose her calm. The game finally ended after four-and-a-half hours. Around 10:30, she walked out of the room, exhaustion all over her face.

Yes, she was tired, but she had won the game in almost a hundred moves.

Latoria won a number of games that way because of her immense concentration and mental stamina. In fact, one of the things we taught them was to stay with the game even if they were tired. The good players all seemed to develop that mental stamina, which was another reason our kids won so many games.

That's an important quality to mention about my chess players. Perhaps another thing to emphasize is that the best players have the amazing ability to compartmentalize their minds. Most of these children came from tough backgrounds. But once the game started, they pushed all their pain and heartbreak aside. They didn't think about personal issues. They gave total concentration to their game.

Even more impressive about the game where Latoria played for four-and-a-half hours was that her mother was extremely ill the day before we left for Parsippany. Latoria had been quite worried about her. Several times she called from New Jersey to get the latest updates on her health.

But when that girl went out to the table and began to play, she pushed aside her personal worries. She was all game, and the others, who knew about her mother, admired her intense focus. In the three years she played for Vaux, Latoria didn't miss a practice or tournament. Next to Denise, she was the best female player with the most natural ability we ever had. A master of the French Defense, Latoria often frustrated male players ranked much higher than she with her vast knowledge of variations.

Demetrius, who had already shown that he was going to be an outstanding player, came through at Parsippany. It appeared almost as if he was playing for his family and that every opponent was that mean landlord back in Philadelphia.

Before they went in to play a game, no one knew who he or she would be playing against. It was only afterward that they learned. Demetrius played a student from Bucknell University. And he beat him. When the Bucknell student realized that an inner-city kid had beaten him, he could hardly believe it.

Our kids defeated a team of students from Bucknell University, which is near Penn State University. That school had been known for having some top-level chess players. More important, one of their players was a graduate student. Bucknell is considered by many to be an Ivy-league-level college. They were extremely good players.

*　*　*

Demetrius's toughest test would come in the next round. When the play began, it upset me to see Demetrius having to face an obviously older and extremely good player. I talked to a couple of coaches about it.

"It will be good experience for him," one of them said. "It will show him how good some of these players are."

"It's good for him to play against the best," a second one said. "Maybe someday he'll be able to use what he learns from this expert and he'll beat somebody at this level."

Expert? Who would match him against someone so good so soon? Surely, they knew he was from the inner city and had struggled with housing only the day before. Forget about *later*, who is thinking of him now? He's only a kid, and I kept worrying that it would ruin his confidence forever.

I stood behind Demetrius where I could look at the play and not distract him. At first I thought Demetrius was sitting on the wrong side of the table because of the position of his pieces on the chessboard. If he made one move with his rook, he was going to force this expert player into a position where he had to sacrifice (give away) a major piece (queen or rook), or lose the game. He made the right move.

This can't be real. The man is an expert-level player. This is a kid who's been playing chess for all of two years. He's only been to a few tournaments.

But that inner-city kid was playing it exactly right.

A friend of that top player was standing next to me. When Demetrius made his strategic move, the friend swore out loud, amazed at what he saw. He raced out of the room and hurried to the hotel bar. A few minutes later, he returned with a beer and set it down in front of his thirty-something friend. He said nothing, but it was his way of communicating that he'd need plenty of time to think about that last move, so he'd better enjoy it.

That guy who sat across from Demetrius stared at the board and didn't make a move for almost thirty minutes. I had gone to check on the games of all the other players on our team. When I returned, he still hadn't moved. As I studied his face, I could see that he couldn't comprehend that a black kid could mastermind a move like that. He finally looked at Demetrius.

I don't know what was going on inside the man's head, but I'm sure he thought something like this: I'm in a bad situation, but this kid from the inner city is not going to be able to come up with the winning combination (a series of moves) that's going to force me to succumb.

The player moved.

Demetrius's hand shook when he picked up his piece. This was the easy part, taking the opponent's most powerful piece. It took every bit of self-control to keep me from taking Demetrius's hand and moving the piece for him. He was worried because he had made some truly great moves and there must have been twenty people watching him. Many of them had left their own games to see this chess whiz from the inner-city of Philadelphia.

Then Demetrius took a big risk in his last move. I cringed, but that's what I had taught the kids all along. "Be risk takers. Don't be afraid!" I cringed because I thought I saw a better move for Demetrius. Later, when we analyzed the game with a chess master, he showed me how Demetrius's thinking on the chessboard was superior to his opponent as well as my own. Just what I wanted for all my students—for them to teach me—and he did.

Demetrius took that risk and it paid off.

A few minutes later, the near-expert player resigned; there was no way for him to win the game.

Demetrius became one of the most famous chess players in the U.S. Amateur Tournament history, in that one final move. The biggest upset ever.

Even more impressive about the game where Latoria played for four-and-a-half hours was that her mother was extremely ill the day before we left for Parsippany. Latoria had been quite worried about her. Several times she called from New Jersey to get the latest updates on her health.

But when that girl went out to the table and began to play, she pushed aside her personal worries. She was all game, and the others, who knew about her mother, admired her intense focus. In the three years she played for Vaux, Latoria didn't miss a practice or tournament. Next to Denise, she was the best female player with the most natural ability we ever had. A master of the French Defense, Latoria often frustrated male players ranked much higher than she with her vast knowledge of variations.

Demetrius, who had already shown that he was going to be an outstanding player, came through at Parsippany. It appeared almost as if he was playing for his family and that every opponent was that mean landlord back in Philadelphia.

Before they went in to play a game, no one knew who he or she would be playing against. It was only afterward that they learned. Demetrius played a student from Bucknell University. And he beat him. When the Bucknell student realized that an inner-city kid had beaten him, he could hardly believe it.

Our kids defeated a team of students from Bucknell University, which is near Penn State University. That school had been known for having some top-level chess players. More important, one of their players was a graduate student. Bucknell is considered by many to be an Ivy-league-level college. They were extremely good players.

* * *

Demetrius's toughest test would come in the next rou When the play began, it upset me to see Demetrius having face an obviously older and extremely good player. I talked couple of coaches about it.

"It will be good experience for him," one of them said. will show him how good some of these players are."

"It's good for him to play against the best," a second said. "Maybe someday he'll be able to use what he learns fr this expert and he'll beat somebody at this level."

Expert? Who would match him against someone so good soon? Surely, they knew he was from the inner city and struggled with housing only the day before. Forget about *la* who is thinking of him now? He's only a kid, and I kept wo ing that it would ruin his confidence forever.

I stood behind Demetrius where I could look at the play not distract him. At first I thought Demetrius was sitting on wrong side of the table because of the position of his pieces the chessboard. If he made one move with his rook, he going to force this expert player into a position where he ha sacrifice (give away) a major piece (queen or rook), or lose game. He made the right move.

This can't be real. The man is an expert-level player. Thi a kid who's been playing chess for all of two years. He's been to a few tournaments.

But that inner-city kid was playing it exactly right.

A friend of that top player was standing next to me. W Demetrius made his strategic move, the friend swore out lo amazed at what he saw. He raced out of the room and hurr to the hotel bar. A few minutes later, he returned with a b and set it down in front of his thirty-something friend. He s nothing, but it was his way of communicating that he'd n plenty of time to think about that last move, so he'd be enjoy it.

*   *   *

When we looked at some of the other upsets at Parsippany, we saw differences of 631 and 850 points. Such an amazing upset rarely happens for players to defeat others rated that much higher. But our kids did it.

When the difference between the rating of Demetrius and his opponent, 1071, was posted on the wall for everyone to see, the place erupted with yells, shouts, and laughter. Who would ever have believed that a thirteen-year-old inner-city boy defeated a player who was rated 1,071 points higher than he was?

The U.S. Chess Federation had considered Demetrius a novice and they had rated him around 900 at the start of the tournament.

This kind of upset had never taken place before in the thirty-five-year history of this tournament. They posted Demetrius's name on the wall for the next two days. He had defeated an expert-level player—something never done before. Even now, years later, people remember and still speak with awe about that game.

After the defeat, the Bucknell player congratulated Demetrius, and then he turned to me and asked, "Tell me the truth. Are they really middle school kids?"

After all of us yelled, "Yes!" he jokingly asked to see identification. He marveled at how good they were. "And this is astounding that you're only *eighth* graders."

I didn't want to deflate him more or I would have told him the truth. They were *seventh* graders and Thomas was in the *sixth*.

"How could that kid play so well?" I heard people ask at the tournament.

I knew the answer, but I wasn't going to tell. It was the same answer then that it always has been. Our kids didn't know they couldn't win and believed they could pull off a victory every time, so they played their best!

*   *   *

Another exciting achievement at Parsippany was that our middle school kids played against a team of experienced men, most of them middle-aged, all of whom had been playing chess an average of thirty years. All were top players. Our team, most of whom had only been playing for two years or less, defeated them. Our kids won the award for the largest upset in the first round!

Just to see Demetrius's name posted as the largest upset at that tournament, a young black child from the inner city of Philadelphia using his mind, filled me with deep joy and excitement. It wasn't his jumping ability, or his speed or his musical talent. This kid did it by using his mind. It was the greatest compliment to the chess program.

When Demetrius received the award, tears filled my eyes. I didn't care who saw them. I was so glad he had insisted on coming when reason said he should have stayed back in Philadelphia. I was overjoyed, yet I was also sad. I wished that all of the kids at Vaux School could have had such a moment as that.

I had decided we'd leave on Sunday afternoon, one day early, as soon as we finished our last match for that day. That last day was our worst day and the children were tired and somewhat discouraged—Latoria worried about her mother, and I wanted to get home to my wife and make peace.

"You can't leave now," one of the coaches said. He pointed to his laptop computer. I thought our team had scored badly, but I had no way of knowing for certain.

We stayed and I'm glad we did.

At the end of the tournament, we received a plaque, four new chess clocks, and a Cross pen set for being the top team in our category in the whole U.S. Amateur East Tournament. We were the number one team in our division.

Just hearing "Vaux Middle School" called out over the PA system was so exciting to me and to the kids. It was one of the greatest feelings I've ever had in my life.

As I listened to the merriment and excitement over the team, I also thought about Shawnna at home. I had a big problem to deal with and it was entirely my fault.

But somehow, Demetrius's win—and especially in view of the fact that he had been evicted and had to buy clothes just to come to the tournament—made the trip totally worthwhile. The entire community had rallied behind him.

One of the individuals Demetrius thanked was a man named Claude Williams, because his financial contribution had made it possible for us to make that trip.

Claude had been my barber since I was a kid. He knew my mom well and was aware of our financial situation. During my school days, he rarely charged me or any of the other poor kids in the neighborhood for haircuts. He was not only my barber but he became my mentor. Even after I went to college, he remained my mentor and friend. Whenever I came home for a weekend or holiday during my college days, Claude would slip two or three dollars into my pocket. He'd say a few words of encouragement, pat my shoulder, smile, and I knew he was totally behind me.

After I became a teacher, Claude asked me to bring my students to the barbershop for a chess game with some of his relatives and customers. I did and our boys didn't lose a single game. Claude had posted articles about the team's achievements all over the place.

When Claude's nephew Dave and another barber in his shop, Mike, heard we needed money to travel to Virginia, they petitioned barbershop customers to sponsor us. And they did just that. Thanks to the guys at Claude's, we were the most famous chess team in the East.

As I stood and watched Demetrius receive his trophy, I knew—somehow I knew—that God was going to watch over him, as well as make sure that things worked out right with my wife.

16

Winners Take All

Because we had scored the biggest upset, our kids earned a gourmet meal at the Parsippany Hilton Hotel Restaurant. The kids felt this was one of the greatest moments in their life. There they were—all inner-city kids—sitting in a beautiful, fancy dining room, and for the first time in their lives, they were able to order anything they wanted. They ordered prime rib and lobster. Those were words they had only read before. Now they actually tasted those dishes.

As soon as we returned to Philadelphia, I rushed home and shouted the news to Shawnna. Then I put down the trophies and said, "I'm sorry. Forgive me." That's all I needed to say. She was in my arms and held me as tightly as I held her.

"I understand," she said and hugged me again. She forgave me for deserting her. Even though I had known she would forgive me, I knew I didn't deserve it. I felt so grateful to Shawnna for being the kind of person and wife she was. I silently thanked God for her.

We spent all of the next weekend together—only the two of

us and didn't have contact with any of the kids. It was also a special weekend for us to be in our new house, which we had recently purchased in the Belmont Village section of Philadelphia, near Wynnefield. It is an integrated neighborhood that borders Fairmount Park and is only ten minutes from Vaux.

(Shortly after we moved there, the people elected me president of the neighborhood association. I felt bad that I couldn't give much time because of my work with the kids, but they seemed to understand. In fact, my neighbors frequently asked about the children and sent money to the school for the team.)

After the upset at Parsippany, *Chess Life* magazine published an article about the U.S. Amateur Championship and they congratulated us for being the top team in our division. The writer called it a truly remarkable and exceptional feat for a team with an average rating of 890 and ranked 230 at the start. *Chess Life* went on to say "Hats off to the team to beat, the Vaux Mighty Bishops."

As I read that article and reflected on it, those words reinforced my philosophy that my kids could overcome anything if they only knew they could be successful. And I was never going to tell them they couldn't be successful.

I made copies of the article for everyone in the school and told every child how proud I was of the team and how proud I was to be their coach.

"Now I don't want you to relax because there's more work to be done. We're just getting started." That had taken place in February. In March we faced the city championships and then the state.

We played in the city championship and marched right into the semifinals. This time I didn't hear any sneers or disparaging remarks about our kids. Everyone had heard about our conquering in Parsippany. We again reached the semifinals against the same three magnet schools. We played five games against Conwell and won every one of them.

The kids were pumped and so was I. We were ready for the finals. As we had expected, we were pitted against Masterman. That was the only team that we had not defeated. Although we'd defeated their players individually, we never did in a team event. It was my alma mater, but I wanted to defeat Masterman's team. The kids wanted to do it because they knew it was important to me.

For the first time, I believed we had a chance to beat them. In the first four games, both teams won two. If we won the final game, we would beat Masterman for the first time for the championship. Our player, Thomas Allen, was winning.

I have no idea what happened, but Thomas made a wrong move. He lost the game to a player he had defeated in Bloomsburg.

The children were upset, and they took out their frustration on Thomas. Victory had been within their grasp and then we lost at the last minute. As they badgered him, he began to cry. I think all of the kids cried. They were so close to victory and then lost it.

Thomas couldn't handle the pressure of his loss. "Just one play and I failed. I let the team down," he said again and again. No matter what I said, he couldn't get beyond the fact that he was the final player, was ahead, and he should have won.

A few days later he quit the team. He didn't tell me directly, but he sent word.

I went to see him as soon as classes were over that day. I called him aside and said, "You've got to understand that *you* took us to the championship. We wouldn't have gotten in the finals without you. Just because you didn't win the last game doesn't erase what you did for your teammates. I know they were upset back then. They said things to you because victory had been close, but it wasn't you they were upset about. Besides, they need you, Thomas, I need you."

Thomas did come back. He was with us and competed for the state championship and we ended up finishing second in the state with Masterman being number one.

Once we got beyond Thomas Allen's game loss, we thought more about it. We consoled ourselves with the fact that we had to take local kids from the inner city. We weren't able to recruit students. Masterman was able to bring in top students from around the city.

We were a different type of school. Parents weren't banging on our doors to get their kids entered in our school. Sometimes we would see as few as five parents at a school meeting. That's not good for a school with nine hundred children. We never let any of those issues stop us. We were proud of our accomplishments. In some ways, I think our kids felt a bit superior, because they were breaking down the stereotypes and proving their ability.

We still felt that we should have been able to beat Masterman. I was glad the kids were upset. Some schools insisted that we shouldn't have to compete against schools like Masterman, Conwell, and AMY that recruited students and attracted parents from throughout the city. But we didn't feel that way. We need those and they provide inner-city parents alternatives for their children. Competing against them would push us to raise our expectations for students. We believed that our kids were good enough to compete and win against any school. Not then, not ever, did we ask to make the competition easier for us.

"This is what you will face when you get out in a world that doesn't care about the underprivileged or the poor. You have to make your own way. You all will have to grow up in this world together."

I was glad that the kids were upset because it showed that

they weren't feeling sorry for themselves, and they hadn't gone in against their nemesis with low expectations. Despite previous losses, they had expected to beat Masterman.

I want to make it clear that we always had a good relationship with the players from Masterman. We traveled with them to most of the tournaments. Our kids usually hung out together. A lot of times they would practice and go over games together. There was and is no animosity, just a healthy, friendly rivalry.

Now it was time to get ready for the nationals in Knoxville. Our expectations were high.

In April we faced the national championship so we had more work ahead of us, but I wanted the team to understand what they had done that weekend. They came out to play, and in their fine performances, they had represented every poor child that has ever had to overcome obstacles or stereotypes. "You came in and you showed people what you can do. You are dispelling myths and you're breaking down prejudices everywhere. Be proud of yourselves, because I'm really proud of you."

Everywhere we went people always asked us, "Are you a basketball team?" Whenever they carried their trophies home to Philadelphia, people they talked to had trouble believing that black, inner-city kids could be as smart as anyone else—and bring home chess trophies.

It offends me that the people who ask if they're an athletic team don't ever assume that they're on the road for something academic.

When we returned to Vaux from the state championship, we learned that everyone knew about our great playing. The kids had become stars. They brought home trophies and awards, and it was a great time at the school because we were able to celebrate success for something that the children had done with their minds.

What made that weekend outstanding for me is that I received a letter from one of the employees at the hotel where we stayed for the state tournament. This was a school trip and the letter actually arrived at my home, so I felt extremely concerned. When I first spotted the Quality Inn letterhead, I became worried. Immediately my mind clicked away, wondering if one of the kids had done something wrong or if there had been a negative incident they'd hid from me.

When I opened the letter, it simply stated: "I am an employee at the Quality Inn hotel in Buckhorn, Pennsylvania (five minutes from Bloomsburg University), and I hope you don't mind that I got your address from your personal information card. I was not sure you would get this letter if I sent it to the school. I wanted to let you know how pleased the staff at that hotel was with the behavior of your children."

She went on to write, "They helped other guests with their luggage, held doors for them, were very orderly, and always mannerly . . . We have never had children stay at our hotel who behaved so respectfully. I felt that I should let you know that these children really behaved in a great way."

She probably had seen kids from all over who came and probably didn't know how to behave properly. These were children who knew how to take care of themselves and how to help others.

That letter filled me with pride. This was one way that went beyond academic achievement. I copied that letter and sent it to every teacher. I wanted them to see what our children were capable of doing outside the school and that they could do the same thing inside school. And just as important, I wanted them to know that people recognized thoughtful and kind behavior.

It was also for teachers to see that these were children who went out and represented them well. The teachers did a good job preparing them to represent the school and the community. We received compliments, many of which were from establishments, restaurants, and hotels.

17

Upset at Knoxville

Going to the national championship in Knoxville, Tennessee, in 1997 would be an extremely big step for the chess team. We knew, and so did the kids, that they didn't stand much chance to win it all. Just because they couldn't win didn't mean they ought not to try. I never said they couldn't win, but I didn't let them think they were going to Knoxville and walk away with all the trophies.

"Don't worry about winning. Don't worry about losing. Do your best. Focus on the game and learn everything you can." That's the way I talked to them—the way I tried to talk to them before every event. This was much more important than winning trophies.

There were people who cared about the experiences of the children, such as employees at Wilkie Lexus in Ardmore, Pennsylvania. When we visited the dealership a couple of days before we left for Tennessee, the employees overheard us talking about practicing for the national championship. They cleared table space in their showroom for us to set up chessboards and clocks. We actually practiced chess moves while sitting next to fifty-thousand-dollar cars, and many of their rich customers watched in amazement. The general manager, Jack Cornish, and the sales manager, Ray Johnson, Jr., generously provided the children with sodas and food. The employees donated money to help us reach the nationals and invited us to their new store in Haverford to film a training video for Lexus.

They believed in these inner-city kids. Our secret as a team lay in our attitude, our commitment, and the belief that we could do anything we set out to do. We also wanted to spread the magic of chess to other inner-city schools.

This time we chartered a bus to drive us from Vaux Middle School all the way to the University of Tennessee at Knoxville. We had already enlarged our plans beyond Vaux to take students with us from Morton McMichael and Robert Morris Elementary Schools, because they had also decided to compete. We felt we had put together a winning combination for children.

We had forty-five people on the chartered bus and that included twelve adults and thirty-three children. We had both boys and girls.

Again, the trip was a significant time for our kids, riding in a bus, seeing farmlands, animals, and unlimited fields of green. The campus overwhelmed them, because as inner-city kids they had no idea that such an expansive place existed.

Shortly after we arrived at the university campus, we learned that our team was already well known across the United States. Ours was the team that couldn't possibly win anything, and yet we were winning everywhere we went.

"We're coming after your kids," one coach said to me. "We were in Parsippany when you blew everyone away and we read about you in *Chess Life*. We have to beat you because you're the team everyone talks about."

He smiled as he talked to me, but I knew he was quite serious.

The tournament at Knoxville started on Friday afternoon and went until 10:00 or 11:00, resumed the next morning at 8:00, and again went until 10:00 or 11:00 at night. It finished on Sunday, usually by 6 P.M.

As soon as we started playing, we knew this was going to be a magic city for us because the kids started out winning. At the end of the first day, we were in first place. After every round I called back to Philadelphia and told the principal and parents how well we were doing, and then whomever I called spread the word to everyone else in the community. We were in first place for the first five of seven rounds over two days. We were so successful that our team was the focus of a cover story in Knoxville's *News Sentinel,* the city's leading newspaper.

By the way, we realized the impact of our wins when a player from another team offered our kids ten dollars to lose so he could claim to be the first to defeat us. No one was interested in taking his money.

In the sixth round on Sunday, our success started going downhill. Earl lost a game and we had been counting on him to carry us. He was the first to finish and just about everyone on the team lost game six.

Demetrius was our only player who didn't lose a game during the entire tournament. Less than 50 players could make this claim out of 4,000 competitors in Knoxville. At that time, we could see that we had dropped out of our chances for winning and had gone from first place to fourth place.

"There's only one chance for us to win the championship," I said to one of the parents. "Every kid has to win every game in the final round." I didn't think that was possible, but I didn't say or hint of that to anyone. This is almost never done in national tournaments. I read somewhere that this has been done less than ten times over a twenty-five-year period. These kids had surprised me so many times; maybe they could work their magic once again.

We were in a great position and we could pull it off, but the pressure was on.

I had never seen the kids looking so disappointed and sad. It hurt me to see how bad they felt. No one blamed anyone. It wasn't that kind of thing, but a general sense of not being able to win every game. They had been so sure they would leave without dropping a game.

I suggested we go back to the hotel so the kids could relax before they played their final game Sunday afternoon. None of them wanted to leave. They were stressed out and a couple of them even complained of being sick. Yet they were so involved in the games, they didn't even want to rush to the restrooms for fear that they'd miss something important.

Just before the final game, I saw how deeply stressed they were. And yet as I figured and refigured and talked to two different coaches who had computers, I realized that we still had a chance after all, I thought. *A chance.* If not the top spot, at least maybe we can make one of the top three spots, and that would have satisfied me. Before we left Philadelphia, I hadn't considered, hoped, or dared to think we could win first place, but after they started out so well I couldn't stop thinking about going home with a first-place trophy.

Now that dream was out of our control.

For us to win a top position—not even thinking about first place any longer—also meant that some of the other top contenders had to lose. There seemed no way for us to tell who did what because we didn't have the computerized programs like some of the other schools did to calculate results. I couldn't run over to them constantly and ask who was winning. Occasionally, I'd go to another coach and ask him for an update, but I didn't do that very often because I didn't want to be a nuisance.

As I watched their anxieties, I felt my heart breaking for the kids. One was in the bathroom sick because of nerves. "This isn't worth what you're going through," I said. Let's pack it in. Let's go home."

"Oh, no, we want to play," said Demetrius.

"We can do it," said quiet Denise.

As I looked around, not one kid was ready to quit.

"It's a long shot," I said.

"We know, but you keep saying we can do it," Latoria reminded me.

"That's right. You're the team that can make it happen."

"There you go preaching again!" Those words came from Earl.

We decided to let them play that final round.

We made the right decision.

Each of the kids started to win their final game. As I moved around, I realized that none of the Vaux kids was losing. Everywhere I looked, our kids were coming through and were all in the stronger position.

"I won! I won!" child after child screamed as he or she ran to me and hugged me.

Our kids did great, but we still didn't think we had a shot at winning because the other teams ahead of us were winning too. Because of our bad showing in round six, we thought we had dropped out of any top spots. We had grouped together and were getting ready to go back to our hotel. Although every one of our kids had won the final game, we assumed that the other top contenders had won all their games as well. I started out by telling my kids how proud I was of them for finishing so strong and not giving up. I began to rehearse my runner-up speech.

"Congratulations, you guys!" yelled a coach of a competing team.

I waved and started hustling the kids away. We were in no mood for jokes.

"Where you going? You're the national champions."

"National champions? Some of the players in this round aren't finished," I said. "Nobody knows who won. They're still trying to—"

"We have ways of figuring these things out with our computerized system. I'm telling you, your kids have won. You scored tremendous upsets on that last round. Most of the kids you beat were on teams that were ahead of you."

I couldn't believe it. The kids were watching my face, waiting for me to respond so they'd know if it was true.

I grinned and they began to jump up and down and scream and cry.

Half an hour later, "Congratulations to Vaux Middle School of Philadelphia!" thundered the voice over the intercom. "They are our new national champions," was all I heard.

It was all I needed to hear.

We stared at each other because now it was official. No one knew what to say. We stared in silence, hardly able to believe the message we had just heard.

Tears spilled down my cheeks. I guess I must have signaled the others because within a few seconds, all of us were crying and hugging. It was one of those powerful moments that I can't ever forget.

Our joyful tears and hugging probably lasted ten minutes. We even missed our team photograph, but we didn't care. *This was our time. This was our cry together of joy.*

I could no longer stand on my feet. I dropped to my knees and thanked God for the victory for these kids. I thought of all the problems and issues these kids had to cope with every day of their lives. They live among drug dealers; they've personally seen murders committed on the streets or in the projects. Family crises were part of their lives. Few of our kids had a stable environment and everything in the world said they ought to come in at the bottom of the tournament.

Never had I felt so proud of these kids.

Never had I been more convinced that I was doing the very job I was supposed to be doing. I couldn't reach all the kids at Vaux School with the chess program, but this was a powerful start. We'd have other programs and find new ways to challenge them.

But for now, I cried.

18

The Taste of Victory

The children had worked hard. They had a chance to give up when everybody lost on that sixth round. Nobody gave up. What they did was use that as their incentive to go back and fight.

Masterman had competed in a different division—the K–8 open division. They also had a team in the high school division. They won the championship in the K–8 open and the high school division, while we won the K–8 championship in the under 1000 division. Each section fielded about 100 schools, the largest chess tournament in world history. They called it the "Super Nationals." That day our two schools—same city but from two different sides of the world—made history. They called it a triple crown win because schools in the same city school district had won all three divisions. The United States Chess Federation said a triple crown for one school district was rare. "We think it's quite a remarkable achievement," said Eric C. Johnson, Assistant Federation Director in 1997.

I was very proud of my kids. As a graduate of Masterman, I was proud of those kids too. It takes plenty of hard work and tremendous sacrifice to become the best in the country.

This says a lot about kids from Philadelphia Public Schools. It also says a great deal about our students because they were able to compete in a division that was filled with many suburban, private, and parochial schools. *One* inner-city public school was able to not only compete, but to finish at the top.

I had always known my kids were winners.

Now the world also knew it.

At the final ceremony we were presented with a gigantic team trophy for winning first place; I received a plaque as the national champion coach. They presented plaques to the top four players on our team. For finishing third best in the nation, Demetrius received a divisional trophy, and it was taller than he was. Charles Mabine, Anthony Harper, and Anwar Smith picked up trophies for their top ten finishes.

Sunday, after the ceremonies, our kids strutted around the University of Tennessee campus, carrying eleven trophies and plaques. "We're the Mighty Bishops!" they screamed. I followed behind them, proud to be with them and always wanting to be sure that they didn't do anything foolish. But I was as excited as they were. These were my kids—and they were fulfilling my dream for them.

"It's finally happening. Thank you, God," I said as fresh tears filled my eyes.

For maybe two hours they marched all over the campus, brandishing their awards as if they were kings and queens with crowns. "We're the Mighty Bishops! We're the Mighty Bishops!"

We went out for dinner that night. Every kid thought of some relative or friend to call at home and shout the news to. I'm sure we would have called the President of the United States if we had known his phone number. We were so excited and wanted everyone to know, so we called anyone we could think of.

On Tuesday morning when our bus pulled in at the school, I began to feel bad. The previous year we had held a pep rally and then we hadn't won the first- place prize. This year we had won, but we hadn't planned anything special for the return of the kids from this trip. I guess everybody had been tired.

What I didn't know was that the administration and staff planned a reception as soon as they had gotten the call about our winning the nationals. They didn't even tell me, the coach. The auditorium was full of kids waiting to see us. They waved signs and displayed a large banner that read:

1997 SUPER NATIONAL CHAMPIONS—
KNOXVILLE, TENNESSEE

What a powerful moment it was for everyone to come to school and see all those kids and faculty waiting. This was something normally done only for football and basketball teams. Some districts close schools for the entire day when sports teams win championships. We must begin to make children feel like champions when they excel academically.

For the entire school to cheer kids who had won distinction in chess was something completely new. They were being cheered for using their *minds*. For me, this moment was the ultimate show of respect. Our kids were being taught to think and the response was overwhelming.

The principal asked me to give a speech, and it took me several minutes—or maybe it only seemed that long—to pull myself together. I'm one of those articulate types who's rarely at a loss for words. But I lost it that morning. I was so touched by the school and seeing the parents who had come out. And to watch parents hugging and congratulating their kids was one of the ultimate joys for me.

The highlight, however, was when the principal called the children by name and asked them to come to the platform with their parents. People snapped pictures, smiled, and laughed the whole time. It was an unbelievable event.

It was an event I'm sure they'll never forget. We had been living in the shadow of the Bad Bishops team of twenty years ago and we had become known because of their achievements. Now we had defined our own era because we won our own national championship.

I thanked the teachers for the sacrifices they made for these kids. Many of them had turned down better pay and better-funded schools to stay in the inner city. It was a sacrifice for them, but they had stayed. Now I could give them a few moments of praise and thanks for their efforts.

"You have made a lot of sacrifices in helping to build and mold children so they can survive in a competitive environment with their mind as the only tool that they can use. In that bigger world, our physical strength means nothing. It takes a true teacher to be able to develop a child like that. So I thank every one of you teachers."

I thanked the students. I thanked the parents. I thanked our principal for allowing us to go out and practice and to do the things we did. He had stuck out his neck by giving us freedom to practice after school.

I thanked the alumni, community, and businesses for giving us the money and resources to do all the things that we were able to.

I thanked my kids for letting me be a father and a brother to them at a time when I needed to do that and at a time when they needed it. They had to open up themselves. "We've been through some hard times together and I said some things that you didn't like and you said some things to me that I didn't like."

There was so much more I wanted to say, but I couldn't. I became so choked up I stopped, held back the tears, shook my head, and walked out of the auditorium.

It was a moment for me to be alone and to cry thankful tears in private.

19

A Chance to Succeed

We were winning tournaments, but that was not the point of the chess matches—at least not from my point of view. I loved it when they won, and they needed to win. But the winning was to show them what they could do. They were talented young people. They were beginning to realize that they had potential. Just growing up in the inner city didn't automatically make them losers.

They needed that one thing—a chance to succeed. That's one of the important reasons I stayed in the inner city—to inspire kids and to help them know that they could succeed in their careers and in life.

Winning brought a lot of praise and recognition to our kids. For instance, on May 12, 1997, after we returned from our national championship in Knoxville, everyone connected with the chess team received an invitation to meet Dr. David Hornbeck, the superintendent of Philadelphia schools, at the school district administration building.

We received several awards from him as well as a plaque signed by the school board president Floyd Austin and by Dr. Hornbeck. Each player received a distinguished achievement award for an outstanding contribution to the school district of Philadelphia.

Wearing our biggest smiles, the children and I stood in front of reporters from all the media. Those reporters helped to make it not only a special event but big and exciting. For me, the best part was the recognition by the school district, which took the time to recognize these young people who brought glory and pride to the schools of Philadelphia.

For so long, Philadelphia schools had received much negative publicity because of all the wrong things that go on in schools. Too often the media overlooks the positive factors. This was one time to shine the light on a positive moment in the history of schools in Philadelphia.

A few days later, Mayor Ed Rendell, then mayor of Philadelphia, invited us to city hall. Mr. Rendell, who later moved on to become chairman of the Democratic National Party, presented each child with a citation from the city and invited all of us into his office for a visit and for photographs.

As I watched the children's reaction, it was obvious that they could hardly believe where they were. None asked, but from their faces, it was as if they were asking each other, "Can this be happening?"

For me, it was a great and humbling experience to be honored, first by the superintendent of schools and then by the leader of our city. The mayor seemed to enjoy being around these children of Philadelphia. He told the entire team that he was willing to challenge them for the keys to the city.

They reminded him of what happened to Ukee Washington when he made a similar statement. These were symbols of what schools can be like and he was proud that we made the city look good.

*   *   *

Later in June 1997, we received a call from the school district. They wanted to televise a live chess match between a Masterman student and a student from Vaux. This would be the first live televised match in Philadelphia history. The children liked the idea, but they were afraid they would lose. Even though this would be a chance for the entire city to see them compete against a team that had defeated them for the city and state titles for two consecutive years, they might lose again.

Earl volunteered to represent us. He had won several games in different tournaments against players from Masterman but he had never played against any of their best. We learned that he would be matched against one of their top players—a boy rated 500 points higher than he. This all but guaranteed a win for his opponent.

"I'll have something to say about that," Earl said to us. I wasn't sure how much was self-confidence and how much was empty bragging, but I did know that he would do his best.

As soon as the game started, Earl used a new opening he had been studying, called the Pirc. That opening not only surprised his opponent, but Earl took over and won the match.

Even today when we talk about chess, Earl remembers it and smiles. And he deserves to! It was the biggest win of his young life.

What impressed me most was that after the match both players talked about the game and shook hands like gentlemen. I marveled at their behavior and thought, what a show of class and sportsmanship. This is what I want. This is the type of behavior I want to teach all the kids.

In the summer of 1997, Demetrius Carroll and Earl Jenkins were invited to a scholarship and achievement dinner at Pinn Memorial Baptist Church, located in the Wynnefield section of

Philadelphia. They were to be honored for their achievements in chess.

The key note speaker, famed lawyer Johnny Cochran, spoke to children who had excelled in schools throughout the city. Afterward, Mr. Cochran invited Demetrius and Earl to chat with him in the pastor's office. Several people took pictures of them together and the boys signed autographs. Mr. Cochran was impressed with their chess achievements and said, "You have become great role models for children all over the country."

It thrilled Demetrius and Earl that a famous man like Johnny Cochran would take time to talk to them.

Not only did the boys receive copies of the photographs, but also their parents have the pictures prominently displayed in their homes.

In August 1997 we returned to Orlando, this time to compete in the U.S. Open. While there, we won the top scholastic prize in every grade category.

We returned home with a whopping eleven trophies, more than twice as many as any other team there.

Of course, we had some problems. When we arrived at the Orlando airport for our return flight to Philadelphia, an airline employee at the check-in counter told us that we would not be allowed on the plane with so many trophies. I asked him if he realized what these children had accomplished? He didn't, of course, and I explained to him who we were and what we had achieved over the last few months. He was so impressed by the kids he told us to go right on to the gate with the trophies.

I thanked him profusely. I couldn't have turned around with all those kids at that point. Hundreds of excited parents and supportive friends awaited our return to Philadelphia.

That wasn't the end of the problem, however. The gate agent

let us on board, but two flight attendants didn't want the trophies on the plane because they weren't easily placed in the overhead compartment, and they worried about passenger safety. They insisted that we could not store the trophies in the overhead compartments because of endangering others and that we would have to check the items or get off the plane. I quietly protested and explained what our kids had won.

Several adults on the plane had already commented on our national champion T-shirts. They also listened as I pleaded with the flight attendants. Once they heard of our outstanding accomplishments, several of them said to the flight attendants, "Let them on."

"They deserve to carry those trophies on board," one woman said.

Before long, almost every adult on the plane knew about it. They even gave the kids a standing ovation.

Oh, yes, they allowed us to stay on the plane. I have to admit that we had to do a lot of creative packing to secure the trophies in the overhead compartment. None of them fell out during the flight.

I was proud of the children for the way they carried themselves and the honor they brought to the inner city. That applause seemed to last for the entire two-hour plane ride. Or maybe the memory of it kept ringing in my ears.

The new school year began in September 1997. It had been five wonderful months ago when we won the national championship, and our kids still felt like celebrities.

A big moment came when they were interviewed and featured on a TV program called *Kids Are Paramount* for the UPN network. The host, a kid himself, was Marcus Paulk, who was then starring as the younger brother of the singing sensation Brandy on the TV show *Moesha*.

We felt so excited and honored to be able to hear him say our name and talk about us being a cool school. He gave Vaux an award for being one of the cool schools in the country.

My big thrill in watching the show was that everyone in the city and nationwide could see us on TV, and I hoped that would enable them to realize that Vaux was a school where soccer, basketball, and football stood in the shadow of chess. I also hoped they'd see this as a powerful game to exercise the mind. Our goal was for chess to become the number one sport in greater Philadelphia.

A number of people contacted us after the telecast—many of them were kids—and they talked about how cool it was that Vaux kids had chosen to take hold of something where they had to use their minds.

During the fall of 1997, the chess team was invited to attend a 76ers' game and to visit with some players in the locker room after the game.

They also met Grant Hill, an all-star player with the Detroit Pistons. He took the time to talk to the kids, which was a lot more than signing autographs. He was there to talk and listen to them. He told them he thought they were special because they had taken the time to learn the difficult game of chess. He told them that many players on the team and in the NBA played chess on plane rides. Although the Pistons won the game, we were glad to have the chance to talk to Grant Hill.

Grant is a great role model. He told the kids that he had left college early and that he wanted to go back to complete his education. He promised his parents that he would graduate from college and he graduated from Duke University.

*   *   *

In November 1997, I turned down the opportunity to leave Vaux. Although I didn't spread the word, the news got around— as it always seems to do in good or bad situations—that I had turned down big money to stay in the inner city. The raise had been $20,000, but it seemed as if every time the story spread, the amount became larger. Once I heard that I had turned down $200,000 to stay. Although not true, I would still have said no regardless of the amount.

The effect of my decision was marvelous. Those kids believed that I was committed to the inner city. No matter how much I had talked before or what I had done, it was turning down the big dollars that convinced them that I was there for them.

My relationship with the kids had always been good, maybe even outstanding. It was even better now. Now I was *their* teacher, even if they were in other classes. That simple act of saying no to money made me a symbol to them.

I loved it that they looked up to me, of course, but it was also a little scary. What if I don't measure up? What if I fail these kids? Those thoughts troubled me—and still do at times. I don't ever want to make them stumble because of my failure.

A few weeks after I turned down the job offer to leave Vaux, we decided to return to Parsippany, New Jersey. Not only was it relatively close, but I liked the opportunities and challenges presented at this tournament.

Students from all over the United States come to Parsippany to compete for the top scholastic honors in each grade. This is the only annual tournament where students actually compete to be the top chess student in their grade on a national level. They compete on an individual basis, regardless of their rank. By contrast, in the national championship, kids compete as a team and also individually for their age group.

Our students didn't do especially well, although we ended up with the fifth-place team trophy in the eighth-grade division. Our big individual winner was Demetrius Carroll, now an eighth-grader and a class champion, which meant he was the top player in his class.

In January 1998, we returned to New York to Manhattan Community College. This time we won a third-place team award—a year earlier we had come in fourth. One of our players, Nathan Durant, was the top non-rated player and class champion. We had no problem getting a cab.

A few days after we returned from the chess tournament in New York, we received a copy of *Chess Life* magazine along with a report put out by the U.S. Chess Federation.

To our amazement, we saw the name of one of our players—Denise Pickard. We didn't know until we read the article that she had been selected as one of the top fifty female chess players in the nation under the age of thirteen.

This is a very distinguished honor, and no one else in our school had ever achieved such an honor in a program that was by then twenty years old at Vaux. For the first time a young lady from our school had been recognized as one of the top fifty females in the nation in her age category. To this day, we have not had that happen again to a boy or girl. To our knowledge, Denise was only one of a few African-American females to win this honor in the United States. Obviously, we were very proud of her.

I made copies of the article and distributed it to every teacher in the school. "Read this. Now we can show what our children are capable of achieving."

She was ranked among the top females under the age of thirteen in every category, and she was competing against top, professionally trained players all over the nation.

This resulted in interviews and publicity. Denise is a quiet, shy girl, and that made me extremely proud. She's the type of child who would have been ignored in a different school. This would soon change.

One month later, I visited the local PAL (Police Athletic League) center. One of the officers had suggested that I bring my kids to their upcoming chess tournament for boys and girls. These were the best players from PAL centers throughout the city. I took middle school students, Denise Pickard and Demetrius Carroll, but I entered them in the high school divisions because I knew they needed a challenge.

Both won first place in their sections.

The officers joked about Denise's dismantling of her opponents in the girls' division and how she would have probably beaten most of their boys. I told them she could beat their best middle-school boy. They laughed and set up the match with the boy who had finished winning his division.

"I'm willing to give up my trophy if he beats me," she said. This was a confident Denise that I would never have heard speak that way even a year earlier. Chess had dramatically changed her life and she spoke with a confidence that I admired.

The match began.

Denise won in less than fifteen moves.

She allowed the young man to keep his trophy, although she was prepared to give him hers if she had lost. She was the talk of the PAL center for quite some time!

On Saturday, February 14, I received a letter at home: ". . . You have been appointed as the new acting assistant principal at Vaux Middle School . . ." That was the important part of the letter. I ran through the house. I hugged Shawnna several times. I called my mom and my siblings. This was the moment I had dreamed about.

In February I became the *acting* assistant principal. This is a kind of trial period. If I did well, in six months I would be *appointed*. Acting meant that I was temporary at Vaux. I could also be moved to another school.

Until then I was a teacher, nothing more—and I loved it. In many ways, I would have been content to stay in the classroom the rest of my career. But something pulled at me. I wanted more for myself and I wanted more for the children. If I rose higher in the system, I reasoned that I could do more good for more children. I had long set my goals to become an educational leader and administrator.

◦ What wonderful news it was being designated as assistant principal. It also meant that I would be able to stay at the same school with children I had worked with for a decade. I felt so deeply grateful and thankful to God.

So honored and so humbled, and it was truly a blessing.

I believed God had worked this out for me. I had felt it was the way to go and had prayed about it often. Only three months earlier, I had turned down a similar position and a raise in pay. I assumed—regardless of what I had been told—that I wouldn't get another chance. I had made the choice to stay because I truly believed it was right. Even so, a small part of me kept asking, "Did you really make the right choice?" And yet, my heart told me it was the right decision. And there were some adults from my school who questioned my decision.

Several friends had laughed at me and told me, "You're a fool for turning down all of that money."

"You'll regret that decision," said a leading member of the community.

That letter promoting me to acting assistant principal validated my decision. As I read and reread the letter, I kept think-ing, this is God's way of saying, "This is your reward for your hard work and sticking by those children."

Part of what amazed me was that the assignment was at Vaux. That rarely happened, to be assigned as an administrator at the same school where you were a classroom teacher. Edu-cators generally have the view that administrators promoted within their own school are not successful. They say it doesn't work, stirs up jealousy among peers, and makes it difficult for the person to assume a different role.

I didn't agree—at least not in my case. I knew I could make the change easily enough and make a tremendous impact on our students. And I felt so grateful to have the chance to do that.

According to the letter, effective February 17, 1998, I would become the assistant principal at Vaux Middle School. I must have read that letter a hundred times. I cried a lot and kept thanking God, because I knew this was a special gift to me.

When I called my mom, she said, "I'm not surprised. I knew this would happen one day." She was so glad that it had worked out because she knew my decision to stay weighed on my mind. She felt this was something great for my family and me.

In May 1998, we competed in the national championship in Phoenix, Arizona. We didn't do anything outstanding—at least not compared to our previous wins. Our team ended up with a fifth-place trophy.

We did have one success story, and his name is Anwar Smith. That boy is a miracle story. His mother had a substance abuse problem, but the woman was determined to beat her addiction (and she eventually did). She voluntarily went into treatment, but it was outside the city. She wanted to take Anwar with her, but he begged her to let him stay in school at Vaux. To her credit, she agreed.

For the next six months, Anwar moved from family to family, from relative to relative. He rarely knew where he'd be sleeping or eating the following week. He never complained about it, and was amazingly resilient. No matter how horrible his situation outside of school, when he played chess that young man gave the game his total concentration.

He was the only player from Pennsylvania who did not lose a match and he won third place in Phoenix. He had also performed very well at the state championship at Bloomsburg University a month earlier. This tournament was a yearly ritual for us now. With Anwar's help, we finished in second place again.

I lived to see miracles in the lives of kids like Anwar. And sometimes, even now, when I hit a low spot and wonder if it's worth it all, his is one of the names I think of.

"Yes, it's more than worthwhile," I tell myself.

The sad part is that there are thousands of unnamed Anwar Smiths out there and they're not getting their chance.

After Phoenix, I took the kids to an open tournament in Hartford, Connecticut, during the summer. We entered their scholastic section. *Open* means that it was open to anyone, but the *scholastic section* meant it was only for students still in school. Our kids competed against students from New York, Connecticut, Massachusetts, and Maine.

We were the only team that traveled from Pennsylvania, and we didn't mind that. We willingly traveled anywhere for a tournament if we could raise the money for the trip. We ended up the top scholastic champions.

Ralph Johnson finished as the tournament champion from our school.

Grammy Award winning singer Lauryn Hill had heard about our great female chess players. She invited us to bring one of our girls to her concert and sit in the front row. We were then invited to come backstage afterward to sit down, eat, and talk. We selected National Honor Society winner Latoria Spann.

Like so many of our players, Latoria is someone who overcame many obstacles. She has ten brothers and sisters and her mother raises the large family by herself.

Latoria applied herself in school and has always been an honor student. She has a younger sister, Christina, who is presently an honor student at Vaux, and a good chess player.

Latoria loved her time with Lauryn Hill. Photographers took several pictures of the two of them together. The singer kept telling her to "stay positive," and "We need more young ladies like you who can send the right message to focus on school and to stay strong."

In our quest to improve our chess skills and academic skills, we sought the help of our alumni association in the purchase of computers. Our school couldn't afford to provide computers for the chess team. Our principal didn't have the budget to buy computers and we had already known that we didn't have computers in our classrooms.

We asked the Vaux Alumni Association for the money, and they were gracious enough to give it to us. We bought three computers, although we needed at least ten. Even so, we were happy to have those.

We provided the computers to students to do their homework, which sometimes required typed reports. Until we purchased the three computers, they had to go to public libraries and wait in line for a computer to become available.

Non-chess-playing students in the school came in and used the computers to do reports and homework. They appreciated the fact that the chess team used their resources to get computers for everyone to use. We allowed the students to come in and use the computers, and it developed a relationship between chess players and non–chess players. Anyone could use the computers before school, during school, and after school. I loved it that, although we had limited resources, we could provide that service for the entire school.

In June 1998, I was appointed by the School Board of Philadelphia as the official assistant principal at Vaux Middle School. No more *acting* as part of my title.

I had another dream for our kids—taking them to South Africa in 1999. I knew it was a dream and probably not possible, but I'd never know unless we tried.

My dream was for Steve Shutt and me to take a racially integrated group of kids from Vaux and Masterman. We could show students in South Africa how we lived, and our kids could learn about their way of life. We would also show them that although we were highly competitive with Masterman, we could also work together harmoniously with them.

That trip would cost us $25,000, just for our six kids and me. We called it our goodwill chess trip to South Africa. Part of our plan was to meet with our hero, Nelson Mandela, and then get an opportunity to demonstrate, play, and teach chess in some of their schools. We wanted to stay between seven and fourteen days.

Yes, it was a dream—one that didn't happen. We had interest from our supportive friends and community, but just not enough.

In fact, we didn't have enough money to attend another tournament from August 1998 until the following March. We had already gotten into the pattern of competing in five to seven tournaments a year, but money was starting to dry up. I think people had gotten tired of giving money to kids and chess.

In March 1999, we competed in the state championship again in Bloomsburg. We won second place. We also brought home trophies for the top seventh- and eighth-grade player.

In late April 1999, I called Elmer Smith, columnist for the *Philadelphia Daily News,* and told him, "We're desperate. We don't have enough money for the chess team to travel to Columbus, Ohio, to compete in the national chess championship." When I called, the tournament was only two weeks away.

Elmer came through for us and wrote a series of articles in the paper about our plight.

Below are segments of the series:

Friday, April 23, 1999: Vaux Team Needs Checks to Retain Chess Title

If they had won eight national titles by catching or kicking a ball, the Vaux Chess Team would not have to worry about losing their title by default. America's best middle school chess team may have to sit this one out—unless they find a way to raise $4,000.

"We made deposits on the bus and we have some money for hotel rooms," Vaux chess coach and assistant principal Salome Thomas-EL said yesterday, "but we are four grand short."

"For some reason corporate sponsors and people who usually help us did not come through. I don't know why, but we
are not giving up." The only thing they're known for giving up
is a good whipping. They have beaten the best middle school
and high schools in the country. They beat a chess team from
Bucknell University.

All they need now is a chance to defend their title, but there
is a $4,000 gap between them and that goal. Anyone who
would like to help them bridge that gap should send a check or
money order to the Vaux Chess Team c/o the Vaux Middle
School, 24th and Master Streets.

Wednesday, April 28, 1999: Four-Grand Masters
Generous Daily News Readers Send Team to Title Match

The phone started ringing Friday morning about the time you
opened your *Daily News* to the Vaux chess team story. They
haven't stopped ringing since. My first call was from Thomas
"Chico" Stafford, a friend of mine and of *Daily News* causes.
"How come you didn't call and let me know those kids needed
money?" he scolded. "That's exactly the kind of program we
are trying to support here. What do they need—$4,000? Tell
them they will be getting a check from us for $2,000." Chico's
not the only one we can count on around here. Since Friday,
we've been fielding dozens of calls and e-mails a day from people looking to send money. "I've had 4 or 5 calls already,"
Thomas-EL told me first thing Friday morning. By Monday
morning the remaining $2,000 had come in, much of it in small
checks from people in the community. "We got checks for $500
apiece from Penn Bottle and Supply Company, from the Miller
Memorial Baptist Church, and from Community in Schools of
Philadelphia. We heard from the Criminal Justice Center and
from the State Police. I have to admit, last night I went home
and shed a few tears because I knew I could come in today and
tell them that we were going. They were getting a little edgy because they knew we were coming up short. But I told you this

would happen. People are generous. We needed you to get the word out."

He knew you better than I did. I said to raise $4,000 in 10 days was a long shot. You did it in five. The story that prompted this outpouring is a column Thomas-EL talked me into writing in an urgent phone call on Thursday. Imagine a Philadelphia Public League baseball or football team recognized for seven straight years in a row as the best team in the country. Now imagine such a team scratching for pennies to try to make it back to defend their title? Hard to imagine? It should be just as unthinkable for this team of scholars who are bringing credit to this city and to a school system that is rarely cited for excellence in any area. Sounds like a plan to Chico. "Leland Hardy"—his partner in New York.com—"and I are Philadelphia public school kids. We did all right. Guys like us need to give something back."

I'm grateful to Elmer Smith and to those he contacted. It was wonderful to share all that information with my chess team and with the whole school. This is the community pulling together. This is what we need more of.

In May 1999, we went to the national championship in Columbus, Ohio. We had raised enough money because of Elmer Smith's articles. We chartered a bus to drive us to Ohio. I wanted them to see the vastness and the beauty of the land and people outside the inner-city. They could hardly believe the green fields and abundance of trees and grass. They saw western Pennsylvania, portions of West Virginia, and then Eastern Ohio. It was a wonderful experience and excursion for those students.

The nice bus driver from the bus company stopped along the way several times so the kids could get off and walk around in the fresh air.

They were amazed at how fresh the air was. Many of them had no idea that there were places in America without tall buildings, noisy cars, and pollution.

We won a third-place team trophy and we brought home trophies for individual first-place and second-place winners. The national champions in our division were from our school, male and female.

At the end of the competition in the convention center ballroom they began to hand out awards. They called the top fifteen players to come up and receive their trophies in our division. They started with the number fifteen and stopped at number one.

A few had won six and a half points, meaning they didn't lose any but had a draw in one game. Thomas Allen from Vaux was one of them and he became a first-place winner.

First they called the second-place winners, who were players who had lost only one game. Almost every player was a male. Denise Pickard had lost only one game and that was on the last round—which put her in that second-place group. Denise got sick only hours before the last round of the tournament. She has chronic asthma and was feeling bad. I thought she probably shouldn't compete, but she went ahead and played anyway, and that was the only game she lost.

Losing that one match made her feel terrible. "I failed the team," she cried out and rushed into the restroom and cried.

I stood outside the door, pleading with her to come out. "It's all right, Denise. You won six games. You did great. You can't win every game. You did fine."

Denise felt guilty because she hadn't been well, and the playing, which takes a lot out of the kids, had tired her. "I wanted the game to be over with because I was so tired. I wanted to lie

That wasn't a problem. I felt overjoyed because I was going to be involved all summer with the chess team at Vaux anyway. I might as well serve as principal of the elementary school at the same time. This would be good training for my future as a school leader.

20

Principal Issues

In the summer of 1999, I was the principal of the summer school program at John F. Reynolds Elementary School. I also ran the Vaux summer chess program at the same time. It was great because I used my chess players to mentor the elementary students of Reynolds. That was good. They even began to teach some of the young people how to play chess that summer.

Just before the summer session ended, I received a phone call from Colleen Wisler, the principal at Reynolds. "I've been offered another position." She would become a principal at an elementary school closer to her home in northeast Philadelphia. "Would you be interested in becoming the principal at Reynolds?" she asked. "If you are, I'll recommend you."

I didn't know how to answer. I told her I had received some other offers from a few schools outside Philadelphia, and also had some opportunities at other Philadelphia public schools. I would let her know. I asked myself the same question several times. Was I ready to leave Vaux?

I thought about it for a while and—once again—I decided that I needed to stay in the community and that I wanted to stay. I had worked hard and this would be a chance to lead an

I also received a call from Allentown, Pennsylvania. I didn't even go for the interview.

The associate superintendent left me several messages at home and asked why I wouldn't return the calls. "We want you to come for an interview."

I didn't even call back. I knew I needed to stay in Philadelphia.

I also spoke to someone from the human resources division in the Cheltenham School District, a suburban district outside of Philadelphia that had been recruiting minority principals. The person told me they had a position open in an elementary school that paid more than $90,000. "Some of our principals make over one hundred thousand dollars a year." I didn't apply.

I belonged in north Philadelphia. That's where I had grown up; that's where my heart and soul were focused. I needed to stay and be able to mentor and watch the kids grow. Be there. Just to be something constant in their lives.

I had an opportunity to begin work immediately when a cluster leader (area superintendent) in Philadelphia called me and offered me a principal position in one of her schools. Dr. Farmbry, now the Chief Academic Officer (CAO) in Philadelphia, was the cluster leader who called me. She's my former teacher and she said she respected the fact that I wanted to stay and was glad that I wanted to work with my children. She then added that if I ever wanted the opportunity, she would love to have me work for her.

It felt good to hear that. She was someone who taught me and instilled in me the kind of quality that she would want in a principal. That made me feel great. She also said she was going to write an endorsement for this book, too, if I needed it.

I went to speak to my cluster leader, Mr. Gaeton Zorzi, and let him know about the offers I received. "I've turned them down because I want to stay in north Philly." I also told him that I'd love to have the principal's job at Reynolds.

"I'll do whatever I can to help," he promised.

A few weeks later, I received a call from Gaeton. "Reynolds is yours," he said. "The letter should be arriving shortly."

I called my mom and Shawnna. They were the two people I wanted most to share this with. This was especially wonderful to Mom. Her long-held dream was for me either to start my own school or to become a principal in one.

"Mom, I finally got the job as principal of my own school."

She started crying and I could hear her sobbing. She didn't say anything for a long time. She was so proud. I waited for nearly three minutes.

Finally she said, "I'm glad I got a chance to live long enough to see you become a principal before I passed away." My mother has been in bad health for the last couple of years and has a serious heart condition.

"Stop talking like that. I have a lot of other things I'm going to do in my life that I need you to be around to see. I need you by my side for every one."

"This was a dream we both had," she kept saying, "and you've made it come true."

Even when I was still a child, Mom told me several times, "I know you're one of the youngest but you are the rock of the family. You act as if you are the eldest son in the family. You have provided a lot for the entire family."

Next to Mom, Shawnna has been my biggest supporter from the beginning. She has also made a lot of sacrifices—and put up with my being away from home or having kids over all the time. Most wives wouldn't have allowed it. She really encouraged me. There had been many times and occasions that she's had to do without her husband so I could be there for some child or some family in need.

*   *   *

Arnold Schwarzenegger is the founder and national chairman of the Inner-City Games Foundation (ICGF). He established the foundation with the motto, "Every kid is a lifetime investment." The Inner-City Games teaches children to make positive choices in their lives. These kids are learning to say no to gangs, drugs, and violence. In more than ten major cities, the foundation provides children with the opportunity to participate in positive activities such as sports, tutoring, computer technology, and chess. Vaux Middle School was one of the first East Coast sites for the Inner-City Games Foundation. The ICGF has the support of stars like Dawn Lewis, Danny Glover, Tiger Woods, Edward James Olmos, Maria Shriver, Shaquille O'Neal, Vanessa L. Williams, Jay Leno, and Gloria Estefan.

One of the sponsors of our summer program is Cendant Mortgage. They targeted Vaux as their first site, because they had heard so many positive things about the programs for children at Vaux. A computer camp (children spend a summer learning how technology impacts the world), a fencing program (one of a few in the inner city), and a chess program were all part of the daily grind every summer at Vaux Middle School. Cendant Mortgage has supported the efforts of these magnificent children wholeheartedly.

When Arnold Schwarzenegger came to visit the school, he said how proud he was that he had some kids who were national chess champions. He also said, "I would be honored to play chess against some of your kids."

I loved him for saying that, because it showed me that he realized how important chess was. He told us that he sometimes used chess on his movie sets. "Chess keeps you alert," he said, "and makes you think."

Arnold sat down and people from the news media took photos of Arnold playing chess with the children at Vaux. That picture ended up on the front page of the *Philadelphia Daily News* and the *Philadelphia Inquirer.* The children's faces were plastered all over the local TV news and they even appeared on *Inside Edition.* It was definitely a shining moment for Vaux Middle School that he wanted to come and visit.

More than his hero status in films, Arnold came to the United States from Austria and has become a self-made multimillionaire. With all his money, it amazed our kids that he would visit the inner city and spend a few hours with them.

"He really likes us," one of the girls whispered. "I can tell by the way he smiles at us."

I honestly couldn't think of a better, more high-profile person to come. I don't think Arnold Schwarzenegger can possibly know how much he inspired our students. His encouragement was one of the major factors to motivate me to write this book.

I was able to talk to Arnold about the chess program and how I was moving on to Reynolds and continuing the program there for younger children. He knew a lot about the chess program and he was very proud of the children. The involvement of the girls especially impressed him.

In September 1999, I began my career at Reynolds Elementary School. One of my first goals was to enrich the reading program. I had spoken with some of the teachers during the summer, and they told me about the reading program they were using. It was a reading cycle where students actually left their home classrooms and went into classrooms according to their reading level. This meant that although they were with one teacher most of the day, when the reading period began, many of them had to leave and go into a different classroom with a different teacher for more than an hour each day. Those teachers often had no relationship with the children who came into their rooms. As good as the idea had been, it didn't seem to work. Reading levels were very low.

It also involved the issue of self-esteem. When children had to leave their classroom—especially if they were the ones who had to go to a lower-level classroom because they didn't read well—it made them feel even worse about their reading skills.

The teachers weren't happy with the present program and wanted to find ways to build up the self-esteem of poorer readers. "We need to build up their confidence," one teacher said. "This does just the opposite."

One of the first things I did was announce that we were going to make changes in the reading program. I wanted the teachers to know that I had the utmost respect for their dedication and commitment, and I was an example of what those children could become. I believe—and I told the entire faculty—that if students are going to read effectively, the best teachers should teach them. And the best teachers are those with high expectations in the classroom every day.

That's when we began to fully implement what we call the 100 Book Challenge Program. My cluster leader, Gaeton Zorzi, has always been fully supported because his wife, Jane Hileman, started the program. He helped me get the program implemented in every classroom from grades K–5.

The 100 Book Challenge Program uses a "book leveling" and coaching system that makes it clear to students what they need to know and should be able to do at each reading level. Teachers learn to coach students in reading and writing workshops as they work at independent reading levels. Every student is expected to read twenty-five hours during each report card period.

The following is a quote from Gaeton Zorzi: "The 100 Book Challenge helps to unify and enthuse our whole school community around our main mission of teaching kids to read well and to love it. Students, teachers, and parents using the system know where each child is, where he/she needs to go and what he/she needs to do to get there."

As part of the program, all children at Reynolds keep a reading log. They have to write down what they read in school and at home. A teacher or parent has to coach or watch the child read and then sign the log indicating their approval. Sometimes as principal, I signed a log after hearing a child read a "book."

All children are responsible to maintain their own logs and report to the teacher. Teachers keep a chart on the wall indicating the children's progress. The chart tells what level they're reading on and how many books each child has read.

It's a great program because every time a child reaches 100 books, he or she gets a medal from the school. I go into the classroom and individually place the medal on a ribbon around the child's neck. The children wear the medals proudly when they walk around the school. If they reach 200 books, they get another medal. Some have already won three. Those with three we call Olympic champions because they're walking around looking like they came back from the Olympics and had successfully run three different track events. When they reach 300, they receive a medal and a gold ribbon that says, "Reynolds Elementary School 300 books read."

We didn't have any resistance to the new program, although it's a lot of work to keep up with the children. During my second year, we were able to get a Reading Excellence Act grant from the U.S. government, and the school district hired a coordinator to keep the program running and make it an effective literacy initiative in the school. Again, we found no resistance. The teachers knew it was a good program and totally got behind it.

Once everybody had bought into the program, we began to

make significant progress. We have consistently been named as one of the most improved schools in our cluster in reading. We've also become a model school for reading. Various school leaders from as far away as upstate New York and Washington, D.C., have visited our school and observed the kinds of things we're doing with our children.

We now have an in-school breakfast program. That started because I noticed that there were students in school who were very hungry. I could look at the students and tell from the way they were eating at lunch, and their energy levels were low.

I also read some research about some schools in the other districts that actually started in-school feeding programs. Within weeks, their students' grades improved and test scores went up. Attendance was better because they found that students who weren't eating properly at home were motivated to attend school after the feeding program began. Most schools have early feeding programs that students don't attend on a regular basis. Kids are not getting to school early enough to eat.

"If we feed these kids when they get to school," I said in promoting this, "we'll know that every child has had a good breakfast to start the day." I promised them it would only take a few minutes each morning and the return would far outweigh the investment.

We fed them hot or cold cereal, or hot cakes, with juice and milk every school morning. Food services were happy because that meant they were feeding more kids. The money came from the school district, so all we had to do was ask.

Most of the teachers were all for our breakfast program, but one teacher at Reynolds was strongly opposed. She didn't object to the fact that they need breakfast—or at least she never said so. She insisted that it was not her job or that of her colleagues to feed her students when they were hungry.

Looking back, this could have been the beginning of my

demise. I was only the acting principal at the time and had not been confirmed by the school board, so my position was in no way guaranteed.

I wondered if I had pushed too much. Would I be able to keep this job? I loved it and adored the children. I pondered that a long time. Eventually I said to myself, "I believe I've done the right thing, no matter how it turns out."

21

New Achievements

"Do you want Mr. EL to stay here as your principal?" Before anyone could answer, or so I heard later, a teacher complained about others feeding the children and stated that she opposed it.

One teacher—and I don't know who it was—said to her, "We don't know how you feel, but we want him here. We want him to be our principal."

Someone else told me that the complainer tried to push them to stand against me, but not a single teacher supported her, so she dropped it.

"We need to hold on to this man," one teacher said. "He's got a lot of good ideas."

Without my having to do a thing, the teacher realized that the staff was focused on doing the right thing for the children. They didn't want to get rid of me and they were willing to spend time feeding hungry children, the way Mrs. Petit had fed me in third grade.

Shortly after that meeting, the teacher apologized, because the staff sent her a message that they were "going to do the right thing."

Their note said, "We're going to do whatever we can for the children and to make this young man our principal because he's moving us in the right direction." That's an exact quote from one of the teachers who came and told me what happened.

Another teacher came to me and said, "You brought a new vision to our school that we haven't had in years."

The feeding program is still going on. The results have justified all our efforts because our students have had some of the biggest improvements in their standardized test scores in the city. I believe a big part of that was because of our feeding program.

The staff voted overwhelmingly to make me their new permanent principal at Reynolds. I relaxed, because I knew I had their full support.

A committee of parents, teachers, and the cluster leader decided that I was to become the appointed principal. The school board approved the decision on January 5, 2000. That was one of the happiest days of my life.

We continued with the 100 Book Challenge Program and it was doing extremely well. Almost immediately I started a chess program at Reynolds. I had Saturday school for kids to come in to get extra help with reading and math. We didn't do it every Saturday, but almost every one. We would usually open the school from 9:00 in the morning to 1:00 in the afternoon.

One of the things we did—and I think it was as important as the reading or chess program—was start a grief support program. This isn't the sort of program that most schools would even think about. But then, most schools aren't part of the inner city. Many of the children in our community have lost siblings, relatives, and friends.

We have a high death rate in our community. I doubt that there is a single child in our school who has not seen someone murdered or at least has lost a friend or relative within the block where they live.

This has been—and remains—one of the saddest things for me about being in the inner city. I'm around so much death. I've already attended more funerals than anyone should ever have to go to in two lifetimes.

After I had heard about a grief support program run by a Christian organization, I investigated it and made sure it was a good program, then I brought it to Reynolds.

This program allows students to talk about troubling issues and find ways to deal with them. Originally it started in the middle schools, but we needed it at Reynolds so I invited them in. The program, is called "I'm Still Here," and it has helped our kids immensely.

In the grief program, we enabled these children—and they were as young as first graders—to talk about their grief issues. This wasn't only involving the matter of death either. A number of the children have relatives who are incarcerated. Most people outside the inner city have no idea what that's like for school children. Some of them have never seen their father without bars separating them. That's a tough way to grow up.

These kids live in an atmosphere of loss. Some have had pets that were accidentally killed, murdered, or simply disappeared. They never have a chance to talk about that kind of loss with anyone. They also see drugs on the streets every day. There isn't a child in our school who doesn't know someone or know of someone associated with drugs. Some kids worry that they'll end up on the street. We're doing everything possible not to let that happen.

Until the program began, our children had no chance to talk about their feelings or find out how to deal with such problems. We didn't want them to block their feelings or act out aggressively. We felt that by offering such a program we were also saying, "It's natural to feel the way you do. And it's all right to talk about your feelings." They meet after school one day a week for two hours.

At the end of the year we had a culminating program where we had a big celebration for all the parents and all the people involved in all the after-school programs and the children involved in the "I'm Still Here" program. They did a dramatization to show how they deal with grief. Almost 300 parents and students attended.

Two major events in the fall of 1999 did more to encourage me and my leadership than anything else. After I had been at Reynolds a few weeks, I still had doubts about the effectiveness of my leadership. I wasn't sure if I made the right decision to leave Vaux and if I had been fully accepted as part of the Reynolds School "family," especially by teachers who had been teaching at Reynolds for more than twenty years. There was one woman who had been a teacher there for thirty-six years and had even been a Reynolds student. What in the world would she want to hear from me? Not only did I feel like the new kid on the block, but I was also younger than most of the people I supervised. Even though I wondered and sometimes doubted, none of them showed any disrespect. They listened to my ideas and helped me implement anything they thought would make things better for the students.

Then I found out how they truly felt.

I walked into my office on October 21, which was my thirty-fifth birthday. I had mentioned it only once in September and I didn't think anyone remembered. After I greeted my secretaries and stepped into my office, the first thing I saw was a large wrapped package. It looked like a big gigantic bottle of orange juice.

"What's this?"

The two secretaries and a teacher watched. "Open it and find out," one of them said.

When I opened the package, I saw a stack of tennis balls and they had come to me as a gift from the staff. The teachers all know I'm an avid tennis player, and Joe Mordecai, my NTA, a non-teaching assistant, is one of my tennis partners. Their knowing it was my birthday and giving me a surprise and appropriate gift made me realize that I was part of the family.

For me, as the new principal, to find such obvious affection and respect from the staff overwhelmed me. Inside was a beautiful card that every member of the staff had signed, with several notes. The card was gigantic with wonderful messages about the vision that I had brought to the school, how much they valued my support and my sense of humor. It was very touching for some people who didn't know me well to be kind enough to do something to lift my spirits.

It was heartwarming for them to do that. I had wonderful messages from the students themselves. This was great for students to write letters and cards to their principal. It was a rewarding experience.

There's one more exciting thing we did in 1999. Our staff met and decided that we wanted to have an event that would bring parents out to the school. After a lot of discussion we decided on a family math night. So we set up a big family fun math night at Reynolds. This was probably the biggest event in our community in ten years. Like most inner-city schools, traditionally we don't get much parent participation. We wanted to design a night where parents would come out and not be intimidated by school. "Come out and have fun and understand how learning math could be fun."

Every teacher participated in this program. I personally provided a dinner. We had a staff dinner as a family together. We ate together first and then we invited the parents to come and join us. Each teacher set up a station. Some of them brought their children from home to help them, for instance, to show parents how computers were part of mathematics. We provided basic math activities that parents could learn and none of them were intimidating or technical.

I bought hundreds of pencils and prizes so that everyone who came would win a prize just for being there. They didn't even have to be successful at any game. If they walked up to a table, and even if they only participated, they earned a prize.

We posted a chart in the hallway. Every time parents came in we put a sticker over their children's classroom. The classroom with the most stickers would win a pizza party.

I went on a campaign throughout the community and told parents that I needed them to come out for this family math night. I told them there were times when they'd come to the school and want to see me, or they needed something, and I would see them right away. This time I needed them to at least make a commitment to come out for their child.

"We'll be there," they promised. "If you have it, Mr. EL, we'll be there."

I had their promises, but I was getting scared. I had ordered enough food for 300 people. We have 350 students in our school, and I didn't expect a large turnout, but I hoped it would be good.

Those at other schools told me that they had tried this sort of thing. "If fifty parents attend, we feel we've had a big night."

"I'm counting on three hundred," I said.

They smiled indulgently as if to say, "You'll have to learn the hard way."

I went around to each classroom the day of our event. I handed out cards listing all the prizes we were going to give away. This was a math night so every prize they won involved some math concept.

For instance, we had a basketball autographed by the 76ers. I didn't tell them how, but the family that came the closest to guessing the circumference of the basketball would win it.

We had an entire Thanksgiving turkey dinner, a basket with turkey and all the sides. Whatever family guessed the amount of calories in that dinner was going to win that entire dinner. Whoever could guess the weight of a jar of candy we had would win that candy.

We had all kinds of prizes and things that we gave away. Participants would come and estimate how much these various things were—weight, calories, volume, things of that nature.

I took that around and showed each kid in every classroom that this is what you have a chance to win tonight if you get your parents to come to family fun math night.

"Are your parents coming?" I asked one third-grade child.

"I'm not sure. My mom said she might not be able to."

"I want to show you what you do when you go home and your mom or dad tells you that they don't want to come," I said. "We're going to role-play and I'm going to be you and you're going to be Mom and Dad."

I called a couple of kids up to the front of each class and said, "I'm you and you're your mom or dad, okay?"

The child nodded when I explained this was a role play.

I played the student and said, "Come on, Mommy, take me to Reynolds family math night." Then the kid would say, "I don't feel like going."

Still playing the child, I grabbed the "parent's" arm and said, "Come on, Mom, you got to take me to family math night because we have got to win those prizes."

Before I left the classroom I said, "I want all of you to do what I did. You do whatever it takes to get your moms and dads here."

*   *   *

I had started to get nervous. It was early, and I waited. And I prayed. And I hoped. "Oh, God, if only a hundred parents would come, I'd be satisfied," I said at one point.

I kept thinking about the food I had ordered for 300 people. What if we wasted all of that?

Within ten minutes after we opened the door, the room was full. Parents came with their children. And more arrived. Within the first hour I ran out of food! Some people told me I needed to lock the doors because the school couldn't hold that many parents. I only smiled. We weren't going to lock out any-one—it had taken so much just to get them there. They came for their children.

My cluster leader was there. He was so proud. It was over-whelming to see so many parents. He read stories to kids and their parents.

"You know those parents are here because of you, don't you?" one parent said.

Her words surprised me.

"Listen, Mr. EL, all of us know how much you care about the kids in the community. That's why we showed up. This is our way to let you know that we support you. So don't be sur-prised. You've supported us. Now it's our turn to support you, and that's why we're here."

Tears filled my eyes. I was so touched by those words. I had consciously not done anything to make them come just for me. My thoughts had centered on the children. Then I smiled. That's exactly what that mother was saying. They knew where my thoughts were. I felt so thankful that they had come.

I sent out for more food. We never did have an accurate count, but we know the total exceeded 400, including children. It was a cold night in November, so I knew some of them had made a special effort to attend.

We probably could easily have had 500 or 600 parents and children in that building. Eventually, we did have to turn some people away from the food because there was no more left and they had arrived so late.

As parents spoke to me and children raced up to me and hugged me, I kept thinking, this is going to define my tenure at Reynolds. We've done the right thing by starting the school year off with a significant event like this. As I walked around, more people shook my hand than at any time I could remember.

"This is so wonderful," a mother would say.

"Thank you for all you and the teachers here are doing for our children," another parent would add.

Teachers beamed when we passed each other. A few paused to comment on how well everything was going. I felt proud of my staff.

Never before had so many people said so many kind and caring things. I felt as if a big grin had been permanently formed on my face.

And something else, I heard myself say, "I belong here." As I continued to walk around, I realized that I had been sent to Reynolds for events such as this. I'm here not only to educate the young but also to educate the old about educating their young.

That felt good.

During my first year at Reynolds we also received some shocking news of the murder of a prominent writer named Russell Byers. He had been a longtime columnist for the *Philadelphia Daily News*—a paper that had been an adopter of our school and helped us in many ways. *Adopter* means they provided financial support and visited our school to mentor and support students. They also asked their writers to visit and talk with the children. Such organizations helped us show positive role models to students so they could relate to them. We also hoped that actually meeting people in such occupations might stir their aspirations. Russell Byers had come several times to visit our children. Many of them knew him by name.

When we heard about his senseless murder, we knew there was something we had to do as a school and as a community. Immediately, our children wrote letters and sent cards of condolence to the family. Our Head Start children made a painting for his widow, Laurada Byers. They called it the "Hands of Love" and used their hands to make designs.

We sent everything to his widow. The gesture touched her so much that Mrs. Byers came to the school to thank each of those children who had individually participated.

When she spoke with us, we learned that her husband had loved gardening and horticulture, so our kids started a coin drive. That is, they brought small coins to school every day—nothing more than a quarter. Within a few weeks, our elementary school children raised one hundred dollars, which they donated to the Pennsylvania Horticultural Society in memory of Mr. Byers. The children took on that project on their own as a way to show their appreciation for his dedication and service to the kids in the inner city.

I remember him as a man who could have gone anywhere, but he chose to come to the inner city and make a difference. And he did make a difference.

Mrs. Byers said she had the "Hands of Love" painting professionally framed so she could hang it in her home as a symbol of the love that the children displayed to her husband and family.

Zack Stalberg, the editor of the *Daily News,* especially touched our kids also. He visited our kids on several occasions at the school. When we visited him, he told us that he wanted to continue the newspaper's commitment. "But that is not the reason for your coming today. My reason is because I want all of you to know how deeply those of us at the *Daily News* appreciate what you young people have done for the name and memory of Russell Byers."

When Mrs. Byers came to visit our school, she read to some of the younger students. After she left, she donated books to our school library and thanked the students for being so kind to the family.

At Reynolds, they have had an annual event, for more than twenty years, where the teachers serve Thanksgiving dinner to every child in the school. Some of our children live in shelters, and others come from such impoverished homes that a full turkey dinner is something they never taste.

To serve them a big meal once a year seems so little in many ways. I wish we could do it every day of the year. But I've reasoned that, at least for one day, no child would go hungry. For one day each child would have a full, nourishing meal.

Each child gets served personally. The teachers cook turkeys and they're assisted by volunteers from Miller Memorial Baptist Church. Parents who are able to do so also participate in this event, because it's done to honor and encourage the children.

Several of the volunteers from Miller Memorial Baptist Church were men. As they served and cleaned up, they would talk to our students. One of them told the kids at one table, "I graduated from this school in 1925."

"I graduated in 1930," said his counterpart at the other end of the table.

Both told the children they were proud to be able to come to the school and to serve them as alumni.

"And one day, you'll get your chance to serve children like we're doing today," said the first man.

*   *   *

In December 1999, I received an award of service to the community from Holsey Temple AME Church. This award honors people in Philadelphia who have dedicated themselves to the community over the years. When I heard that I was on the list, I was so pumped and felt so honored that I told my secretaries and then I called my wife and my mother. This award goes to people who have spent years and years serving the community. I felt I hadn't been there that long or done that much to deserve such recognition. Even so, the news still excited me.

When I went to the awards ceremony, I could hardly believe it when I saw several tables with more than twenty people who had come from Reynolds and Vaux. It was a great experience to receive such a prestigious award, and it made it even more special because I certainly had not expected to see any of those people there. They made sure it was a surprise.

I expected that one or two friends from the community would come, but for me to stare at twenty people boggled my mind. And not only from Reynolds but there were many there who represented Vaux School. I had already left Vaux and yet there they were, including Harold Adams, my former principal.

It took a long time to get to the head table because everyone wanted to shake my hand. Actually, I wanted to shake theirs, because I appreciated it so much that they had come.

Once I was seated, the pastor of Holsey Temple, the host church, came over to me. "I want to shake your hand, Mr. EL," he said.

We talked for a minute and then he said, "You know what I'm more touched by than anything else I've seen tonight?"

I shook my head.

"All of these people have come out for their *principal*. I've never in my life seen a staff come out on a Saturday night in December to support their principal." He didn't mention that they also paid twenty dollars a plate to come and honor me. He also commented, "And about half of them are from your former school. That's even more amazing."

That evening and that experience made me realize that there were people who appreciated what I was trying to do in the inner city. Sometimes I hadn't known if people understood what I was trying to do or if they grasped the impact we could make on the lives of our school children. I had tried so hard to make it clear that together we—the community—were the ones who were helping our first- through eighth-graders make decisions that would affect them for the rest of their lives. I wondered if people got tired of hearing me talk that way.

More than once I'd stood before the staff and said, "This is a team effort. I can't do it without you." When I said *you,* I meant everyone from the building engineer all the way up to my secretaries, classroom assistants, and lunchroom assistants. It's a full effort.

When I thanked everyone for coming and the leaders of Holsey Temple AME Church, I said, "It has become popular to say, 'It takes an entire village to raise a child.'" I truly believe those words. It takes a community—our village—and we have that village here. We're proud of the things that we've been able to do with those young people. And we're looking forward to being able to do even more."

During the spring of 2000, we took the fifth-grade students of Mrs. Hensford's and Ms. DeBrow's classes to spend an entire day on a college campus. My alma mater, East Stroudsburg University, totally financed the trip because they wanted to expose inner-city students to college at an early age. They reasoned that many times the students don't understand how important it is to see what a college campus looks like. They wanted words like *college* and *university* to have strong emotional associations and to become part of their thinking about their future. It was part of their way to help us impress on elementary-age children that a college education was not only important but that, even for inner-city kids, it was possible. I especially did not want any of them to visit a campus for the very first time as college freshmen as I did.

Before we made the trip, the two teachers asked our students to e-mail and write letters to students of the North Courtland Middle School, which is in the city of Stroudsburg, Pennsylvania—and a predominantly white community. Before we took the bus ride to East Stroudsburg, our kids had been learning about their counterparts and telling them about themselves. I don't' think they were aware that we were also taking advantage of this trip to try to break down racial barriers between the two diverse groups.

When our fifth-graders arrived at East Stroudsburg, the children to whom they had been writing came to meet them. It was a great experience for everyone. This surprised some of the people who watched, but several of our students had never actually met a white child. But then, some of those white children had never met a black child before, either.

It was a splendid opportunity for them to meet, talk, and play together. Just being together in an informal structure helped both groups of students to be at ease and to enjoy each other as children.

"You know, he looks a little different," one of our boys said as he pointed to a white student he had corresponded with. "But he's cool, you know."

I laughed. What an appropriate comment from a fifth-grader. That was exactly what I had hoped they would understand. During the noon hour, they discovered that, despite racial differences, they enjoyed the same music, videos, food, and clothes. I smiled. They were all cool.

The students from North Courtland Middle School had

learned about our 100 Book Challenge program. Before we arrived, they had already collected books in their community to donate to our school. They called it the "100 Book Challenge for the Year 2000." They also knew that we operated on a tight budget and there wasn't much money for library books.

Working with students at East Stroudsburg University, they collected and donated slightly more than two thousand books to Reynolds Elementary School. They wanted to do this to help our kids improve their reading levels. Our children then made history books for the children of North Courtland, profiling the history of Philadelphia. It does take an entire community—a global community.

On January 5, 2000, I was appointed principal at Reynolds school—my permanent appointment. That was a great day at Reynolds. It was a wonderful time for me to know that I had been approved by the staff and the community and my cluster leader. The school board made it official when they read it into the minutes of the school board meeting that I had been officially appointed principal of Reynolds School.

22

Big Names and Inner City Games

Arnold Schwarzenegger returned to Philadelphia in the summer of 2000 for the Republican National Convention. While in the city, and accompanied by Mayor John Street and several other local politicians and businessmen, he visited Vaux School and wanted to see our chess program. I was there along with several former Vaux students who had played on the chess team. Because of funding from the Inner City Games, Arnold and the others observed inner-city children at computer classes, tennis, fencing exhibitions, creative writing workshops, and of course, chess competition. Not only did he play chess, but he spoke to the media and community about his philosophy on the game. "Chess is a fantastic game," he said. "When children play chess, they must learn to keep calm and resolve conflicts."

The kids' eyes lit up as he spoke, because I had been telling them the same thing for years. I smiled at them, because they paid rapt attention to his few sentences. Maybe it was his dazzling smile. Or maybe it was his reputation as the Terminator. They stared as if hypnotized.

"These children here are learning crucial lessons for life, and they make very sophisticated moves. It is great for them to play at this age. I played with my parents as a kid."

All of us smiled and clapped as we listened to this advocate for chess. "The players on this team make wise moves and decisions under pressure. It is like the fear of a test, math, English, or writing. Here you learn about pressure." Now was the moment the kids had been anticipating since first hearing about Arnold's plan to visit. "That is why you are one of the top teams in the country."

As the chess players listened, they felt special. Empowered. A rich and famous person told them they were great.

He was being videotaped, and one of the filmmakers asked if he would play one of the students. We had expected this and had selected Denise Pickard as his opponent.

When they started the play, Denise didn't cower, but seemed to us not to be intimidated by his fame or size. In fact, she made a number of smart moves. They didn't finish the game because it was time for him to go into the auditorium. As he got up, he said, "You cornered me. I know your tricks."

A reporter asked Denise, "How does it feel to play the Terminator?"

After a long pause, she said in a soft voice, "Very exciting."

"No, that is not the right question," Arnold said. "The right question is, How do I feel as the Terminator being terminated?"

Almost everyone in the room broke out in laughter. The other children smiled, especially Denise. I was so glad to see that smile on her face. Her mom hadn't been feeling well lately and she had seemed kind of down. This was exactly what she needed—a large dose of truly deserved compliments from one of the world's nicest men, who could also play chess.

The "match" with Denise was videotaped and telecast on Arnold's website, www.schwarzenegger.com.

We hurried Arnold into the overflowing auditorium. It was a big event because many of our children were waiting to receive certificates from him and the Philadelphia co-chairs of Inner City Games, Nicholas DiNubile, M.D., and John Daniel. Coleman Walsh, a Cendant executive, had already addressed the media and community, assuring everyone that Cendant would continue to fund activities for the children.

What impressed me the most was that before Arnold left the school, he asked me how my younger students were doing. His question amazed me and made me realize that he had remembered our conversation from a year earlier. It also showed me that he cared about the children. His thoughtfulness so surprised me that I blurted out, "You didn't forget that, did you?"

"Of course not. I remember you and your kids very well."

I told him that our elementary and middle school students had spent three days in July on the campus of the University of Maryland, Baltimore County (UMBC), competing in the U.S. Junior Open Chess Championship. One of our students won a top prize.

He didn't seem surprised at the news and showed genuine pleasure at hearing it. He became excited when I told him that Cendant Mortgage had financed our entire trip. They even provided travel bags and suit blazers embroidered with our Mighty Bishops emblem. All of this was done for inner-city kids.

In the fall of 2000, someone from the Community Partnership Program of the Philadelphia Eagles contacted me at Reynolds. "We've heard about you and the outstanding things you're doing at your school."

I assumed she meant the chess program, but I was wrong.

"That 100 Book Challenge program is one of the most exciting things I've heard of," she said. "Please tell me more."

Only too glad to talk about our programs, I must have spent ten minutes explaining how the program worked and how responsive the children and teachers had been. Then she said something that surprised me. "We know about your turning down the opportunity to leave the inner city and make more money—you chose to stay there. That fact impressed us here and also one of our players."

Her information took me aback. I had no idea how she found out and I didn't ask.

"Here's the reason I'm calling," she said. "Cecil Martin would like to visit Reynolds School." He was a running back for the Philadelphia Eagles. "He's a graduate of the University of Wisconsin." She told me other facts about him and I knew he would be an inspiration to the kids.

The following week Cecil Martin came. He pulled up in a gigantic van filled with books for every child. Hugh Douglas, an All-Pro defensive lineman for the Eagles, spent $50,000 of his own money and bought the book van. Then his teammates filled the van with books, such as those written by Dr. Seuss, and Cecil Martin personally delivered them to Reynolds School.

That wasn't all. After he had distributed a book to each child and had shaken the hand of every one, Martin himself went into the school library and read to forty kindergarten, first-, and second-grade children. It was a nice story about the relationship between a grandfather and his granddaughter.

Cecil Martin also spoke to our older students in the auditorium. His most impressive and stunning comment began with these words: "At one time, my family and I were homeless."

The kids stared at him. They knew he was a big-name football player. It had never occurred to them that he had lived in a shelter or didn't always have money and a nice home to live in. They were shocked.

Then he talked about overcoming obstacles and said, "It was because of teachers who believed in me—the kind of teachers you have here. My teachers mentored me and made sacrifices so I could succeed.

"I hope you children appreciate having someone like Mr. EL

and the others here who have turned down better-paying positions so they can stay and teach here. They care or they wouldn't stay."

Martin impressed me immensely because he was intelligent and highly articulate. The kids loved listening to him, and when he finished, after about twenty minutes, they began to clap. I didn't think the applause would ever stop.

"You are truly inspirational!" I thanked him, hugged him, and thanked him again. We took pictures with the children. It was a great day for all of us.

"Mr. EL, you have a call," my secretary said.

"Take a message" was my usual response when I was busy, especially with the children. A few minutes later, when I looked over my messages, I realized that I had missed a call from Elease Gindraw, a former student. I had last talked to Elease over the summer about her refusal to leave the inner city and accept an offer of admission from Indiana University of Pennsylvania (IUP).

"There's nothing there for me," she said. Her room and financial aid had already been confirmed. I always thought she was afraid, but I didn't want to pressure her. Her younger, elementary-aged brother had recently been killed in a neighborhood accident. She never acted the same after that tragic incident. I understood.

Just as I began to think about the opportunity she was missing, I noticed that her area code was 724. I remembered that was a Pittsburgh area code. I called her immediately and thanked her for getting in touch with me. She had taken my advice and started her freshman year at IUP.

"That's one more former student who's going to make a difference," I said as I hung up the phone. "One more. And each one can make a difference."

*   *   *

I began my work toward a Ph.D. in educational leadership as well as a superintendent's certification at Lehigh University. Lehigh had offered me the opportunity to study on a full scholarship. That would have meant taking a leave of absence from Reynolds. I considered the offer and met with the Dean of Education, Dr. Ron Yoshida, and two other professors, Dr. George White and Dr. Juan Baughn. I explained to them that I truly appreciated and needed the scholarship, but I could not leave my students.

"I really want to get into Lehigh, and I know this may hurt my chances for admission, even if I could afford to pay. But I have to be very honest with you." The *U.S. News and World Report* magazine had featured Lehigh University as one of the top fifty graduate schools of education in the country. (The following year they climbed eleven places in a similar report.) Lehigh had an excellent reputation as a school that encouraged the study of how leaders change organizations to make them work more efficiently and how individuals from different backgrounds can work together more effectively.

"It would be a dream that came true for me to get my doctorate here, but I can't afford it. And as I said, I can't leave my children to go to school full-time."

The interviewing professors told me they respected and admired my decision to stay in the inner city with my students. To my amazement, they offered me a scholarship that would pay half of my tuition.

I almost blurted out, "You have to be kidding," but instead my tongue got tied up as I tried to express my thanks.

"This type of scholarship is rare at Lehigh," said Dr. White, the program coordinator.

Dr. Yoshida and Dr. Baughn both added that they had high expectations of me.

That happened during my second year as principal. This was probably my toughest time as an educator. Lehigh is located in Bethlehem, about an hour's drive from Philadelphia, and I would have to drive to classes one night a week. One night didn't seem like much, but I was already heavily committed and kept wondering how I could find more time to be with Shawnna.

We were seeing results with various programs at Reynolds, but they also increased the pressure to do more and to refine what we had set up. I wanted more programs to help students, and I didn't want the chess program to die.

As I was going through all that stress, Shawnna had her own load of stress. She was pregnant with our first child. Almost from the beginning, she experienced problems and stayed sick most of the nine months. At first, she tried to work, but she couldn't do it and had to spend a lot of time in bed.

Every evening that I stayed away from home, guilt clawed at me. I wanted to be with her. There was nothing I could do to make her feel better physically, but I wanted to be with her. I thought that it would be so much better if we could spend each evening in the same room—just the two of us and no one else around. Because of my already overcrowded schedule, those evenings alone rarely happened, and I felt bad about that.

At 7:00 A.M. on November 27, 2000, I took Shawnna to the hospital after she began to have regular labor pains. I was under such stress that I took my laptop with me, figuring I could get quite a bit of my course work done while I waited. I'd been told that it would probably take hours. I set up my computer at her bedside and tried to work on an important paper for my organizational administration class with Dr. White at Lehigh. We were there all day, but I couldn't focus on the paper. Finally, at 8 that evening they took Shawnna into the delivery room. At 11:19 P.M., the nurse shouted "You have a daughter."

I was glad I had decided to be present in the delivery room for the birth and I cut the cord.

"Is she all right?" I asked. "Healthy?"

"She's fine, and your wife is also doing well."

I thanked God. My wife and baby were fine. I couldn't ask for anything more.

I jumped up and down and grinned as my mother-in-law snapped numerous pictures. I felt as if I were in a press conference.

We had already chosen her name. *Macawi* is a Native American name that means "motherly and generous." Her middle names are Delores Amena. She is named for my wife's mom and sister (who passed away), who share the name *Delores*. My mother's name is Amena.

Obviously, I never finished the paper. I was so overjoyed at the new life that Shawnna and I had brought into the world. For the next day or two I spent as much time with both of them as I could. It was one time when I tuned out the world and focused totally on my family.

Dr. White did give me a few extra days to turn in my paper. I received an A in the course.

*   *   *

On December 18, 2000, the Philadelphia school district honored our school for making vast improvements in reading and math. Reynolds was one of only forty-nine schools in a district with over two hundred fifty that met or exceeded targets set by the district. Many of the schools were magnet schools but there were quite a few from the inner city.

Over the past decade the news media kept telling the public that inner-city schools weren't making improvements in reading and were, in fact, going downward.

I've seen the statistics and I knew about all the reports. I also know those figures did not reflect the progress made at Reynolds and other schools. Ours is one of the few, but not the only inner-city school to break that negative stereotype. We're making progress and the commitment of our teachers to teach every child to read is one of the big reasons. Students at Reynolds had not only reached the goal set for them, but they exceeded it.

I'm proud to be the principal of such a caring, progressive school, even though we received some of the most limited funds in the state. We have something more important than dollars—we have teachers who care.

In early 2001, the staff of Reynolds school nominated me for the Leon J. Obermayer Award, which is given annually for an outstanding graduate of a Philadelphia public school. Also, I later found out I was nominated for the annual Marcus Foster Award, the award given to the outstanding administrator in the school district. A school district central office administrator called me and asked, "Are you aware that you are the only person in Philadelphia nominated for both awards?"

I didn't think I deserved either award, although I was honored and flattered to be nominated by my staff. It's not always easy to be a school administrator because the staff and I don't agree on everything. In the end, however, we try to make decisions together that benefit our children.

I didn't win either award. Congressman Chaka Fattah received the Outstanding Graduate honor, and the Outstanding Administrator award went to Edward Williams, a long-time school district administrator. They were both deserving winners and role models for me. I felt highly honored to be considered for the same awards alongside such great committed Philadelphians.

The next day when I walked into my office, the first thing I saw was a huge banner that my secretaries had made: YOU ARE OUR WINNER!

That gesture touched me deeply. It showed that the true honor was in being recognized and appreciated, and not only in winning. Of course, I had been disappointed. Even though I didn't feel I deserved either award, I felt sad in not winning.

Over the next couple of days I used my experience as an opportunity to teach my students how to find victory and accomplishment even when they are not declared the winner.

Many times during the next few days, child after child would come up to me and say something such as, "You deserve every award in the district."

I know they were trying to cheer me up. And I must admit, it worked.

23

Other Voices Speak

My name is Cecil ("Cec") Murphey, and I'm the writer who helped Salome Thomas-EL with this book. Salome initially contacted me in late October 2000 after he had read the autobiography I had written for Dr. Ben Carson of Johns Hopkins Hospital called *Gifted Hands*. "You're the writer I want," he said.

Despite some skepticism on my part that he had enough of a story to fill a book, I agreed to listen to his pitch.

"No, I want to meet you," he insisted, "and spend time telling you the whole story."

I realized even then that I was dealing with a dynamic and persuasive person. "I'll come to you," he said. "A parent of one of my students that I helped attend a prom gave me a free airline ticket as a gift, so I can fly down and spend a couple of days or even a few hours if you'll let me talk to you."

A week later, Salome flew to Atlanta to spend the weekend with me and to talk about the possibility of the book. After listening to him only a few minutes, I believed I had an exciting book project before me. In all candor, however, another part of

me kept questioning what I was hearing. Salome is a charis-
matic individual and I've met a lot of his type before. Too many
of them have the silver tongues, the warm, wholesome smiles,
and they seem never at a loss for words. Too often, there is
more noise than substance.

As I listened to story after story about the chess club and the
kids, and scanned half a dozen photocopies of news articles, I
nodded. Despite all the excitement in his voice and the enthusi-
astic gestures, every once in a while the cynical part of me questioned what I heard. I needed to find out the truth for myself.
Was he really doing all those things? Were these kids honestly
being helped or was he trying to make a big deal out of a few
chess games and the visit of a few celebrities?

On December 13, 2000, I flew to Philadelphia to see his
school, meet some of the people involved, and verify that all of
his stories rang true.

Salome met me at the airport and drove me to the Gen. John
F. Reynolds Elementary School. This was a typical inner-city
area with a school in an older neighborhood, surrounded by
closed businesses and a few boarded-up brick buildings. I could
see the tall buildings and housing projects from miles away.
The school, estimated to be about seventy-five years old, bore
marks of being a beautifully constructed building. Beautiful
mosaic designs above the front door showed what was once its
glory.

Although I didn't think it would be the case, that doubtful
voice wondered if Salome had prepared the teachers and staff
to make a good impression on me. I've been around enough to
know that if he had, I would have been able to see through the
veneer.

As we walked inside and up a flight of steps, the first person
we came to at the front door was an elderly woman volunteer
who sat at a table and greeted everyone who came through the
doors. I saw no metal detectors or any sign that they feared vi-

olence. There was no one else except an unarmed school police officer at the sign-in desk.

Once we stepped inside, the cleanliness of the hallways and the orderliness of the children impressed me. Another thing struck me: It was quiet. Just then a second-grade classroom filed out of their room to go to the library. A boy broke out of line, raced up to his principal, and waved his report card. "Mr. EL! Mr. EL! See my report card!"

The little boy hugged Salome and waited while Salome read the grades.

"That's good, very good. But you got one C. Bring that up next time with those A's and B's."

"I will, I will."

Just then a girl hugged him and also showed him her report card. It was the first time she had all A's on her report card. Several children waved as they filed into the library.

Salome took me into his office and introduced me to his two secretaries, Mrs. Bridges and Mrs. Brooks. Their cheery voices and warm smiles greeted me, as well as anyone who came into the office. Mrs. Brooks spoke on the phone to someone who was long on words and short on understanding, but she didn't argue or sound ruffled. For the third time, she explained how important it was for the parent to meet with the child's teacher. "I really think you need to come. This is not only for your daughter's benefit, but for you as well."

Meanwhile, the other secretary, Mrs. Bridges, spoke to students with a friendliness and warmth that was as effective as if she had been the top sales clerk in a department store.

I marveled at the casual spirit and yet no one took advantage of their good natures. As my gaze scanned the outer office, I saw that although it was quite small and extremely crowded, they had framed aphorisms or mottoes in several places. For example, taped just below the clock were these words: ATTI-TUDES ARE IMPORTANT: CHOOSE A GOOD ONE.

A few minutes later, Salome took me through the school into each classroom. It's a five-story, fairly narrow building. The structure forces children and staff to trudge up and down a lot of stairs—and these included the youngsters in Head Start as well as kindergarten through fifth grade.

Every classroom we visited was orderly. Again, I spotted positive statements displayed on various walls. In every room, I noticed signs about the 100 Book Challenge program. Tacked on the walls below the posters were hearts with children's names and lines showing the number of books they had read. I thought it interesting when I visited the fifth-grade classroom, which was the first one. Then I realized that every room had a poster.

In one fifth-grade classroom, taught by Cathy Hensford, the children were studying Spanish when we walked in.

"The teacher wanted to enrich her class, and so this is her idea," Salome said. "We can't afford a Spanish teacher but the kids need the language."

She stopped the students and smiled at me. "Mr. Murphey, we have a special welcome for you in Spanish."

One by one each of the children stood and spoke a few sentences in Spanish—some of it I understood, but most of it went beyond my meager vocabulary.

When they finished, I smiled. *"Muchachas y muchachos, gracias."*

"De nada," said Mrs. Hensford.

The children laughed and beamed at each other.

From there, we went down the third-floor hallway and into another classroom. Near the end of the twenty-five-minute tour, we came to the auditorium, where I saw the kindergarteners waiting for their parents to pick them up. I met both teachers and two volunteers and chatted briefly with them. The children sat quietly. Several of them were reading books.

"What's this 100 Book Challenge program?" I asked the

kindergarten teacher, Mary Ann Mulvihill. I had not yet interviewed Salome.

The 100 Book Challenge program, she explained, was used for children even in kindergarten. "Our goal is to have all children reading on a first-grade level when they leave kindergarten—not all of them achieve that level, but we try," she said. She showed me one of their books—mostly pictures but they also contained a few words. "They learn to associate simple words with the pictures and we teach them a few phonics and a few sight words."

I shook my head in amazement. Even more surprising, one of the kindergarten girls was wearing a ribbon and medal. She held it up for me to look at. "I won this!"

This was an inner-city school, but I saw no trash on the floor and the floors had been carefully polished. In the five minutes I lingered in the room, no one ever asked the children to be quiet, yet they spoke softly among themselves. I heard no loud voices. Of the twenty or more children waiting for their names to be called, five of them were reading their books, oblivious to anything else.

For lunch, Salome ordered and paid for a display of sandwiches, cole slaw, potato salad, and four large pizzas. He invited the teachers to come in and eat when they had free time. Today the children went home at noon because it was report card day. The teachers had arranged for a large number of parents to come in for appointments in the afternoon.

We sat in the library, but I observed that whenever a parent or a child saw Mr. EL, they stopped to wave or say hello. Several times, Salome beckoned them inside the library and offered them a sandwich or a slice of pizza.

Emily Perrin, who brought her grandchildren to enjoy some pizza with us, whispered, "God has sent Mr. EL to Reynolds."

I stayed in the library for the next four hours. The night before, Salome had called several of his former students—those who had played chess during his days at Vaux School.

Salome's grin widened when he introduced me to Rodney Veney, a former Alternative Learning Center student who had also played some chess. Rodney would graduate in June from Cheyney College with a degree in therapeutic recreation.

Rodney had grown up on the tough-and-rough streets of north Philadelphia. Salome said that Rodney had lived in drug-infested neighborhoods, on drug blocks, and sometimes next door to a drug house. "He's had to deal with having friends who were murdered at a young age. He's coped with drug dealers living in the same community and often in the same block."

When I asked Rodney why his life had turned out differently, without hesitating he talked about chess. "That's what chess does for these young people. Teaches them to make the right decision." He smiled at me and nodded at his teacher. "Mr. EL, for one, was one of the guys who helped me adapt to become what I am now. He helped me mature, become a man, and learn how to take things nice and slow. He helped me to know that there are better things out there than the streets and where I come from. For me to overcome that was a big change in my life. Mr. EL helped me. Two other teachers named Ken Hamilton at Ben Franklin School and Reuben Mills also helped me. But mostly Mr. EL. He was the biggest reason for change in my life."

Just before I spoke with others, Rodney said, "There's one important incident when I was really, really down. I was in the sixth or seventh grade and I knew I had to determine where I was going with my life. I had to decide if I wanted the street life or if I wanted to get an education. What brought me to make the choice of education? Mr. EL explained the options to me and what I have to do and what I can do. He said, 'If you want, you can go ahead and do the drugs. If that's what you want to do, go do it. You're your own man.' He brought me to that crossroads and helped me make that decision. He didn't tell me you got to do this and you have to do that. He let me work it out as a man."

I also met Kenyetta Lucas, who had graduated from high school five months earlier. She still wavered about going on to college. Several times in the conversation Salome said to her, "You need to get into college."

Her major resistance was because of lack of money. Kenyetta also expressed fear of leaving Philadelphia, the only place she had ever lived. Salome had already started to help her get into his alma mater.

"She'll go," he said as an aside to me.

Kenyetta had been an A student in high school, but had never taken her SAT test. Salome encouraged her, and although she hadn't prepared, she scored 900.

For reasons never made clear to Salome, Kenyetta's mother refused to sign the college application or the request for financial aid, but Salome encouraged her to send the application in anyway. (A few months after my visit, Salome e-mailed to tell me that East Stroudsburg University had accepted Kenyetta for the fall semester.)

Shy Denise Pickard had been the best female chess player Salome had ever coached. When she did speak, she kept saying that although she loved playing chess, it was more than a game. "It taught me to think, and I learned to analyze."

She beamed as she recounted that she was the one who had played with Arnold Schwarzenegger in 2000 when he visited Vaux for the second time. When he walked into the room, Denise was playing against one of the coaches and Arnold took the coach's place. Salome, Denise, and the others were impressed with the actor's chess skills. "We've been around enough players we can spot those who are good, and he was good," she said.

"We never finished the game, but he was pretty good," Denise said.

I spoke with three other male students that day, all of whom are now in high school. Salome informed me recently that this group of guys finally won a state chess championship title together as high school students. Their love and admiration for their mentor was obvious—not only from their words but from the undisguised admiration in their eyes.

"He's more than a teacher and a coach," said Nathan Durant. "He's been a mentor and father figure."

Nathan told me of the time in 1998 when they played in Washington, D.C., and they put him in adult competition because he had barely turned fifteen and fourteen years old was the cut-off. "So I was in there with all the adults—all old guys twenty-four or thirty, and even fifty. I was the youngest person in that adult section, and I'd been playing only two years. I was undefeated until the last round then I lost. But I still came out with a third-place trophy. It made me feel real good about myself, and Mr. EL had helped me. Even if I hadn't done that well, he had taught me to feel good about myself."

Nathan also said, "Mr. EL has played a positive influence in my life like a role model. He set standards that we had to comply with. In order to play chess we had to have good grades. And if we didn't, we wouldn't be able to play. So throughout the whole eighth grade I got one B. Everything else was an A. That's basically because of the chess club. In seventh grade I wasn't doing too well. Eighth grade came and chess came and it prepared me. It made me set high standards for myself. Because I said if he [Mr. EL] thinks I can do it, I know I can do it. It made me feel good about myself."

A slightly embarrassed Salome Thomas-EL listened when Nathan said that the year before he wanted to go to the school prom but he didn't have any money. He's the oldest of five children in a fatherless home and a mother who tries to support them all. Nathan had tried to get a part-time job but he couldn't find one.

Not only did Salome give him money for the dance ticket, but paid for a suit for Nathan—the first new one in his life—and then drove the young man and his date to the prom. "I felt happy that he would do something like that because there's not many people that would do that for you. I was in a time of need and I wanted to go and he kind of fully helped me out there."

"He's all of that and he's a friend," said Demetrius Carroll. This is the boy who, in 1997, scored the biggest upset in tournament history when he defeated a player who was ranked 1000 points higher, at the U.S. Amateur Championship.

"What made me outstanding was that I studied a lot and all of us were just good. We gave it our all in tournaments. We played every day and we had some good coaches.

"I was an "A" and "B"" student. Chess keeps me thinking right. It helps me exercise my mind, and the mind gets stronger. It teaches me, because chess takes a lot of patience. It's not a game that's over real quick. And we sometimes played professionals.

"I beat a college kid when I was about twelve years old. I felt great. It was like the biggest accomplishment during that tournament. Because that was the major thing I did. He congratulated me on it. You go in there and you learn a lot. It's a good game. A lot of people don't know that but it's a good game to play."

*   *   *

Earl Jenkins spoke about his finest moment on the chess team. A student at Masterman had previously beaten him. In 1997, one of the cable TV networks contacted Salome and wanted to film a game with one of the Vaux students. Earl had been elated that Salome chose him to play for Vaux. At the time he didn't know he was going to play against the same Masterman opponent who had once defeated him. Earl overheard the boy tell one of his friends, "I can beat Earl. I did it before and I can do it again."

Earl had recently learned a new opening. "So I decided that's what I'd try. I started moving and watching to see if he knew what the play was. He didn't know it and I beat him. I beat him so bad he resigned from the game."

Earl talked of other games during his three years with the Vaux team, such as the time he won second place or when the team won the nationals. He'd excitedly tell me of a game and then pause. "And Mr. EL, he was right there. Even when I lost, I'd feel bad, really bad, but he never did. He just kept saying that I could do better the next time."

Salome also let me read some of the letters and cards he had received since coming to Reynolds. They're highly complimentary, of course, but I was also quite impressed with the variety of the responses.

Letters and Notes from Teachers and Students

The first note I read came inside a card sent to Salome by Mrs. Kathy Donovan-Suavely a sixth-grade teacher at Vaux Middle School before he moved to Reynolds. She told him that he was extremely dedicated and cared deeply about her children. She rejoiced in their successes and assumed some blame for their failures, always wondering how she might have done more.

Salome told me she often reminded him of Mrs. Pincus, who had cared so deeply about him.

Her note ends: "I just want you to know what an encouragement it is to see you in the hall with the children, and to hear you say 'good morning' each day. Thank you for making yourself available when I have a concern. Thank you for spending time with Larry's mother.

"I admire your vision and your determination—and am rooting for you from Room 414."

Thanks for all of your support. Please stick around, we need your vision.
—Robin Parke, first-grade teacher

Continue to be the individual our children need and deserve. As you ascend the ladder of success, always look back and remember those who loved and helped you.
God's Blessings,
Gertrude Dunlap, teacher for thirty-six years at Reynolds

You are an inspiring and energetic leader. Your love and concern for children shows in very creative and insightful ways. You have won the hearts of your students, the trust of their parents, and the respect of your staff. May God keep you!
("Somewhere in your youth or childhood, you must have done something good.")
—Cathy Hensford, fifth-grade teacher

God has truly blessed you to be an integral part of the lives of our young children. You are a great model of success and you provide the positive guidance our children so desperately need. May God continue to bless you in all that you do.
—Gail Gay, third-grade teacher

*   *   *

Below is a sampling of letters he has received from students since becoming the principal at Reynolds.

You are a wonderful man. Really, I think you are more than wonderful. I think you are magnificent. I love you and I know you love me and my class too because almost every day you come in and watch my teacher teach us a lot of stuff. Then you leave and come back. I know what you are thinking. You are thinking I can't leave without saying Hi to room 304.

—Kionna, third grade

I want to thank you for being a nice principal to me and my class. You are a wonderful principal. I love you like my dad.

—Tamika, third grade

You started Saturday School, a chess club, you gave us a pizza party and other things. You are the greatest principal yet.

—Danielle, third grade

You are a super principal. You are a hero to me. You wear suits everyday. When you come in our class you help us with our work. You help us when we are up or down.

—Maurice, third grade

I look up to you and at Vaux they speak highly of you and thank you for teaching us Algebra, it was fun. You love your students and you want us to graduate and go to college and be something one day.

—Lovesha, fifth grade

You love to teach. I like the way you do things for us. I want to thank you for working with us. You are a loving and caring principal to me. I love you with all my heart.
—Ashley, fifth grade

You took time out of your job to set up a chess team. I see you as a role model for children. You have done so much at this school and every school you have worked at. It is like you have met every famous person that I have ever heard of.
—Darnell, fifth grade

Below is a copy of a rap song written and performed by Reynolds students about their principal:

There's a brand new day at the Reynolds School
We've got a new principal and he's really cool.
He goes by the name of Mr. Thomas-EL,
And here's a story we're about to tell:
He always uses common sense
To help us strive for excellence.
He's not afraid to "talk the talk."
And it seems like he can "walk the walk."
He knows that he can really rhyme,
And every day he takes the time
To let us know we can be smart.
(And he really says it from the heart!)
He wants us to do our very best
With every assignment, book, and test.
This man expects us to expand our minds.
With Mr. EL, everything's fine.

*   *   *

Here are excerpts from the nomination letter Salome's staff submitted to the School District of Philadelphia:

Walking down the corridors of General John F. Reynolds Elementary School is a well-groomed and meticulously dressed young man who slows down his energetic stride, and stops to talk to a child whom he calls by name. He smiles and exchanges with that child in an affirming manner, blending his gifts of poetry and praise, that the child realizes that he is known, that his life has worth, and that there are high expectations for his life. The man who stops to speak to the child is our Principal, Mr. Salome Thomas-EL; the child with whom he is speaking could be any child at Reynolds. He knows them all, and they all know him. Mr. "EL," as the children affectionately call him, is accessible to them. His smile says to them, "I used to be like you." Their smiles say to him, "You give us hope that we can be like you."

Though Mr. Thomas-EL walked public school hallways as a child, he doesn't have to walk them as an adult. His feet do not have to pound the often-hard urban vestibules of academia any longer. Attractive offers from elsewhere have sought to exploit and reward this former Gratz High School student who has "done well." The influx of charter and other school offers would seem like an attractive lure, and a prime opportunity to promote his philosophy for children; however, in spite of all that beckons him to greener school yards, he has made a decision to stay. The courage of his choice to remain in public schools, in the community from which he came, continues to evoke positive responses from many.

It is impossible to say anything about Mr. Thomas-EL without mentioning chess. The chess club is a favorite activity for Reynolds' students. One teacher describes the chess experience at Reynolds by recognizing that, "Extended Curricular Activities (like chess) develop and expand intellectual and creative abilities, and talents; develop self-worth; establish a bridge between school and the real world; and develop team spirit and cooperative effort . . ."

It is with great pleasure, pride and sincerity that we, the proud staff of the General John F. Reynolds Elementary School, nominate our outstanding young, gifted, and dedicated principal Mr. Salome Thomas-EL for the Leon J. Obermayer Award.

The day after I interviewed the students in the Reynolds School library, others came to Salome's house to meet me. Their eagerness to talk about their teacher, their mentor, and above all, their friend, amazed me. It was obvious that they hadn't come at his prompting but they came to show their appreciation of him.

One of those students, Shawn Murphy, a college senior, finished his last statement with these words, "I just love that man."

All questions about Salome Thomas-EL had been erased. I, too, had become a believer.

24

"I Need More Graduations"

The first time I visited Mrs. Ella Travis, the principal of the High School for Engineering and Sciences (HSES), was in June 1998. I went because I wanted to get Harream Purdie entered in that outstanding high school. The boy had been a National Honor Society student. George Washington Carver High School for Engineering and Sciences had denied him admission because of his below-average standardized test scores. What the test did not show was that his grandmother, also his guardian, was terminally ill at the time. She died only days after my visit.

I was afraid to visit Mrs. Travis because of her reputation as a hard-nosed administrator and as a person who had no problem saying no. I took Mrs. Lewis and Mrs. Young, teachers from Vaux, with Harream and me. They were as eager as I was to influence her.

Harream was armed with a letter written by his grandmother begging Mrs. Travis to listen to the Lord and allow Harream to attend HSES. We made our case and gave her the letter. Mrs. Travis agreed to think about it for a few days and I reminded her that graduation was only days away. We needed to make a decision on a high school before the school year ended.

Several days later, she asked Harream and me to come to her office. This time Harream and I went alone. I didn't want the other teachers to see me fail this kid.

"I have decided to accept you as a student," she told him before I could present my argument.

Sad to say, Harream's grandmother had died only hours before we visited Mrs. Travis. She never heard the words "I've been accepted" from the boy's lips.

Three days later, as I sat at her funeral along with hundreds of others from the community, I believed it was her prayers and her letter that had gotten Harream into HSES, not me.

The day after the funeral, I visited Mrs. Travis and thanked her one last time for accepting the boy, and informed her of the passing of Harream's grandmother.

The news saddened her, and then she talked about how important it was for educators like her and me to provide positive opportunities for young men like Harream. I agreed.

Harream did not play championship chess like Nathan or Demetrius. He went to Vaux so, of course, he played because everyone at Vaux plays chess. We sometimes say, "At Vaux, even the mice are good chess players."

(Harream is headed for a college scholarship and is on the honor roll.)

Demetrius had already been accepted at HSES, but Nathan didn't have the necessary test scores. I begged Mrs. Travis to give Nathan a shot, just as she had given Harream. She said it would be tough because there were so many important people in Philadelphia who wanted their kids in HSES. I promised her Nathan would not let her down.

"In that case, I'll admit him," she said.

Nathan did not let her down. He went on to become an honor roll student and was offered a place in their medical program for students who aspire to be doctors.

Nathan and Demetrius also led the HSES Chess Team to a State Title in 2001.

Mrs. Travis died before she could see their success. They have dedicated their lives to making her smile in Heaven.

One of my goals is to impact the lives and careers of young people. In this new century, I've been able to see some of those kids I taught a dozen years ago enter college and a few of them have graduated. I swell with pride over every one of them, because I know that I was one of those individuals who helped to make a difference in their lives.

I'd like to make a difference for kids like Akeem Carter, who was a second-grader when I first met him. "So you're going to be our new principal, huh?" Akeem said as I walked to my car from Vaux for one of the last times before going to Reynolds.

"Yes, I am, and who are you?"

"I'm Akeem, and you know me—my dad washes your car for you sometimes."

"And do you go to Reynolds?"

"Yeah, but I was left down [retained] this year."

"Why?"

He shrugged. "I don't know. I guess I don't really like school."

"My job is to make sure you like school. If I can do that, will you promise to try harder?"

He left me standing on the sidewalk with "I can try."

After two years Akeem is moving into the fourth grade as an honor roll student and a member of the third best elementary chess team in the state championship in Bloomsburg. He now mentors and tutors second-graders.

At a recent tournament where his teammate won top unrated

player in the state, a player from a rival school asked Akeem if Reynolds was a new school.

"It is now," he said, "because we have a new principal."

Some of those dreams for my students are starting to become reality.

"It's a little late to tell you, and you probably have other plans anyway," Otis Bullock said.

His phone call had come during a busy Friday afternoon the first week of June in 2000. I did have other plans and told him so. "But I'll see if I can change them. I'd like to be there."

"It's just—well, I just wanted to let you know that I'm graduating Sunday. You've always encouraged me to stay in school. You're one of the biggest reasons I'm graduating. I wouldn't have stuck it out if you hadn't encouraged me."

Nearly two years had passed since I'd heard from Otis. When he first started his studies at West Chester University, he contacted me regularly. As in most situations with kids going off to college, as time went by he called less frequently.

"I didn't want to walk down that aisle on graduation day," he said, "without having a chance to thank you for everything you've done for me."

I barely remember my response because I kept thinking of Otis graduating. During my early days of reactivating the chess team at Vaux, I had seen the possibilities in that kid. He was one of the older ones who already knew how to play and was better than most adults. Otis was shy and quite studious. One thing, though, all through high school he called or came back to Vaux to let us know how school was going.

"I'd like you to come to the graduation, but I know it's a long drive—" and he kept making excuses for me not to attend.

I wanted to be at his graduation, but I wasn't sure I could make it, so I couldn't promise. I did tell him how excited I was that he was going to graduate. "You're the first of my kids to make it through college," I said. "That makes your graduation special, you know."

After I hung up the phone, I paused and thought again about Otis Bullock. I felt warm inside after that call. It was finally happening! All those years of urging kids to stay in school and to keep on. Yes, I felt proud of him—the first of *my* kids to graduate from college. Others would graduate in 2001 and the years ahead, but Otis would be the first.

I had seen just as much promise in a number of kids who had dropped out of school after they left Vaux. Some had been murdered; a few had gotten into drug use and disappeared. Others had moved away and I lost track of them.

These inner-city kids face obstacles that middle-class Americans can't understand. It's more than a lack of money. Some get little support from their families and even less from their peers. Many of those kids have never known a father and few of them have been inside a two-parent home.

Every day of their lives those kids live in the projects or near one. They know about drugs, violence, prostitution, and they can tell you where to buy a handgun. Most of them either had had someone murdered in their family or could name half a dozen kids in their neighborhood who never lived long enough to reach college age.

"Oh, God, it's so hard for these kids," I heard myself praying as I sat at my desk. "So many pressures from their peers and the pull of being like all the other people in their community."

Then I thought again of Otis.

He had done it. He had paved the road that others could follow. Rodney Veney and Shawn Murphy were both studying at Cheyney University, and they would graduate in 2001. I smiled as I thought of them and how much I loved those two kids. Samirah and Blair would be right behind them.

Then I remembered some of the others who were no longer

alive—kids like Willow Briggs and Stephon Copper. Willow "Fu" Briggs was one of our first chess players. He was our first player to be successful on a national level in Orlando, Florida, in 1996. When a seventh-grader, he was rated one of the top twenty-five players in the nation in his division. He was a kid who whenever his former teachers in elementary school would read about him in the newspapers or see that he was a successful chess player, they would always talk about how they were so surprised that Willow had become successful. In elementary school they predicted that he would drop out.

All he did was gamble and play around before he got to school. But they were proud that with the support of his family he turned his life around. He had some mentors in his life and he was becoming a champion at chess and doing better in school.

What was sad was that when he moved on to high school, he went to a school that didn't have a chess program. Willow got into more trouble in high school. I don't know all the details, but one day Willow was standing on a street corner talking to a younger kid. They began to argue. A third kid came by and said, "I'm coming back and you're dead if you're still here."

Five minutes later the kid came back and Willow hadn't moved. He shot our former chess player and killed him right there on the corner.

Willow's death was one of the hardest deaths I've had to face. He was one of the most talented kids I've ever taught.

Another senseless death.

Those not-yet-forgotten kids will never have the opportunities that lie ahead for people like Denise, Latoria, Demetrius, Nathan, Earl, and Thomas.

I reflected on the teachers who had influenced my life. I had made it, but where would I be today if it hadn't been for the encouragement of teachers like Mrs. Smithey and especially Mrs. Pincus?

Throughout the rest of the day, my thoughts kept returning to Otis's telephone call. In my mind, I could see him lined up with gown and tassel, waiting to receive his degree.

"I have to go to his graduation," I said aloud.

Shawnna and I had plans to spend Sunday after church with some good friends. I called her at work and told her about Otis. "I'd like to go to the graduation." As I spoke that sentence, I realized that my breathing had constricted and my muscles had tightened. This graduation meant a lot to me, but I didn't know how she would feel about riding in a car for two hours. She was in the early stages of her pregnancy with our first child, and she was sick most of the time.

"I think that's a wonderful idea," she said. "I'd also like to see Otis graduate. It's a big thing for him—and for you."

"You don't mind then?"

I could hear her soft laugh on the other end of the line. "I'm proud of Otis. I'm even more proud of you. Of course, we're going."

For the past seven or eight months, Shawnna and I had been attending Calvary Baptist Church in North Philadelphia, which we enjoyed very much and felt that was where we belonged. This was an integrated church in the Fairmount section of Philadelphia, less than five minutes from Reynolds and Vaux. It reminds me of Masterman at times with blacks, whites, Hispanics, and Asians all worshiping and learning together. Shawnna had already become a member and I was getting ready to join.

To go to the graduation ceremony for Otis, however, meant we'd have to miss the worship service that Sunday. We loved the congregation's involvement in the community. Pastor Sean Wise lived a life of service and sacrifice that I found inspiring.

Two weeks earlier, he had started a series of sermons on dedicating ourselves to God and proving it through our service to the church and the community.

I wrestled a few minutes about not being there, but I knew I had to go to West Chester University. Finally, I realized something else. I wanted to see Otis graduate—to walk alongside those other graduates and receive his diploma. But even more important, I needed to be there—for me.

It was one of those dark times when my mind focused on the deaths of kids within the community. There had been another one only the day before. Not from Reynolds or Vaux, but from the inner city. Death crept around all the time. Two of my former female students recently had been killed in separate incidents. Both only nineteen years old, and one was a college student. I needed to go where there was life. I had to see hope fulfilled through Otis.

On the drive up, I kept thinking about inner-city kids. As long as they're alive, they have a chance to turn their lives around. As long as there are teachers and leaders out there giving of ourselves, we can make changes. Sadness filled my heart when I remembered those we hadn't been able to snatch from destruction.

I wasn't the only teacher or leader. There were others—a lot of others—and each of us carried the same burden. We cared. And because we cared, it hurt deeply when we lost a child.

I kept thinking of the funerals I had been to during the past ten years—more than I wanted to remember. Some of those we buried were young—elementary and middle school kids who happened to be playing in the wrong place when a fight broke out.

When I was a boy, I had gone to funerals—but they were

only for old people. I'd stare at their lined faces and gray hair and it felt peaceful. They had lived their lives, but these kids were eight, ten, or fourteen years old. They'd never know what life really is. Too many inner-city kids grew up too fast—if they grew up—seeing the harshness of life on the streets every day. We had been a poor family, but I hadn't seen or been through what so many of those kids went through every day.

I thought of Anwar and his mother's drug problems. They had beat the neighborhood pressure, but his mother had fled to Lancaster to do so. I thought of Denise and the struggle she lived with every day, and her mom still wasn't doing well. There was Nathan who longed for a relationship with his father that seemed as if it would never develop. And there was Demetrius, who lived a thousand miles away from his mom— in his third house in two years.

The world is larger than north Philadelphia and bigger than the ghettos, I kept saying to myself. Education is their passport to another world. As I drove toward the university, I vowed afresh that I would give every child a passport to go wherever he or she wanted to go.

I know I'm impacting lives and careers—and that's encouraging, but I'm just one person. My mind kept going back to those kids who wouldn't ever stand where Otis would stand today. They'd never graduate from college.

For the ten-year period beginning in 1990, I mentally ticked off almost twenty of my former students who had been murdered. That's something I never thought about when I was studying to be a teacher. No education classes had ever mentioned coping with such grief.

One day on the morning news, I wept when the TV showed pictures of two of my former students. One was from Strawberry Mansion and the other from Vaux. They knew each other and were in the same house when a robbery took place. Both died there.

That morning had been one of the first times that I had thought about whether I wanted to continue teaching. I didn't like that feeling of loss and ongoing pain. Each time I'd hear or read of a murdered child, I'd ask, "How can I go through this again?"

Too many funerals.

I would have such a short time to impact each of these children. At most, I'd have six years to point them in new directions. That didn't seem long enough.

Too many funerals.

I had debated about calling Otis before we left Philadelphia, but I decided not to. I wanted to be there and to watch his face the moment he spotted us.

Shawnna and I sat in the shade near the stadium stairs. It was almost one hundred degrees that Sunday, and several people collapsed from the intense sun and heat.

I fidgeted and squirmed until the graduating students marched in procession. It took me a few seconds to spot Otis. I stared at him, hardly aware that tears had filled my eyes.

When he saw Shawnna and me, his eyes lit up and he grinned. I couldn't hold back any longer. Tears streamed down my cheeks, and I didn't care. Otis had made it! He had beaten the poverty and the drugs and the peer pressure. He was alive and graduating from college. Between the pride and the tears, I paid little attention to the rest of the ceremony.

As soon as the graduation was over, Otis rushed over and hugged us.

We made him pose for pictures alone, then with other classmates, with me, with Shawnna and me, with professors.

I couldn't get enough pictures of him in his graduation gown.

Somewhere in the middle of the picture taking he asked if anyone else had come.

"No, none of the others could make it," I said, "but I'm representing them, because we're all proud of you."

This was a totally selfish moment for me. I wanted—and needed—this time with Otis. "I'll call them when I get back to Philadelphia."

"We don't have that many inner-city kids graduating from college," Shawnna said, "so they'd be thrilled to hear how things went. We'll send them pictures and that will make them feel proud of you."

At least four times Otis thanked us for coming. He couldn't seem to get over the idea that Shawnna and I would drive all the way from Philadelphia to see him graduate.

"When I called, I really didn't expect you to come," Otis said.

"I'm not sure you understand, Otis," I said. "I needed to come to this graduation. I *had* to come. I've been to too many funerals. I needed to go to a graduation. I need to go to many of them. I hope that many more of my students will give me the opportunity to come and see them graduate and reach their goals and continue to hold to the commitments that they've made to themselves and to me."

As I spoke to Otis on that sweltering-yet-beautiful June day, I knew I wanted to write a book. I didn't want the book to be about one exceptional teacher. There are many exceptional teachers out there. Today I am who I am because exceptional teachers took time to work with me.

When I attend funerals, I weep over those kids and I ask

myself and God how I can go to another one. Almost immediately, I find comfort in one thought: If I quit teaching, if I left the inner city, if I stopped reaching out to these kids, how many more funerals would take place that I might have prevented?

Then the pain eases. I know I need to keep teaching.

More than ever, I know why I still choose to stay in the inner city.

entire school and it was in the inner city. An entire school would be mine to run and to get great teachers like the ones who taught me. I would be able to procure materials and resources for the school and the children.

I called and said yes, I would like to take that job at Reynolds. "I'll make sure I let the district know that you are my choice to replace me," she said, "but I can't guarantee anything."

By now the word had gotten around and school districts were actually coming to me. I interviewed for a job in Chester, which is outside of Philadelphia. They offered to top any salary that Philadelphia offered me by $10,000. In fact, one of the interviewers made it clear that I could be their superintendent in a few years. The interview panel requested that I build a chess program in Chester similar to the one I had in Philadelphia.

I thought seriously about the offer. It would lighten the financial burden at home. Shawnna and I were thinking about starting a family. My tuition for my future doctoral studies program would be paid for. It was no secret in Philadelphia that suburban districts paid for educators to further their education. That attracted many qualified teachers and principals to the suburbs from the city. It was tempting, but I turned it down. No matter how much money was offered, I knew my work wasn't finished in Philadelphia. I had chosen to stay a year earlier. That commitment hadn't changed.

"I still have a lot of unfinished work," I told the human resources director at Chester, "even though I'm flattered by your generous offer."

It hadn't been a difficult decision.

By staying, I could continue to mentor the students who had been under my tutelage for so long.

Initially my wife asked, "Are you crazy?" Once we discussed everything, however, she agreed I had done the right thing.

20.

Principal Issues

In the summer of 1999, I was the principal of the summer school program at John F. Reynolds Elementary School. I also ran the Vaux summer chess program at the same time. It was great because I used my chess players to mentor the elementary students of Reynolds. That was good. They even began to teach some of the young people how to play chess that summer.

Just before the summer session ended, I received a phone call from Colleen Wisler, the principal at Reynolds. "I've been offered another position." She would become a principal at an elementary school closer to her home in northeast Philadelphia. "Would you be interested in becoming the principal at Reynolds?" she asked. "If you are, I'll recommend you."

I didn't know how to answer. I told her I had received some other offers from a few schools outside Philadelphia, and also had some opportunities at other Philadelphia public schools. I would let her know. I asked myself the same question several times. Was I ready to leave Vaux?

I thought about it for a while and—once again—I decided that I needed to stay in the community and that I wanted to stay. I had worked hard and this would be a chance to lead an